To Fly By Night

The Craft of the Hedgewitch

Edited by: Veronica Cummer

To Fly By Night

The Craft of the Hedgewitch

Edited by Veronica Cummer

PENDRAIG Publishing
Los Angeles, CA 91040

To Fly By Night: The Craft of the Hedgewitch
Edited by Veronica Cummer
First Edition © 2010
by PENDRAIG Publishing

Cover Design &
Interior Typeset & Layout   Jo-Ann Byers Mierzwicki

PENDRAIG

PENDRAIG Publishing
Los Angeles, CA 91040
www.PendraigPublishing.com
Printed in the United States of America

ISBN: 978-0-9827263-7-2

Table of Contents

Dedication

This anthology is, as ever, dedicated to the Muse.

In addition, I would like to thank all the authors who contributed to this work and shared their thoughts, insights, experiences, and advice. It's a brave thing to put something of yourself out into the world, especially when it means so very much to you.

I would also like to express a debt of gratitude to Peter Paddon of Pendraig Publishing for choosing to support this work and to sacrifice time, money, energy, and even *(sometimes)* a smidge of sanity in order to provide many forums for furtherance of the knowledge and the on-going evolution of the Craft.

Blessings and best wishes. May all your journeys end in divine gold. May you always return with something most needed.

Now I go, now I fly,
Malkin my sweet spirit and I.
Oh, what a dainty pleasure 'tis
To ride in the air
When the moon shines fair
And sing, and dance, and toy, and kiss;
Over woods, high rocks, and mountains,
Over seas, over misty fountains,
Over steeples, towers, and turrets,
We fly by night, 'mongst troops of spirits...

Hecate
From *"The Witch"* by Thomas Middleton
early 1600'

Introduction

Up hors
Up hedik
Up will ridn bolwind
And I kin I's reyd among yu

*F*ar from the glow of the cities, out in the true darkness of the countryside, you can still stand and gaze up at the night sky and see the nearest thing to infinity. To see stars layered upon stars, darkness upon darkness, and the gleam of the Milky Way as it spills across the heavens. It's a familiar vision for we know this track, this starry road. After all, it's the way that witches and spirits are said to ride, to travel, to fly. That far-flung road beckons and we long to take it, to go where it might lead us.

It's an ancient dream—to fancy that we can fly. In truth, flying and witches go hand-in-hand, extending into the unknown and exotic world of the distant past. Who has not seen the fabulous image of the witch soaring across the sky on a broomstick, usually silhouetted against a full moon. Of old, witches have been linked to the ability to fly, a gift that many still long for. Yet, what is this gift? Why are stories, myths, and legends filled with the idea that witches have this power? And since we don't tend to literally see witches zooming around in the air against some fateful full moon, where does the idea of the flying witch come from?

Well, for one thing, *"flying"* is a term used not just to describe a physical act but a *spiritual* one. You *"fly"* by leaving your body, leaving your physical form behind, while you go elsewhere. Sometimes, this happens naturally in certain states of sleep, but the witch or worker of the cunning arts seeks out that state through more conscious and deliberate means. We concentrate on gaining the ability to *"fly,"* to travel beyond what is known and to go out into the wilds, be it called Faery, the Otherworld, or any of those strange, beautiful and dangerous lands beyond the boundaries, beyond the Veil, beyond the Hedge.

It's a place we still remember, a world we dream of and long for, and seek to rediscover and claim for our own. Which makes perfect sense, because it is our own, our secret, sacred heritage—the world of our beloved ancestors, of the beautiful and enigmatic Faery, of the strange ancient Gods of the land and of the land itself.

It's the world of the past, when witches and cunning folk of all flavors, and with as many different names as there were cultures that required them, lived to serve the land, the Gods, and the people. To do this, they underwent a physical, spiritual, and psychological death and rebirth into a brave, new form of existence, that of someone who existed neither here nor there, someone who stood between the land of the living and the realm of the dead. Someone who was the eternal loved, hated, feared, desired *"outsider."*

They became what one particular land of the North would call a *"shaman."*

From the North to the South, from the East to the West, all across the Old World, there was an undercurrent of these outsiders, these cunning or *kenning ones,* just as they existed and continue to exist in other parts of the world. Yet, beneath the differences of name and practice based upon where they lived, there exists a commonality that binds them all together as one.

There is the night-flight, the spirit journey, the ability to shapeshift, the power to heal and to harm, and congress with all sorts of spirits, Gods and Goddesses, the dead, and the powers of the Earth. There is the thin edge that needs to be walked between magick and madness, between life and death. There is the boundary that must be leaped or walked or stood upon, always a chancy business at best. There is the going-there and the coming-back-again with lost souls, healing knowledge, gifts for the community, new insights and ancient revelation.

There are battles to be fought, quests to be undertaken, sacrifices to make, and seeds to be sown for the future. There are angry and hungry ghosts to be dealt with and Gods to be courted or appeased, each as required and all necessary to the proper functioning of the land and of the community to ensure that both continue to live and grow and evolve.

And yet...what happened to these *"shamans"* of the Old World?

The very same protectors of the land, the servants of Gods and humankind alike, were accused of being evil and in league with evil spirits and Gods who had come to be called *"devils,"*—most often those very same Gods and Goddesses who had once been the benefactors of the community and were now demeaned and demonized. Witches and cunning ons became the cause of every kind of ill luck, disease, and hardship imaginable.

Instead of being seen as those who walked the line between this and that, able to bestow healing and fertility and bounty as much as being capable of taking it away, they were seen as primarily working against the good of the community, as those who cursed and poisoned and caused illness and hunger. They became wicked, wrong, and worthy of persecution, torture, and death.

Sure, a few *"white witches,"* cunning folk and faery doctors, remained accepted here and there. Depending upon the culture and the region, some pockets of these ancient outsiders endured and managed to keep on doing their work. Some even have held on to the present time, though mostly by being somewhere where older beliefs and thoughts have not been entirely destroyed or by keeping a very low profile and pretense towards fitting in with everyone else. While others chose, of necessity, to go deeply underground hundreds of years ago, hiding away to pass down what they knew as best they could, until the seeds they buried in keeping for the future could blossom again in some hopeful springtime.

Eventually, the persecution gave way to denial as the beliefs of our ancestors were lumped under the name of fanciful superstition, ignorance, and even outright lie. The past became an alien world we of the now can only peer at dimly through the narrow lens of science and reason, of history and archeology. None of which can see the whole picture, let alone hope to truly comprehend it without the missing pieces of faith, revelation, and kenning, what some might call the Second Sight. Without the insight and understanding of the Gods and the spirits and the Fey, who all played and continue to play an intrinsic part in the unfolding drama of the Earth.

Without those who stand with one foot in this world and one foot in the Other, what some today would call hedgewitches and hedgeriders.

And yet...the wheel spins. Times change and Ages rise and fall and, as they do, paradigms shift and what was old becomes new again and what was lost becomes found. Misrule turns everything on its ear, and that is the lesson of time and of the trickster Gods, those who are also of this and that, night-riders, shape-shifters, hedgewalkers. Faery threatens to return, the old Gods to awaken, and the witches to fly free once more. The Hedge remains, the Otherworld beckons, the Gods of flight and furious fancy call, and the hunger has grown at last too great to deny. The hunger to know what we once were, where we sprang from, what we are or could be, and where we can yet go.

The hunger to once more walk with spirits, commune with Faery and the dead, to laugh and sing and dance with the Gods, and be as one with the land. To make the leap not just between supernatural realms, but across the very boundary of time and reality, and be reborn once more. Creatures of the now, of the modern world with all its wonders and problems, and of the past and the future all.

We are outsiders who once more may become acknowledged for the part we have to play, for all that we have to offer. For the necessities we might well fulfill and the hopes and dreams we can seek out and realize for our own good and the good of all. Balance-keepers and tricksters and healers and explorers who not only endure, but who overcome and always endeavor for the more, not only walking upon the boundaries of possibility, but pushing them ever outwards.

What is a hedgewitch? What are the ways that a hedgewitch walks? What tools do they use? What dangers do they encounter and what mysteries discover?

The essays in this anthology are a glimpse into that world and those practices. They build upon the knowledge and speculation, the history, legends, and stories of the past, and out of what has been reclaimed and renewed in the present. They show us what it is to live today as one who walks the between, who rides the boundaries, and counts themselves as a resident among many worlds and none. They lift a torch into the unknown darkness and allow us to catch a glimpse of the ever-changing future. Whether of the Old World or the New, the authors speak to us of what they have discovered, what they are still discovering, and how we can learn to discover for ourselves.

Contained within are the diverse insights of a hedgewitch from Ontario, Canada, a conjure-man from Mississippi, of witches and cunning folk of many persuasions from Strega to Traditional Witchcraft to Wicca. We have Magisters and Druids and magicians. Teachers and artists and researchers. Priests and Priestesses and *"staff-carrying"* women who are busily rebuilding the heritage of the Volva through song and experience with staff, body, and voice. We have walkers of all sorts upon the Witching Way, the Crooked Path, the Crimson Thread, who have chosen to share the words, courage, wisdom, and dedication of those who have sought time and again to go beyond.

One foot in this world and one foot in the other. Shapeshifting, changing, daring and dreaming...unwilling to give up that feeling and that delicious freedom once we've had a taste of it. And who could blame us? Who doesn't want to fly? Who doesn't want to rush, jubilant and wild and so very alive, high against the moon and sky and once there go beyond the edge, past that last boundary.

To fly upon the road of stars and spirits. To travel the night. To ride the Hedge.

The Hosts

We are the ragged vagabonds
Travelers on unknown shores
Where worlds meet, there we go
Where worlds end, there we fly
Neither here nor there
Black nor white
Alive nor dead
We are the patchwork promise
The diamond shards of the mirrored gate
Harlequin jesters
Balancing out tomorrow on the back of the past
Our hands are the hands of Gods
Masked fools
The shadow-side of kings and ghouls
We are born with the caul
We are born to be called
By blood sworn true,
Wayward and free
Flame-wise weavers
Spider's children and Fate's blessings
We could no more deny the wilds
Than our own hearts greatest desire
By soot and by snow we go
On geese, hounds, goats, wrens
Broomstick and pole
Sweeping above in rushing flight
The sleeping land
With its dimmed and dreaming lights
Condemned to the night
Lonely, yet never really alone
No matter how far or fast we go

What the Heck is a Hedgewitch

Juniper

Hedgewitchery, or hedgecraft, is a kind of combination of witchcraft and shamanism. For the most part, this path comes from the traditional witchcraft and cunning folk traditions of Europe from ancient to modern times. It is something of an eclectic tradition, but just how much so depends on each individual practitioner.

The basic modern definition of hedgewitch is comparable to older definitions of wisewoman, cunning man, medicine man, shaman, herb healer or folk healer. It is loosely based on the old wise wo/men, cunning folk, herbalists, faith healers and actual witches throughout history. Hedgewitches are involved with herbalism and healing, along with a deep love for and understanding of nature added to the mix. If you think *"hedgewitch"* and picture the strange old lady who sold herbs and magickal charms, acted as midwife and healer in the ancient times, you are not far off. Nor are you far off if you picture the wise sage who would cast bones to divine the future or journey in the Otherworlds to heal members of his community.

Throughout history, shamanic, wise-woman and cunning-man traditions have risen and fallen all over the world. These kinds of traditions have never truly died out. In recent years, more and more people within the Western world are turning to them and adapting them to modern times. Modern hedgecraft is the study, adaptation and practice of these ancient nature-based, spiritual, shamanic and healing traditions in our modern lives.

Hedgewitches can come from any cultural background, but the majority of hedgewitches seem to come from European ancestry. This means that most hedgewitches will practice based on the folklore and traditions of the ancient Celts, Vikings, Romans, Greeks, Slavs, Anglo-Saxons and so forth.

Most hedgewitches look to their own heritage to find inspiration and lore. Yet some are drawn to the traditions of other cultures. Some may seek to learn from other cultures to gain a better understanding of their own heritage, as well as a greater respect for others. Hedgewitches are not opposed to the study of modern tradition as well, for they strive to bridge the gap between old and new. To blend old traditions with a modern lifestyle in a workable and practical manner is a hallmark of hedgecraft.

The shamanic aspect is the most important of all in hedgecraft, for to call oneself a hedgewitch is to call oneself a shaman. A shaman is a person who traverses the *axis mundi* and who enters the Otherworlds to commune with ancestors, gods and spirits for many purposes and using many different techniques. The word *"shaman"* comes originally from the Turkic word *"šamán"* and translates as *"one who knows."* This word has been used by peoples of the Turkic-Mongol and Tungus cultures of Siberia for many centuries. It was introduced to Europe from Siberia to Russia and then into Germany.

Later, white colonists coming to the New World and Africa applied the words *"medicine man"* and *"witch doctor"* to the healers and holy people of tribal cultures. These titles were eventually replaced by *"shaman."* This is why people of European decent are often told by *"shamans"* of other races and cultures they should not call themselves *"medicine men"* or *"shamans."* Those of us who have white skin need not borrow words from other cultures for such practices. For we do have our own traditions and words, and names, for such people, and we can *(and should)* use them with pride.

"Hedgewitch" comes from the Saxon word *"haegtessa"* and the Old English *"hægtesse,"* which can roughly translate to *"hedge-rider,"* with *"haeg"* meaning a *"hedge," "fence,"* or *"enclosure."* However *"hægtesse,"* and the shortened *"haeg,"* not only translates to *"hedgerider"* and *"hedge,"* but can also be translated as *"hag," "witch,"* and *"fury."* From this we have the modern English word *"hedgewitch."* Since we take the name for this form of Witchcraft from the word *"hedge,"* let us take a look at what a hedge means to the hedgewitch.

The concept of a boundary hedge in a spiritual and magickal sense stems from the tradition of hedge laying, or growing hedgerows. Hedgerows are carefully landscaped intricate layers of plant-life. The European landscape has been crisscrossed by hedgerows since the time of the Roman occupations and possibly before. The Anglo-Saxons also used hedgerows extensively, and many of these ancient hedgerows still exist today. The early European colonists in the New World put up hedgerows, though often with different species of plants. In Europe the most common species growing in hedgerows are the hawthorn and blackthorn, whereas in North America cedar and juniper hedges are more common.

These often-large rows of shrub, herb and tree are boundaries for farmsteads, pastures, villages, ditches and roads. In ancient times, at the very edge of a human settlement, there was a sturdy hedgerow keeping the wilderness and wildlife out of field, pasture and garden. Crossing a hedge means crossing a boundary of some sort, such as walking into the wild, going from wheat field to cow pasture, or entering another person's property.

A hedgerow is not just a boundary, but is also a protective home and shelter to all kinds of wildlife, such as rabbits and birds. They provide shade and act as a windbreak. The hedgerow is also a place where foxes and hares being hunted may hide and where hunters will send their hounds to flush game. Hedgerows were also very important in keeping the herds in and the predators out.

Berry and fruit bearing trees and shrubs are grown in hedgerows, making them a source of food for both animals and humans alike. They may also have both healing as well as baneful herbs and plants growing within them. While beautiful, these hedgerows will typically sport thorn bushes and other plant life that can be hazardous if you are not respectful of the hedge and what grows and lives within.

For the hedgewitch, *"the Hedge"* is not just a physical boundary but also a metaphor for the line drawn between this world and the next, between reality and dreamscape. It represents the threshold between the many worlds. In short, the Hedge is what many Pagans refer to as the Veil. It is also the boundary between civilization and the wild, the place where the wildwoods and the urban jungle meet.

The more one learns of the tradition of laying hedgerows, as well as about hedges themselves, the more the use of *"hedge"* for this Craft becomes clearly appropriate.

In a 13th century Icelandic text called the Poetic Edda, we find a long poem called *Hávamál,* and in that poem the god Odin recites a list of Rune-spells he has learned while hanging upon the World Tree *(axis mundi).* This part of the *Hávamál* has come to be called the Song of Spells. The tenth of these spells particularly interests and inspires hedgewitches. There are many translations of this verse; here are four of them.

For the tenth I know,
if I see troll-wives
sporting in air,
I can so operate
that they will forsake
their own forms,
and their own minds.
~ Benjamin Thorpe

"A tenth I know, what time I see
House-riders* flying on high;
So can I work, that wildly they go,
Showing their true shapes,
Hence to their own homes."
~ Henry Adams Bellows

"If I see the hedge-riders magically flying high,
I can make it so they go astray
Of their own skins, and of their own souls."
~ Nigel Pennick

A tenth I know: when at night the witches
ride and sport in the air,
such spells I weave that they wander home
out of skins and wits bewildered.
~ Olive Bray

*House-riders: witches,
who ride by night on the roofs of houses,
generally in the form of wild beasts.

A hedgewitch is thus a person with some shamanic qualities. They can "ride," as in travel through and over, the boundary of this world and into the Otherworld. They can leave the *"enclosure"* or *"hedge"* of their own body, experience soul-flight and send their spirits to wander in the night. It also appears that at least one God knows how to confuse their shamanic travels and send them packing back home!

The true origin of the term *"hedgewitch"* may never be known. It is a modern English term, likely to have originated in Great Britain within the last century. Yet a word does not have to be old to be legitimate. English is still a young language; it is changing and growing all the time. Our ancestors had their own names, in their own languages, for such traditions. *"Hedgewitch"* is for our culture, in our language. There can be variations in its spelling, such as *"hedgewytch,"* and a few related terms, such as Hedge-Riders, Night Travelers, Myrk-Riders *("myrk" being the old spelling for "murky," or a kind of darkness)*, and Gandreidh *(wand-rider)*. Cunning folk is sometimes used and also Walkers on the Wind.

Throughout history and in many cultures the hedgewitch *(wisewoman, cunning man, shaman, etc)* lived at the edge of the community, often amongst or just beyond the outlying hedgerows. Hedgewitches in history were typically folks who lived somewhat on the fringes of society, not just by actually physically living beyond the township, but often by being outspoken women and men who did not follow societal norms. Just as shamans in other cultures often live somewhat apart from the people they serve, so did many of the folk healers, wise women and cunning folk in Europe and its colonies. For one of the causes that these shamanic-type practitioners take up is to speak the truth, even when the truth is ugly. Also they will do what is needed for people, even if it goes against the grain or wins them no popularity in the community at large.

A wonderful example of this is Biddy Early, a folk healer who lived in Ireland from 1798 to 1874. Biddy served her community not only with herbalism but also by using her intuition and utilizing magical charms. She had a bottle containing a mysterious dark liquid which she would peer through. By some sort of scrying method with this bottle, she would divine the necessary cures for her clients. This bottle went everywhere with her and was on her person when she died.

Biddy was outspoken and would often speak strongly against the abuses that the peasant folk around her endured. She was also known to have many unkind words for the Catholic Church and its parish priests, as well. In 1865, Biddy was accused of witchcraft and taken to court. Despite her reputation as a troublesome and strange woman, few people were willing to testify against her and she was released. Biddy died of old age some nine years later.

These folk healers, spirit healers, and *"hedgewitches"* served the community in many ways. They earned a living through such means as midwifery, healing, protection spells, house blessings, crop and livestock blessings, herbalism or wortcunning, understanding nature, prophecy and divination. One of the most common practices was the selling of magickal charms and spells of protection from curses.

A hedgewitch might sell one member of her community a small curse or ill-wish one day, and then charge its victim a fee to break the curse the next. Therefore, people who followed such traditions were respected and likely a little feared because of these abilities. They were also looked upon as a little strange because they had such a close relationship with both the natural and spiritual worlds.

In modern times, a hedgewitch is usually (but not always) found outside the city, perhaps on an acreage or farm, often practicing by herself or within the family. They work much as the cunning folk of old, helping neighbors, friends and family with ailments, shamanic healings, and even blessing the odd field. Hedgewitches will work in cultivated gardens and farmsteads, but often prefer time spent in the woods and other wild areas. They may very well be the only modern witches you can find tromping through ditches and vacant lots or even climbing out of a stinking culvert.

A cottagewitch, hearthwitch, greenwitch or kitchenwitch works mostly in her garden and in her home. A hedgewitch will practice largely in the home as well, but will likely spend more of her time gathering her herbs and practicing her craft in rural or wild places than many other witches. A cottage or hearth witch, greenwitch or kitchenwitch may use some trance or shamanic techniques in her practice, but has probably not received the call to shamanize. To shamanize is to be called by your spirits or the gods to become a shaman, to serve your community, spirits and Gods as a hedgerider. A hedgewitch has the *"fire in the head"* also commonly known in this Path as the Cunning Fire. A hedgewitch is *"one who knows."*

Although many of the traditions that a hedgewitch draws from have changed—after all, lore is lost and knowledge changes over the centuries— you will find most hedgewitches prefer to practice as close to traditionally as possible. Yet still in a manner practical for these modern times. Hedgewitches are very adaptable. You may find a hedgewitch casting a spell on a modern tractor that comes right out of a book on Cornish folklore, for an example. Another hedgewitch might play a drumming CD on his stereo while he performs a traditional rite to bring about a much needed weather change.

The typical deities of a hedgewitch, should she have any at all, will be the Witch Queen and the Master of the Craft. Not exactly the Wiccan Lord and Lady but close enough that many Wiccans feel comfortable taking up the work of a hedgewitch. Working with the Mighty Dead and their own ancestors is also a very important part of this Path. They will also work with familiar spirits, land and nature spirits, totems, their fetch and the like, all to assist in their work. Hedgewitches look to these spirits to provide bits of lost lore and also for inspiration.

Hedgewitches use herbal concoctions known as flying ointments, as well as shamanic techniques such as drumming and meditation, to induce altered states of consciousness. This is not something that hedgewitches take lightly, nor do they use such techniques and ointments as a short-cut to the Mysteries. They understand very well the dangers of this practice and enter into such rites and workings with eyes wide open. They will experiment with their ointments and techniques, often for years. They increase the potency gradually, rather than simply *"jumping in to the deep end."* Many foolish young pagans have done that, and then learned the hard way the consequences of such actions.

Hedgewitches often refer to shamanic journeys as *"Walking the Hedge," "Riding the Hedge," "Oot and Aboot,"* or *"Crossing/Jumping the Hedge."* They also have a tendency to spend much of their lives with one foot on either side of the Hedge, which makes them eccentric to say the least. It is said that being called to become a hedgewitch and then answering that call can make you a shaman, a poet or a madman, or some mixture of all of the above. Hedgewitches are known to be outspoken and to be less interested in fitting-in. They also will often see and experience things whilst Walking the Hedge that changes the way they perceive the ordinary world around them. Giving them different and often opposing views on everything from politics, to social rules to fashion sense.

A hedgewitch walks freely into *caol ait,* Gaelic for the *"thin places"* between one world and another. They learn not only to find such places, but how to use them effectively. More experienced hedgewitches can open them even when the Hedge is at its thickest between the Hallowed Feasts. The Hallowed Feasts are the holy days that fall between the solstices and equinoxes, and are often called High Days by modern pagans. The most well known of these days would be Samhain, or Halloween.

Spirituality in hedgewitches varies and depends on the individual; usually they look to their own heritage and ancestry. The only tradition hedgewitches typically follow is a reverence for nature, though some may come from a more formal pagan path originally. The majority of hedgewitches will also practice a form of Traditional Witchcraft, such as that which is based on the work of Robert Cochrane. More and more Wiccans are also taking up the work of a hedgewitch, perhaps because Traditional Wicca lacks a strong shamanic element. Hedgewitches commonly do practice some form of paganism, but many make no claim to any practice but that of hedgecraft or hedgeriding.

The main distinction between hedgewitchery and other forms of witchcraft is that hedgewitches have less interest in the heavily scripted and ceremonial aspects of some types of modern paganism and witchcraft. For they have a highly individual and often unique way of relating to life, spirituality, magick and Creation. A hedgewitch prefers the freedom and joyfulness of spontaneous workings that come from the heart. For the hedgewitch there is no separation between normal life and their magickal one, for their normal life is magickal. The Craft they practice strongly reflects this belief.

Hedgewitches do whatever comes naturally to them; they follow their instincts, and their heart. This does however charge the hedgewitch with the need to know themselves and their own hearts well. It also does not free them from the need to properly research and study. Rather it means each hedgewitch must work to achieve a balance of intuition and research, instinct and study, spontaneity and script.

Most hedgewitches do not cast circles in a Wiccan sense. They may either have other methods to mark sacred space, or not bother at all. After all, hedgewitches believe that all space is sacred. Some hedgewitches may Lay a Compass Rose or Plough the Bloody Furrow in their practice. But whether they do or not, and how exactly they go about it, will vary. With these methods hedgewitches attempt to *"dig down"* into the magickal, natural forces and energies of the Otherworlds and draw them into their working space. The center, usually marked by some symbol of the *axis mundi,* is the focal point and other directions lain out ritually. At the center a gap in the Hedge is created so that hedgewitches can interact with, or enter into, the Otherworlds.

These witches do not typically follow one particular moral code, but rather their own personal ethics and often some version of the credo to *"do only what is needed"* and to *"Know Thyself."* Until they can face who they truly are and who they wish to become, they cannot create a functional magickal and spiritual practice. Hedgewitches do not take up the Wiccan Rede of *"harm none"* for they understand that sometimes in order to heal one must do harm, and sometimes to harm is to heal.

Hedgewitches walk the Crooked Path, the path that winds and twists its way between the right-hand and left-hand paths, between right and wrong, between light and dark. Hedgewitches walk all borders and prefer the grey areas, having little interest in all black or all white magick or spiritual workings. The Crooked Path also refers to a path that twists and turns within a landscape, not a road that cuts straight through it and thus damages that very landscape.

Most hedgewitches use few synthetic objects in their spells and rituals. Their tools are typically very practical, such as a walking stick. Often they will use a stang, even pruning shears, and their tools are handmade by them as much as possible. Most hedgewitches use only what is needed, meaning they do not clutter an altar *(if they should use an altar at all)* with items that will not be actively used during a working or rite.

Hedgewitches usually study herbalism, wildcrafting, rootwork and wortcunning with gusto. They seek knowledge and understanding of the ways of nature, such as the cycle of the seasons and the wildlife and plant-life in their area. Hedgewitches may know how to grow herbs in a garden, but are more likely to study where and how they grow in the wild and how to gather them. They usually have a great deal of lore on trees and plant life, animals, and the wilderness in general.

Hedgewitches tailor their path to suit themselves. Some may focus on wortcunning, while others study midwifery, or focus on animal husbandry. Others may be well versed in healing with crystals. Many hedgewitches choose to be a jack of many trades, but a master of none or few. This means that a hedgewitch must learn wherein their own talents and abilities lay, also to accept their own limitations and not take on more than they can handle. Here again we find the need to apply the axiom *"Know Thyself."*

Hedgewitches are called to serve their communities, whatever shape that community may take, and will use their natural talents and the knowledge they have gained to do so.

While hedgewitchery is something of a solitary path, this is not always so. Some of their practices, especially the shamanic ones, require a trusted friend or group to watch over their body while their soul is elsewhere. Even the most hermit-like hedgewitch can still be found at the local pagan event now and then. Some may have friends or domestic partners who follow another pagan, heathen or witchcraft path, and they will often happily join in any ritual or activity if invited. Yet most hedgewitches may just be rebels and rabble-rousers; this is after all, an Outsider Path.

The daily spiritual practice of a hedgewitch will be adapted to her individual abilities, interests, and lifestyle. One hedgewitch may start his mornings offering up prayers of thanksgiving as he collects eggs from the chicken coop. Another hedgewitch may spend her mornings in quiet meditation on her patio; sipping tea and watching the deer graze in her lawn. A third hedgewitch may say a quick prayer at the household shrine before racing off to work. And a fourth hedgewitch spends his day fasting and preparing for a trip across the Hedge that night.

So what the heck is a hedgewitch anyway?

You may prefer rural or wild settings and may be a little wild yourself. You might be looking for a tradition that is adaptable and practical, one that combines *"old school"* witchcraft and a modern life. You may be seeking tradition that adds a focus on European-based shamanism and the practical application of folklore to the mix.

Are you looking for a tradition that leans heavily on natural magic, understanding the land and the practice of healing lore? Do you want a tradition that focuses on personal experience, experimentation and doing-it-yourself? Perhaps you wish to blaze your own Path, like the witches of old? You might just have that Cunning Fire burning in your head, heart and soul.

You may just be a hedgewitch.

> *The tenth Rune-spell I do know*
> *Is to gaze deep into the murky night*
> *And spy the hedgewitches flying high,*
> *Sending their spirits far and wide*
> *I see their true forms*
> *I can confuse their wandering souls*
> *Then turn them 'round and send them home*
> *Back into their bodies, back within their own skins*

Biography

My name is Juniper and I am a proud Canadian. I am closing in on thirty, but eternally youthful. I have been a farmer and a city girl, a homesteader and a gypsy. I have worked in animal rescue and occult shops, art galleries, liquor stores and bead shops. I hunt in thrift store jungles and gather in the wildwoods. I practice in groves and ditches, hedgerows and seashores, basements and vacant lots.

I wasn't raised in a normal family. I wasn't raised to be normal. I wasn't raised in the church. I wasn't raised to conform. I wasn't taught that women should be demure, modest, and wholesome. I wasn't raised to wear the same clothes as everyone else. I wasn't raised to drive the same kind of minivan as everyone else. I was not raised to be a sheep person. I was encouraged to wear socks that don't match if that makes me happy. I was allowed to wear my PJ's out in public if I wanted to. I was allowed to dye my hair purple and go to school in a tutu.

My name is Juniper and I am just a messy little hedgewitch who speaks her mind.

Between the Yard and Yonder: A Cosmology

Papa Toad Bone

The yard. The four squared world that our lives unfold within. Some people have large yards and others have small ones. Regardless of the size of one's yard, the function is always the same. One must keep back the wilds surrounding their yard from encroaching. The grass must be mowed, bushes trimmed back. In my part of the world, if one does not keep their grass down, and piles of debris out of their yard, one can expect to find a very large rattlesnake, copperhead or moccasin hiding, waiting for you to find it. In order to keep these creatures in their world and outside of mine, yard maintenance is of the utmost importance.

There is no hard and fast rule that one must cut back their yard, and keep its corners free and clear. By all means, let the grass grow, and in no time, trees will be growing, driveways busted by roots, spiders in your home. All around, entropy will flourish. But if safety is desired, then the yard must be kept.

Some people prefer the woods, and well they should. The woods are fascinating places, with all manner of hidden surprise and wonder. In today's world, camping and hiking are common past-times, with its enjoyment stemming from our primal roots, and revisiting them, in a seemingly safe way, is enough to satisfy our old fashioned urge to be out in nature. With its beauty, the wood also holds the same dangers that will creep in on the unkempt yard. Rarely do people need fear a wild animal in the safety of their clearing, but in the wood, man has left his safety net, and stepped in to the element of wild things. These things may not mean him intended harm, but in acting within their nature, they may do harm. Because of this, even when visiting the wild wood for recreation, one will clear a small yard, and use that most primal tool of ordering our world, fire.

Regardless what yard one might dwell in, it is a fact that once it was covered in wild growth, populated by wild animals, and organically rooted in a cycle that was growing and rotting since an unknowable beginning. Once these roots are dug from the ground, the timber cut down, and the animals banished to the borderland, a fruitful, safe world can be developed. It is also a fact, that one day, this safe haven of man will be taken over by the plants and animals that grow and prowl the wild wood surrounding, and sometimes breach the perimeter, testing their fate against the developed order. Much like the *Etin* race of Elder Lore.

The Gods, as illustrated in the many legends of old, built for us the first yard. Out of that great forest of potential, this primal clearing was cut and forged. It is the role of these first Gods, who defeated the great beings of the wildness, to defend the very perimeters that they set forth in those early days. Just as man today must do, with his own yard.

Some men never leave the yard, and hold with a clinched fist to the ordered, and day lit world of safety. This is as it should be. The Gods never intended for us to dwell outside of this yard. It is not our world. But, there are many who take advantage of our liminal existence, and step out into the wood, leaving, temporarily, the safety of their yard, for the adventure across the Hedge, and into the chaotic wilds from which the Gods molded the land, and set the stars on their paths.

Those who stay long in the yard run a great risk as well. This risk is their inability to see that the wood is there, and a necessary part of the dynamic that allows for their dearly loved yard to exist to begin with. These men, out of some unwise attempt to make things safe and happy, will take the rationale of the yard, and apply it to the whole. They believe that since the yard is safe, then everything should be in it. This is not so. Without the wilds to support it, their world would swiftly wither and die away.

As those who are yard bound cleave to their clearing, there are those who would rather eschew the yard, and embrace those beings of entropy and wilderness, hoping to be welcomed among them. They quickly find out that the gifts of the yard do not carry over into this world. There is no control over their food supply, no great shelter. Nothing will ever be theirs, safety most importantly. They will find the world that they sought, sure, but their life will be severely cut short. Just the same as one leaping the Hedge and staying to long. Leaping or not, this condition is called death, by the living.

In normal, day to day living, out of safety, yard dwelling is a must. Even the sorcerer must take precaution so that they can go about the day, working, running errands, taking a walk, etc. It is a good thing to regain the confines of the yard to go about these normal undertakings, lest one become too out of touch with the ordered world, and become incapable of doing the most mundane of tasks. Wearing of symbols of order, from the Latin cross to the swastika, protect one from the otherness they may have opened themselves up to. Crossing oneself, regular cleansings to remove the conditions that build up from this vocation of ours, and even clearing the home with sweeps and washes are recommended. Anyone who seriously jumps the Hedge knows the danger that one runs by doing so, and would agree that precautions must be taken to keep our worlds separate, as they should be.

Outside the Yard and What You Find There

Anyone who has ever been in a deep wood, a swamp, or even a desert, knows how far away from the world of roads, lights, squares, and steeples one can be by simply taking a short walk outside the yard. If you are more than an hour's walk from the confines of our civilized world, you are closer to death than you may realize at the time. If you were bitten by a snake, away from the roads, with nothing but the thick between you and help, you may not survive. Imagine being that close, yet so far away, from not only a road and a hospital, but the entire world of light and living. As dangerous as the deep swamp can be, the dark watered otherside is unfathomably more so. There you will not find snakes of flesh and cold blood, or hard skinned alligators, beady eyed possums. You will find unearthly, unlit shades of these beasts of the bog, where every fear that man has ever had dwells, waiting for manifestation as bedside monsters.

Everyone will walk through this macabre terrain one of these days, or as the fatalist knows, one of these *"nows."* When you cross over, by way of intention, or unexpected demise, you will find a dark road, like the ones of dirt you find cutting through a Mississippi cotton field, where shadows dance and change shape, unformed thoughts hide in the distance. If you meant to be here, you must be insane, and if you find yourself there unexpectedly, you are in for a long journey, that may be terrible, or beautiful.

As I have mentioned, this Underworld is filled with every terror, but is also filled with every joy. These things are found in the same place, but it is through awareness that the difference is perceived. Not in the cliché of one making their own heaven or hell, but in that you only see what you are capable of seeing. What was at a moment a twisted horned devil can become the light bearing angel that will redeem you from hard Fate. The cold waters can either sweep you away, or make you new again. It is through awareness, and the clarity of awareness most importantly, that will keep you from becoming overwhelmed by this River Styx that is the truest bounds between our world and the other.

If you fall into these waters, clinging to the illusion of your separated ego, you will find yourself slapping furiously at cold deep waters, and will forget all that you ever had hoped to retain. Essentially, your precious ego will be swept away, out of your hands, and washed down deep into the knots and roots of that great cosmic tree. With the proper clarity, however, you will flourish in these great waters of potential, without panic, but rather with calmness. You will not be swept away into the darkness of potential, manifesting without your being aware, but will instead experience all that could ever have been, while retaining the awareness that you are aware. You will *"be one"* with everything in either occurrence, but only one way will you actually *"know"* it.

Clarity of awareness is essential to jumping the hedge. In Robin Artisson's excellent work, *The Witching Way of the Hollow Hill,* there can be found everything one needs to develop and nourish this gift, that we all have. These exercises are beyond needful. It is a must that one, regardless of source, finds a way to develop their awareness of their world, and how to maintain a clear vision of it. To let down one's protective veil, yet not be inundated with stimuli to the point of being overwhelmed, takes great practice. Some are more prone to it by nature, and have a bit of a head start, but everyone's clarity can become greater that it is already. In this case, as they say, every little bit helps.

Potential and What is Between

What one really finds when jumping the Hedge, and manipulates when working conjure, is the world's potential. The great river mentioned earlier flows both to and from a mighty wellspring. Everything that is, was or will be, comes from and returns to this well. Like the oroborous, it can not be said whether it is consuming or producing, and is in an ever present state of both. In every *"now"* we stand at this liminal place between the ever becoming. This well is the Well of Potential, that is at the deepest root of the Underworld. Every action in the manifest world goes back into this well to produce the next manifestation. This is illustrated in the World Tree with the drops of dew keeping the well full with water, so that the roots of the tree can drink from it. This reciprocal dynamic was called *"ghosti"* by the Indo-Europeans.

When working conjure, or leaping the Hedge to work directly at the source, one is making a focused, willed attempt to manipulate the materials that Fate has to weave with. By acting in your now, with intent, and calling to you the powers sympathetic to your desires, you are in effect changing the past in order to manipulate the future. Everything in the well is past and future, with now being the middle result of these potentials. The past is simply that which we have become aware of, and the future being that in which we haven't. They are both in the ever becoming, and have never truly existed as something separate from each other. In the Underworld, in its holy timelessness, there is no past, present or future. There exists all at once, with everything that ever *"has"* or *"will"* being *"is."*

When one experiences the Otherworld, either in trance or awake, one is simply becoming aware. It is not that something is not there, simply because you are not yet aware of it. This is the explanation behind many *"haints"* that people experience. As everything is happening in the now, and awareness of it is the only veil between, then all of time occupies the same space. Therefore, when one walks into the parlor of a Victorian home, and hears the clank of dish and spoon, music and chatter, with spectral guests, it is not the ghosts of the dead one sees, though granted, these folks are surely *"dead"* now, yes? What they are experiencing is a glimpse into a seemingly by-gone event. It is no more by-gone to them than your now is by-gone to you. Whereas you see an entire party of ghosts, perhaps even having a séance, they see a solitary phantom, standing before them, possibly as affright as they themselves are.

This is the layer between now and then, here and there. There is no separation between worlds, truly, for the separation exists only in our perception of the world. If you peel back this veil, a needful veil at that, you will see the world in a whole new way. To quote Blake's *The Marriage of Heaven and Hell*, "*If the doors of perception were cleansed, everything would appear to man as it is, infinite. For man has closed himself up, till he sees all things through narrow chinks of his cavern.*"

One must remember that all of the things of the yard are in place for due reason. If it were not there, well, there would be no living thing to even worry with it. The Gods created the yard for the living, and separated it from the world of the dead. It was this chaotic outside that our world was created from after all. If you find the church pew a comfort, then by all means, sit there. If you find safety in the daylight, then bask in it. If you find protection behind a cross, then hide in its shadow. But, if you, like the rest of us, are a little off kilter, and feel the urge to plunge deep into the mysterious otherness, then go about your business under the sun, in like fashion, but when the sun sets, and Old Night returns, then it is *"horse and hattock, away we go."* Just be sure you go prepared. Be Well.

Biography

Papa Toad Bone is a South Mississippi native who grew up along the Gulf Coast. His magical journey began as a teenage in New Orleans, where he still goes on the occasional pilgrimage, to visit ancestor burials, burn candles, and seek out new contacts, living and dead alike. He is the proprietor of Toad's Bone Apotheca, a teacher, writer, and Magister Cassuc, Summoner to the Heth-Bucca, of the Red Thread of Heth.

Italian Witchcraft
and the In-Between Places

Raven Grimassi

In the old forms of Italian witchcraft, practices are associated with the night, the moon, and the stars. In particular the night of the full moon is the realm of shadows, night shadows (*as opposed to shadows in the daytime*). Just as there are *"shadows"* on the face of the moon, there are shadows on the Earth as well when the moon is full. These are considered to have power and to be associated with spirits of the night. It is on the shadow's edge that the witch performs magical rites.

Ancient philosophers such as Plutarch and Plato mention the shadows on the moon and refer to them as the caverns of Hecate or Proserpina. Plutarch wrote about the souls of the dead being drawn in to the moon where they abide for a time and are then reborn on the earth. The circle of the moon in the night sky symbolized the cycle of rebirth and the dwelling place of certain souls.

In the tradition of Italian witchcraft that I practice we have an oral teaching that a ritual circle traced upon the ground, beneath the full moon, becomes the counterpart of the moon. To enter this circle is to enter the moon on Earth. In this realm one can commune directly with the dead, spirits of the Otherworld, and deities linked to the lunar realm.

The ritual circle of the moon is a place between the Earth and the moon in the night sky. It touches the three known realms of existence: the Overworld, Middleworld, and Underworld. Each of these, and their inner mysteries, is symbolized by a colored cord. The Overworld cord is black, the Middleworld cord is red, and the Underworld cord is white. Traditionally these cords are tied together with three knots, one near each end and one in the center. This is known as the Witches' Ladder (*in its simplest form*).

The Witches' Ladder serves as an inner planes device that is worn or carried as a talisman. It connects the witch to forces that are linked to mystical themes. It declares the bearer as one who can traverse the realms. In Italian witch lore, the witch rides to the Sabbat *(in Italian it is known as the Tregenda)* on the back of a goat as opposed to traveling on a broom. The latter is more typical of northern European witchcraft legends. Both are metaphors for the passing between the worlds.

The Witches' Ladder is, in essence, an alignment to the *in-between* principle within occult philosophy. It is a tangible link to the momentum of the past. This teaching tells us that when something is done in the way it has always been done, a wave of energy rises and moves from its memory to its stimulus. Activating the ladder calls forth the dynamic power of this metaphysical principle.

To activate the ladder, simply press the center knot between the thumb and index finger of the left hand. Become aware of the navel area and take in a deep breath, hold it for a moment. and then exhale. Release the pressure on the knot. Then repeat the sequence again with the bottom knot, but this time bring your attention to the genital region. Lastly, do this again with the top knot, focusing on the forehead.

To complete the process, cup the cords in your hands between both palms, and raise them from genital area to forehead while singing the vowel sounds E-A-O. Stretch the sound out: *eeee-aaaa-oooo*. Find your own note or key, but use a rising tone *eeee-aaaa-oooo* as you sing. Following this, you can perform mental journeys or guided pathwork. During such times you can carry the Witches' Pouch with you.

The Witches' Pouch

Just as the Witches' Ladder is an alignment to power, the Witches' Pouch is, as well; but, in addition, it serves as enchantment on the mind, body, and spirit.
Exercise One:

The Alignment Pouch

Required items:
3 fava beans
1 sprig of rue herb, or dried leaf
1 small vial of oil *(natural plant/flower scent)*
1 pinch of salt
1 red pouch

Assemble the following items and place them in a small red pouch: rue *(herb)*, salt, oil, and three fava beans. All of these items feature prominently in Italian witchcraft. On a mystical level, salt represents the mineral world beneath the earth. Salt is the crystallized essence of the secrets that reside in the Underworld. In this regard salt is connected to the ancestral memory, and its inclusion on the family table is no coincidence. In old Italian culture the act of offering salt displayed closeness, familiarity, and in this context demonstrated affection. Such are the type of bonds that tie the generations together.

In your pouch, the rue herb is the center of alignment. Charms symbolizing rue appear as early as the ancient Etruscan civilization. They are most frequently used for protection. Rue also has a long association with the goddess Diana in Her triple nature. As such She was known in ancient times as *Trivia*. The natural division of the branches of the rue plant symbolizes the triple nature of Diana. This made rue of special importance to witches, and in time the witches' charm known as the *cimaruta* came into being. The charm is shaped like a sprig of rue and it bears sacred symbols to declare the wearer as one who follows the triformis Goddess: Hecate, Diana, Proserpina.

The oil is derived from plants, and its scent symbolizes the essence of the inner mysteries that the roots of the plant drew from Underworld. In other words, the scent conveys the mysteries to our senses.

The last items in the pouch are three fava beans. The fava plant has long been associated with wisdom and knowledge in its connection with the ancestors. Fava beans were used for divination, and the dark marking on the bean was said to be its mouth. Through this the ancestors were said to whisper when called upon.

To begin working with the alignments, take out the items from your pouch and lay the pouch flat before you. Next, arrange the items on the pouch so that you can see them clearly. Use the following alignment exercises:

Rue Alignment:

Place the piece of rue on the palm of your left hand. The left hand is the hand of receiving. Recall that since ancient times rue has been connected to the Goddess Diana as a triformis deity. By connecting yourself to the rue, you in turn connect yourself to the Goddess and Her ancient rites. Through the rue alignment, you join yourself to the spiritual lineage of witchcraft.

To establish your connection, recite the following while holding the rue:

This charm I hold of sacred rue,
its power always ringing true.
The past and present do I embrace,
and meet as one in sacred space.
The Triple Goddess of moon and night,

I join myself to ancient rite.
In light and shadow I fix my gaze,
a follower of the ancient ways.

Salt Alignment:

Place the salt on the palm of your left hand. Recall that since ancient times salt has been connected to the mysteries and magic of the Underworld. By connecting yourself to the salt you, in turn, connect yourself to the secrets of the Underworld. Through the salt alignment, you join yourself to the spiritual lineage of witchcraft.

To establish your connection recite the following while holding the salt:

This salt that slept beneath the soil,
drawn and brought by human toil.
Memories within the deep dark sleep,
revealed to all whose mysteries seek.
The purity of these crystals tell
of power to guard the circle well.
All phantoms flee for you they dread
not to remain where you are spread.

Oil Alignment:

Place the vial of oil on the palm of your left hand. Recall that since ancient times oil has been connected to magic and ritual. By connecting yourself to the oil, you in turn connect yourself to the essence of ancestral wisdom and knowledge. Through the oil alignment you join yourself to the spiritual lineage of witchcraft.

To establish your connection, recite the following while holding the oil:

From meadow, garden and forest deep,
The essence of all to blend and steep.
Secrets of the Old Ways this oil does bear,
lifted and carried upon the warm sacred air.
Potion and tincture each in their way,
call dark sacred night and bright blessed day.
The powers arise to grant magical boon,
to the kindred of sun and mystical moon.

Fava Alignment:

Place the beans on the palm of your left hand. Recall that since ancient times the bean has been connected to things that are hidden in the Underworld. By connecting yourself to the beans you in turn connect yourself to the hidden mysteries of the Otherworld. Through the bean alignment you join yourself to the spiritual lineage of witchcraft.

To establish your connection, recite the following while holding the beans:

Ancient's the memory of this sacred bean,
blessed by the power of Underworld Queen.
The ancestors whisper their mystical song
to the world of the living from a realm far beyond.
The roots of the plant entangle and bind,
the rites and the wisdom that travel through time.
Generations are joined to all that has been,
in the world of the living and the one in-between.

Once all of the alignments have been activated then your pouch becomes a tool that connects your to the inner mechanism of witchcraft. This means that you possess a power pouch that helps keep you in alignment. Put it under your pillow when you go to bed to enhance dream work or have it on your person while engaged with pathworking. You can also have it with you when performing ritual or magic. Your alignment pouch is an intimate link, and ideally no one else should ever touch it. Keep it special to yourself.

Next we will look at mental or spirit travel. The ladder and pouch should be with you on your journey. The following pathwork is among the first ones provided to the seeker. The idea is to connect to the momentum of the past through memory-chain association. Such techniques can open beneficial and empowering occult centers in the mind, body and spirit. But the seeker must be prepared to encounter light, shadow, and darkness. Without them there is no balance. Balance is found at the sacred where the three worlds meet. To go there we must fly.

The Witches' Flight to Benevento

The traditions of Italian witches are very old. Among them is the theme of spirit travel to the legendary walnut tree. The walnut tree is sacred to deities of the night and shadow. In Benevento, the tree stood at the site of the Grand Sabbat gatherings, to which witches from many regions were said to travel. At its core such legends speak to realms between the worlds of mortal kind and spirit beings. Techniques did, and still do, exist for crossing over into the hidden land. Although some things have changed, some things remain the same. The ways of the witch are ever ancient and ever new.

The tales of witches flying to the Sabbat at Benevento and gathering at the walnut tree are things of an astral nature. The word astral means "star-like," and it is noteworthy that in the earliest tales of witches they call upon the stars while performing ritual and magic. This appears in the invocations of Medea, and the incantations used by Canidia to draw down the stars:

> *Diana, who commands silence*
> *when secret mysteries are performed,*
> *I invoke you.*
>
> *Night, faithful keeper of my secrets,*
> *and stars who, together with the moon,*
> *follow on from the fires of the daylight,*
> *I invoke you.*
>
> *Hecate of the three faces,*
> *who knows all my designs,*
> *and comes to help the incantations*
> *and the craft of the witches,*
> *I invoke you.*
>
> *Earth, who furnishes witches with powerful herbs,*
> *and you Breezes, Winds, Mountains, Rivers, and Lakes,*
> *and all the gods of the groves*
> *and all the gods of the night,*
> *be present to help me.*
> *Proserpina, night-wandering queen,*
> *I invoke you.*
>
> *Hecate, Diana, Proserpina,*
> *look kindly now upon this undertaking!*

The five-pointed star is also a popular symbol connected to witchcraft. In this light we see the star as a gateway to *"other-worldness"* – a portal that allows us to slip between the barriers that confine reality to a material world experience. The *"in-between"* places have always been associated with the practices of witchcraft, for this is the access point to non-material reality. Crossroads in particular have been the special place for the gatherings of witches.

In Italian witchcraft, the crossroad is the also the gathering place for the spirits of the dead who have not moved on to the spirit realm. The goddess Hecate presides at the crossroads and is the gatekeeper. To gain passage between the worlds we place offerings to the dead and offerings to Hecate.

The classic and time-honored offering to the dead is spelt grain and some red wine mixed with milk and honey. A timeless offering to Hecate is the meat of a pig. These should be placed on separate plates or in separate bowls. If possible, the offerings should be set at the crossroads at midnight. Once offered, you then ask that the portal between the worlds be opened to allow you safe passage and safe return.

To begin the journey requires an altered state of consciousness. This can be produced with alcohol or some other substance in conjunction with the following technique. Mark out a five-pointed star on the ground, oriented so that you are facing west. At each point, set a candle. In the center of the star, place a key *(preferably a skeleton key)*.

Light all the candles and then gaze at the key in the center of the star. As you look at the key blow gently across the flames of the candles three times and then say the following words, repeating the process three times:

> *Sotto aero e sopra vento (sow-toe air-o a so-prah-vent-oh)*
> *Sotto acqua e sotto vento (sow-toe ack-wah a sow-toe vent-oh)*
> *Menami a la noce Benevento (May-nah-me ah no-chey ben-ah-vent-oh)*

English translation:

> *Under the air and over the wind*
> *under the water and under the wind*
> *lead me to the nut [tree] of Benevento*

Immediately following the last repeated phrase, your third and final time, pick up the key in your left hand. Close your eyes, take in a deep breath, and then exhale slowly. As you exhale, see the five-pointed star as a doorway that swings open to offer passage. Allow your breath to carry you into and through the portal.

See the stars in the night sky and feel yourself moving through them. See the land below you as you move over fields and woods. There is a clearing lighted by torches where a large tree stands alone. Descend to this place below by cupping your hands at the forehead and lowering them slowly to your chest and then your genital area. You come to rest at the sacred walnut tree of Benevento.

See a banquet table set with food, and then sit at the table. Others come and sit at the table. Observe the feast taking place and join in. This is the essence of the mysteries, the secrets of the seed that is the harvest returned in grain again. Sit and observe for awhile.

See a procession of torches coming. Rise from the table and follow the lights. Figures accompany you as you walk. In the distance there is a throne set by the great walnut tree. The torch light falls upon the throne and you see the black goat seated on the throne. There is a lighted torch on the crown of his head, flanked by his two powerful horns.

See your banquet companions gather in a circle with you. Feel the dance begin; move you head sideways, back and forth. Rhythmically trace a "S" in the air with the movement of your head, and then reverse and trace it backwards. Do this for awhile until you feel ready to stop *(you can enhance the dance by moving your arms in "S" patterns as well)*. When you feel ready to stop, take in a deep breath, hold it for a moment, and then release. Repeat this three times.

See the black goat again. A person stands behind the goat. The person leaves the goat and moves toward you carrying a reed basket. See the basket set in front of you. Open the lid and see a fig inside, which is the symbol of the hidden mysteries. Take the fig and press it to your lips in a sacred kiss. Then eat the fig *(you can have a real fig for this step, or simply imagine)*.

Sit quietly for a few moments and observe. At some point you will be ready to leave the experience. When it is time to return, see the five-pointed star in front of you, appearing as a portal. Say the following words:

Sotto aero e sopra vento (sow-toe air-o a so-prah-vent-oh)
Sotto acqua e sotto vento (sow-toe ack-wah a sow-toe vent-oh)
Portami via da Benevento (port-ah-me vee-ah dah Ben-ah-vent-oh)

English translation:

Under the air and over the wind
under the water and under the wind
take me away from Benevento

Take a deep breath in and then exhale, long and slow. As you exhale, allow your breath to carry you through the star portal. Once through the doorway, cup your hands at the genital area, and then move them to your chest and up to your forehead. Rise up into the starry night.

See the stars in the night sky and feel yourself moving back home through them. See the land below you as you move over fields and woods. See the familiar sight of your neighborhood. Descend to this place below by cupping your hands at the forehead and lowering them slowly to your chest and then your genital area. You come to rest back where you started from in your journey. Physically touch the ground with both palms flat against it. Affirm that you are back and fully conscious in the material realm. Have something to drink and a small snack.

You can return to the tree at Benevento anytime by using the described techniques. Experiences will differ from time to time. They will not always be pleasant, which is a sign of successful pathwork. The value of the Benevento journey is that it can take you to a realm wherein you can connect with things that can transform you. The walnut tree at Benevento is not an imaginary place or an astral setting. It is a folkloric realm existing in the fabric of magic itself.

To journey to the walnut tree is to awaken the primal conscious through which the ancient forms reconnect. It is a return to the Old Ones known to our ancestors before the world was reshaped by human minds. In ancient times the serpent was venerated at the site of the tree. The serpent has always been the revealer of truth, the enlightener, and the guardian of the seed of light. The seed that lies under the protection of the serpent gives way to the grand harvest. Thus are the cakes and wine featured at the Sabbat banquet. For it is here that one comes to know that within, which is of the eternal Gods.

The inner teachings of the seed are reflected in the following prayer used in my tradition in preparation to the Sabbat supper:

"Blessings upon this sacred meal,
which is as our own body.
For without this, we ourselves would perish from this world.
Blessings upon the grain,
which as seed went into the earth where deep secrets hide.
And there did dance with the elements,
and spring forth as flowered plant, concealing secrets strange.
When you were in the ear of grain,
spirits of the field came to cast their light upon you,
and aid you in your growth.
Thus through you we shall be touched by that same Race,
and the mysteries hidden within you,
we shall obtain even unto the last of these sacred grains"

To Be Taught in Dreams

One of the key tenets in my tradition is the belief that we are taught in the dream state. This belief is tied to another regarding two equal components of our consciousness: the conscious mind and the subconscious mind. In my tradition we call the conscious mind the guardian mind, and the subconscious mind is called the dream mind. The role of the guardian is to deal with the finite world of material existence. The role of the dreamer is to deal with the limitless potentiality of non-material reality.

In dreams we can do things that are impossible in material reality. We can breathe underwater without gear, we can fly without machines or devices, and objects can transform in our hands and all around us quite unexpectedly. This is the realm of all possibilities and all potentials. This is the definition of magick itself.

In material reality, the *guardian mind* dismisses or argues against anything that doesn't agree with material reality. It analyzes, debates, judges, organizes and resolves. It accepts the limitations of material reality. The guardian mind keeps us from fully understanding the dream mind.

It is for this reason that the Gods and spirits teach us in our sleep. Here we can accept anything and everything as part of the experience we are having. There are no limits to what can happen and what can be accomplished. It is here that we truly encounter the creative power of the divine spark within us that religions call a soul or inner spirit. The *dream mind* does not reject experiences or try to explain away the incompatible. The dream mind integrates all that it encounters. Therefore it is in the dream state that we are most open to the metaphysical and to the greater truths of non-material reality.

I will close now with a prayer that is used in my tradition. It is a call to be taught in the dream state. The prayer is part of the full moon ritual, and the full moon is the symbol for the dream mind in its fullness, just as the sun represents the guardian mind its fullness, as well. Here is the prayer:

"O' Great Night Queen, Queen of all witches,
hear our songs of adoration.
Hear our voices when we speak your praises.
Receive our words as they rise heavenward
upon the smoke of our incense,
when the Full Moon brightly shining
fills the heavens with your beauty.
See us as we gather before you,
when we reach our arms up towards you.
When the Full Moon shines upon us,
give us all your divine blessings.
O' Great Goddess of the Moon,
Goddess of the Mysteries of the Moon,
teach us your ancient mysteries,
ancient rites of invocation
that the Holy Strega spoke of,
for I believe the strega's story;
when she spoke of your shining glory,
when she told us to entreat you,
told us when we seek for knowledge
to seek and find you above all others.
Give us power, O' Most Secret Lady,
to bind our oppressors.
Receive us as your children;
receive us though we are earthbound.
When our bodies lie resting nightly,
speak to our inner spirits;
teach us all Your Holy Mysteries.
I believe your ancient promise
that we who seek your holy presence
will receive of your wisdom.
Behold, O' Ancient Goddess,
we have gathered beneath the Full Moon
at this appointed time.
Now the Full Moon shines upon us.

> *Hear us.*
> *Recall your ancient promise.*
> *Let your glory shine about us.*
> *Bless us, O' Gracious Queen of Heaven"*

You may incorporate this prayer into your own full moon rite. Feel free to modify it as needs be. If you are sincere in being taught in the dream state, your call will be heard. In time you will find that you know things you didn't know before. The dreamer will speak through the guardian, and the two separate halves of your consciousness will join as one in common cause.

Biography

Raven Grimassi is a Neo-Pagan scholar and award-winning author of over twelve books on Witchcraft, Wicca, and Neo-paganism. He's a member of the American Folk Lore Society and is co-founder and co-director of the Crossroads Fellowship *(formerly the College of the Crossroads)*. Raven is currently directing Elder of the Arician tradition of Witchcraft.

His background includes training in Italian Witchcraft, as well as several Wiccan systems such as Pictish-Gaelic Wicca and Celtic Traditionalist Wicca. Raven also studied with the Rosicrucian Order, as well as a study of the Kabbalah through the First Temple of Tifareth under Lady Sara Cunningham.

The Bird-Foot Goddess and the Werewolf God

Veronica Cummer

Midnight and still. The stars seem to stand frozen in time, and the snow gleams faintly by moonlight. Suddenly, a shadow swirls past the stars and the moon appears to dim. There's a rush of damp, cold air, sweet and sour together, and with it comes fear and a sense of the sheer fragility of flesh, of just how near to death we are at all times. Sensation tightens, sharpens, and you are never so alive as in that moment when the darkness rushes by, carrying with it the sound of hounds and half-heard voices, of shrieking and wailing. Bearing with it, half-seen forms as though riding on shaggy beasts and too-tall horses, on poles and ragged broomsticks, on spinning wheels and wolves and cats with hands instead of paws, and on milk-pale deer crowned with wreaths of woven thorn and decaying leaves.

And then it is past, gone like a dream, and you are left alone in the night, left shivering and shaking, the breath yet caught in your throat and your heart beating painfully fast. What just happened? Was it real or not real? Had you just experienced something that was an expression and reminder of life and ecstasy or something formed of terror and death? Something in or out of time or, somehow, somewhere in-between. No matter, it was and is the Wild Hunt.

The *Wilde Jagd,* or the Wild Hunt is known in many counties. It is associated with times of change and its troop may be said to made up of the dead, the Fey, witches, or those unfortunate enough to be swept up with it as it passes. Sometimes, a female figure leads the chase and sometimes a male figure. It happens around the transition points and is made up of the wild powers, the forces of nature, that which cannot be controlled by mundane means. It is the wilderness from beyond the Hedge, past the boundaries, impinging upon the material world.

The witches, the Fey, and the dead are all emblem of the outsider, of the supernatural beyond the knowledge and control of the human-made version of reality. This human world needs to both court and placate the powers of the beyond, the powers that it cannot easily contain. These forces are essential to the future and the well-being of the community and of the land, yet they can be dangerous and chancy to work with. That which can heal can also harm and so the Wild Hunt can bestow good luck and bounty or it can take it away.

The idea of the beneficial or dangerous outsider goes back to the beginnings of history. Perhaps, one of the first outsider Goddesses was Lilith. She has been, of course, dedicatedly demonized over the centuries, but once She was worshiped. She stares out at us yet from across the divide of the ages. She is flame and She is darkness. She is the First Wife, the First Mother. She is a furious one, a fury not necessarily of anger but of shrieking, impossible ecstasy. She is Queen of vampires and of witches, the seducer of dreams, the black-winged lady of storms and the keeper of oaths. Charms were made to protect children against Her coming for them in the night and yet She also knew the secret and most powerful name of God.

To be a creature of the wilds is to be outside the bounds of convention, or to at least have one foot in the outside. Lilith is a Goddess of the wilderness and mother to spirits, including those spirits which reside within the bodies of witches. Since we remain a part of Her, She can call our spirits out to fly to places in this world or in the Otherworld. She can summon us to the *"outside."* Witches are sometimes called weird, a word which springs from Wyrd. Strange, spooky, outside of the norm, outside of the boundaries, creatures of the wild and desolate, the unknown places. Lilith's places.

Lilith is associated with mirrors—to look into them gave the ability to see into Her realm since mirrors have long been considered doorways to other worlds, including the land of the dead. Still pools and wells hold reflections, as well, and are known to be gates to the Underworld. From this, we get the idea of scrying in black mirrors or bowls of water. To gaze into Lilith's mirror is to have the gift of Sight, to glimpse what lies beyond the mere physical world we all live in. Her mirror is also the moon, the same moon that the witches of ancient Thessaly seduced down from the sky in order to steal Her blood and work their arts. No one, not even the Gods, could stop them. The blood of the moon is Lilith's blood, the blood shared with Her witches.

Lilith is also linked to owls, cats, and serpents, witch creatures all. She may also be shown as a Sphinx-like creature akin to a harpy. She was connected to the *lamia*, a being sometimes depicted as half-bird and half-woman and or half-woman and half-snake. Some Medieval depictions of the seductive snake in the Garden of Eden have the face of a woman and that woman is Lilith. At other times, Lilith was both woman and flame, an attribute that She shares with the old Basque Goddess, Mari.

Indeed, like Mari, Lilith is wed to the great serpent-dragon God, and associated with the passage of storms, the same storms that may occasionally accompany the Wild Hunt. These storms *"impregnate"* the ground and make it fertile, giving rise to the growth of the red-capped mushroom of Otherworldly journey, the amanita muscaria, considered both a emblem of luck and of the Fey. A mushroom of ancient use in the shamanic practices of the North and in European witchcraft, it opens the doorway to the worlds beyond. Its elements can even be found in the old stories wherein people would put on red or white caps and abruptly vanish from sight, having gone *"flying."*

Like many later Goddesses of Europe and Their witches, Lilith has the power of shapeshifting and often chose bird-like forms. In some of Her images, she is depicted with wings or, at the least, sporting the feet of owls or other birds of prey such as the Zu-bird of ancient Sumer. But then Lilith's name comes from *lilitu*, *lil* meaning *"air"* in Sumerian. The *lili* were storm spirits, spirits of the wilds, and capable of causing disease and killing unprotected children. They were also associated with the night and seduction. Witches have long been connected with the same capabilities, especially the ability to travel on the winds of night. Italian witches are still associated with owls, turning themselves into *strigoi*, or screech owls in order to fly through the night.

Lilith is not the only Goddess that embodies the powers and aspects and, more so, the contradictions of the witch. As She is both bright fire and eternal night, seduction and terror, so the Norse Goddess, Hel or Hela, is half-alive and half-dead, half-black and half-white. The Goddess of the Winter Solstice, the Lussi, also has a night and day aspect to Her. She led a troupe called the *Lussifuda* through the air, one that was dangerous to encounter. The *"evil"* Lussi was called *Lucia diedunkle* and the fair Lussi, *Lucia die helle*. They represented the forces of chaos and darkness and order and light, and the Winter Solstice was definitely a time when those powers were in flux. To hold vigil that long night was to keep safe the last remnant of the light, and the world of order and community, until the Sun could return again. Over time, the Lussi became known as evil, while Her other counterpart, Her other Self, continued to be venerated as St Lucia or St Lucy.

But then many lands in Old Europe had their stories and myths of a female leader of those who ride the night. She has been called Mother

Berchta, Frau Holle, Holda, Nicniven, Selga, Herta, Herodias, Madame Oriente, Irodeasa, Diana, among many other names. Often, She was said to be the Queen of the Witches or the Queen of Faery and had the power to shapeshift into bird or animal forms and to be either old or young as She willed. She could be associated with storms and the weather, as well as with the wilds and the beasts of the wilds such as wolves and deer. She might bestow fertility and bounty or withhold it, very much a Goddess of birth and of death, a Goddess of two worlds. In particular, She was often linked with geese—the sound attributed to the Wild Hunt as it passed unseen through the night—and Mother Goose is a relic of these old, wild Goddesses.

Frau Holle would lead Her troop through the night and finally end up at the sacred mountain of the witches called the Venusburg or the Horselburg. Irodeasa was in command of the Fey known as the *Ielle* while the *Hulden* followed Mother Hulda. The women and Fey who followed Mother Berchta were called the *Perchten* or *Berchten* and could be helpful or harmful. Mother Berchta or Frau Faste was in charge of the Ember Days, one of the times that people would be called out of their bodies to fly in spirit to fight for the fields.[1] On Twelfth Night or *Perchtenacht*, people would dress up in fur and with horns and wear masks to both bless and cause fear the same as the Wild Hunt.

The land and the weather were at Their command as living embodiments of the natural forces and the future of the land and of the people who relied on that land were in Their hands. Snow was said to come from feathers escaping from Frau Holle's bed and the smoke off of Her hearth fire was mistaken for fog. The depths of the forest, the mountains, the caves and deep wells and pools might all be doorways to Her realm, from which She flew and to which She returned from the flight. And wherever this furious host flew, the community would be assured of a good harvest. For not only could the Goddess of the Hunt give plenty and fertility if She so chose, but the Fey and the witches and the dead who rode with Her also held the same power and were potential benefactors or destroyers.

Not to be outdone, Freyja led Her Valkyries, Her Volvas, those who wrapped themselves in feathers and catskin to fly elsewhere in spirit. Some stories hint at the Valkyries also having other shapes, calling them swan-maidens or even ravens. Surely, both the Valkyrie and the Volva are connected to the *flygia*, the shadow of the fate of each man which commonly takes the form of a woman or an animal. In ancient Thessaly, the only divinity that the Witches could not control out of all the Gods

---

1. Carlo Ginzburg, *The Night Battles: Witchcraft and Agrarian Cults in the Sixteenth & Seventeenth Centuries*, Penguin Books, 1985, pp 44.

was that of Fate Herself. The intimate connection between Witches and the Fey—the word Fey springing from fata, or Fate—shows that those who follow this path of flight and transformation are expressions of Fate and hold many of Her powers within themselves.

All of these Goddesses are related to the idea of treading the road between, the same road that carries you along the boundaries, making you half of this and half of that. Or, rather, allowing you to see what was there all along, both inside you and all around you. Finally, the picture becomes clear and you can see both the shadow and the light that casts it and know that one can't exist without the other. A Goddess who can both bright and dark, kind and cruel, old and young, alive and dead, is a Hedge-Goddess. She is if two worlds and this nature is reflected in Her followers, those who come to Her call and ride or fly out at night into the human land or into other worlds as Her followers.

The sense of excitement is akin to the nervous electricity in the air when a storm is coming and this is a storm in a way, a sign of transformation, of mingled creation and destruction. The Faery and the dead and the witches fly free in the night, sweeping the old world away before them and making way for the new. Not always a painless process, but a necessary one. For we are both flesh and spirit, fire and clay, and must not just reconcile the two, but learn to revel in it. How else can we become a bridge, a doorway for possibility to enter into the physical world, for the old powers to flow free. Riding with the bird Goddess, the bone Goddess, the feather and serpent Goddess, grounds us in the past and helps us usher in the future. We touch ecstasy in Her arms, pleasure beyond the ability of the flesh to hold, so that once you have felt it you can never forget it.

If this is truly the Goddess of original temptation, then what She tempts us with is *knowledge*. She gives us the chance to see what is otherwise Unseen, worlds upon worlds, past the restrictions of time and the physical senses. All She asks is that we open to our spiritual senses, to be free and to come dare the wild places, to taste of the fruit of knowledge and to not only consume it, but to be consumed by it. She asks us to fly with Her. She asks us to dare to not just leave our bodies, but our limited understanding of the workings of the world.

But it wasn't always a female figure who flew through the night and inspired ecstasy and terror and knowledge of the Unseen. At other times, the Wild Hunt was led by a male figure, most often by the God known as Odin or Wotun. Odin Himself is an enigmatic sort of God. He leads the Wild Hunt both in His capacity of a warrior and as a traveler, a God who goes between worlds. He sacrificed Himself upon the World Tree in order to gain knowledge, dying and being reborn much as any shaman must. In so doing, He became a God of neither here nor there, a God who can see into two worlds, another name for having the Second Sight.

The two wolves by his side, *Freki* and *Geri*, "ravener" and "greed," represent his war-like powers and *Hugin* and *Munin*, "thought" and "memory," are his traveling ravens, those could could go and bring back knowledge across all the worlds. In Nordic belief, He could change His shape from human to *hamr*, a non-human shape used to travel. This could entail wings and feathers or fur and animal skins. There was a clear relationship to the berserks who in their ecstatic fury were named *hamask*. But then Odin gave His powers to those who swore themselves to him, even if that was not always the safest road to take. The strength and ferocity of the bear and the wolf and other creatures were theirs to call upon. Like their God, they took on other shapes and could travel and battle in those shapes and, once they died, they joined the ranks of the *Einherjar*, Odin's sworn band of warriors.

Other male leaders of the Wild Hunt besides Odin/Wotan, included King Arthur, King Herla, Herne the Hunter, and the Harlequin/Hellequin or the Erl-King/*Erl-Konig*. King Arthur and Herne are said to ride out as a sign that England is under threat and so, clearly, are seen as protective spirits. Arthur springs from beneath the tor of the King and Herne from his oak tree and as they were in life, so they have remained in death and in legend. They lead the dead and the spirits of the land into battle to protect what is held as their responsibility.

The Harlequin—or Hellequin in French—is as complex figure as Odin. He leads a troop called *"la maisnie Hellequin,"* a crew of *"demons"* who chased after lost spirits. Not surprisingly, the black-masked or painted Hellequin was said to be the very messenger of the Devil, a suspiciously close tie to the idea of the Black Man of witchcraft fame. For the Black Man was also a harbinger of the *"Devil,"* and was even sometimes named as a title of the male leader of the coven. Quite possibly, the Black Man and the black mask of the Hellequin—and, indeed, the Wild Hunt itself—has links to the *Harii*, German warriors who painted themselves black and fought at night, fancying themselves to be the dead.

The Harlequin was frequently depicted wearing a melange of patchwork clothing, much like the mummers of old wore rags and tatters, an outfit that slowly evolved into the traditional bright diamond-patterned outfit still seen today. Often, he wore a cap that had feathers attached to it or the tail of an animal. He eventually became a fool figure, comedic and athletic, sometimes shown as a bit slow of wit, but who could also work magick when necessary. He was very much a trickster kind of figure, both King and Fool.

On the other hand, the Erl-King was seen as a lord of death, such as in the poem by Johann Wolfgang Von Goethe from 1782, when a boy sees the Erl-King, feels His touch, and dies for it. The Erl-Konig *(Elle-Konge in Danish)* is the king of the alder tree. Another name for the wren was the "erl-king" and the wren was traditionally hunted as a sacrificial victim at Yuletide. The *"elle"* is the alder and alder was sometimes used to make whistles to summon up the North Wind, the North sometimes being the place of the Gods and sometimes the land of the dead.

King Herla was also a wanderer from the land of the dead. He made a deal with a small strange man riding on a goat and ended up in the Otherworld for what he imagined would be but a short while. Unfortunately, as is often the case, when he returned from his sojourn in the Otherworld, he found that hundreds of years had passed since he had gone away and he was king no more. Instead, he became a leader of the Wild Hunt, a haunted and haunting figure, belonging to no world and yet capable to journeying the between realms.

What these figures have in common—the same as with Odin Himself—is their link between this world and the Otherworld. But then death is transformation, one form into another, as is birth. The power to shapeshift is dying to your old form and being born anew as another, if only for a while. Yet this sort of transformation leaves a mark.

Odin is the God of the hood, the shroud, the shadow, the tree, and yet He is also battle-fury, ecstatic rage, and had the ability to shapeshift for battle or for journey. He is a God who can loosen or bind magick of all kinds, including the greatest loosening and binding of all and that being of spirit to flesh. He is both an agent of and an opponent of Fate, traversing an uneasy boundary between chance and destiny as all shamans must. He is the wolf God who will, in His time, be consumed by the great Wolf, showing Himself to be both hunter and hunted, a God of two natures like those who followed Him. The *berserks* or bear-coats and the *ulfhethnar* or wolf-shirts can never go back to what they were before, not entirely anyway, after they have tasted the battle-fury and madness of the God. Part of them will always remain in the ecstasy, one with the beast.

Wolf-like beasts have long been seen as protectors of boundaries and guardians of the borders. The spectral *"black dog"* is one of these and another prime example of this is Cerberus, the three-headed dog who patrols the bounds of Hades, the Greek Underworld. The Etruscan God of the Dead wore the skin of a wolf and the story of how Rome came to be founded by Romulus and Remus, twins suckled by a she-wolf, clearly has some relationship to another old Roman God, Soranus. His followers were called the *hirpi*, descendants of wolves and protectors of the secret name of Rome, by which they kept the city safe. Odin was also said to have descendants who were both His children and the children of wolves, the Volsungs.

Like witches, the berserks were outsiders, yet they could serve a vital role in protecting the community. This protection came not just through the vehicle of battle against enemy armies, but also by fighting for fertility of the fields and the orchards. They were part of it, yet because of what they were and who they served they remained forever separate. Warriors, their brotherhood fought in body and in spirit. They were men of the noose and the spear point, of the shaman war-god, Odin or Wotun. They were men of the battle fury, the ecstasy that transformed them not just into terrific fighters who felt no fear nor pain, but into their *"beast."* They had great power and paid a great price for it, the same as their *"father,"* the All-Father.

The community needs protectors and who better then a predator to set against other predators, whether man or beast? Wolves turned into dogs and became companions and guardians. Men turned into wolves and became companies of warriors that could not only fight on the physical plane, but battle and protect across the planes. They didn't just take on the spiritual persona of wolves and bears, but in many ways became the spirits of wolves and bears in human form. Not so much donning the shape, physical or symbolic, of the beast, but allowing their true nature to shine through. At one point, witches were also said to transform themselves into wolves and were far more associated with them than hares and birds or even the traditional black cat.

A *vargr* was both an outlaw and a wolf, what can also be called a *wulfes heafod* or *"wolf's head."* They were also sometimes considered *"Godless"* men or fiends with ties to the *"Devil."* For example, in France, a boy named Jean Grenier was out in the woods when he met a *"black man"*—undoubtedly, the same one of witch fame—whom he called the Lord of the Forest. This enigmatic figure gave him an ointment and a wolf skin by which he could then transform himself into a werewolf, one both human and beast. He would change his *hamr* or garment of flesh.

The *eigi einhamir* were those who had two shapes or two skins. This was obtained via a special ointment or the donning of a skin or both as in the case of the French boy. The change into a wolf could so be accomplished by putting on a belt made of wolf skin or even the skin of a hanged man. In fact, the gallows where men were hung was sometimes even called the Wolf Tree. This clearly shows a link back to the power of Odin who hung on the World Tree to gain knowledge. As Odin was a shaman, someone who walked both the edge of the Seen and the Unseen and went beyond the bounds, as He was the *"outsider,"* so those who became werewolves were outlaws, those who existed beyond the bounds of the known world and of society.

The outlaw's tree, the tree of the wolf, was not just a sign of punishment, but one of sacrifice. Dead men were the *"fruit"* of this dire tree and they hung and died upon its branches the same as we each live and die upon the World Tree. They would fight and die to protect their lands and the people. Which doesn't mean that the outlaws, the bear-coats and the wolf-shirts, didn't sometimes do things outside the bounds that was bad for the community. Like all powers, the ability to shapeshift and to fight in a state of ferocious ecstasy could be put to good use or to ill. Just as wolves were sometimes considered dread enemies of humankind, so their cousin, the dog, was a necessary and beloved friend, protector, and companion. The berserks, like the witches, could use their talents and knowledge to help or to harm, the same as the old Gods.

The werewolves who protected and fought for the good of the community, the same as the witches who lived at the edge of the village, shared in the powers of the Gods and Goddesses of the wilderness beyond. To give and to take. To heal or to curse. To frighten or to seduce. To travel across time and boundaries otherwise impassable to mortal humans and there to meet with strange spirits and with the beloved dead, the Ancestors. To have the ability to change shape and to divine the past and the future. To speak sooth, the Divine truth of prophecy, and to propagate as needed between the people, the Gods, the land, and the Fey. To fight in the air or in other worlds for the fertility of the fields, the orchards, the beasts and the tribe or village itself.

The power of the werewolf, of the warrior, springs from that deep well, one that goes back millions of years. Odin, as the God with the ability to loosen bonds, could unfetter the chains of civilization and society, even of convention, and so He is rightfully lord of the wolves and of the werewolves. He is the First Fruit of the World Tree, the one who sacrificed Himself to be reborn as something other, to journey elsewhere and come back again with great gifts of knowledge and abilities beyond the norm. He became two-natured, a King and a trickster, a warrior and a shaman.

Shapeshifting, flying, seducing, with the ability to curse or to heal, the Gods and Goddesses of the troop of night reflect the same power of the witches and werewolves who came at Their command. Just as the full moon is said to cause the transformation of man into wolf, so the Moon Goddess calls forth the chosen to fly to far places, to the battle, to the feasting. As the Goddess could give life or take it, so Her witches had the same authority. They walked as She walked, between worlds and as a part of the cycle of nature. While those who were called by Odin, who sworn to Him, walked the dual nature of man and beast, partaking of both and belonging to no world and all worlds. They were both within and without the rules of law, the so-called *"natural order,"* by obeying an even greater and more mysterious natural order that had little to do with human rules. They could protect or they could consume, just as nature can give bounty or death.

These are all powers outside the pale, making those who bear them outsiders and dwellers in the unknown wilds, the desolate places, the Old Forest of myth and legend, the world of Faery. Half here and half there, a living bridge between two very different and yet intertwined worlds. This is the natural shamanism of the *wicce, hexa, bruja, berserk, striga, sorgin, volva*...the shared mystery of the night-flight and the transformation and the knowledge and power that it may bring.

In today's time, it remains to be fully acknowledged and accepted once more, its roads undertaken by those who have the courage and who hear the call. The White Ladies, the bright Goddess, the keepers of Fate and choosers of the slain, the half-dark and half-light Queen of the Underworld. The hooded lord and His wolves, the ancient hunter, the giver of the battle-fury and the power to be a predator in order to protect what most needs protecting. And, finally, the terrifying cavalcade of the dead, the Faery, and those who have passed from life to death and back again to become hedgeriders...they are all part of the secret, ancient landscape of Old Europe and England. They are part of the heritage of the Craft.

It lingers still, this great pool, this secret well, this hidden current of the Craft of Old Europe. To reclaim this heritage and once more be called out into the night by the Bird-Foot Goddess and the Werewolf God gives us back not only who were are, but why we are here. We fight for bounty and plenty. We mediate between the land and the living and the dead and the Gods. We are healers who also know how to harm, but strive to maintain the balance. We are servants of greater forces than our own, including that one of the greatest of all powers, Dame Fate.

The night beckons, the grand and glittering track arching across the sky, even as the old Bird-Foot Goddess whispers in our souls—arise, awake, transform, follow and be free. Even as the Werewolf God calls, come to me, change, unleash the power, the beast within. Its not simply that you know the proper nights, the nights that you are supposed to *"ride out,"* but that it begins deep inside you. The need growing stronger and more insistent until it becomes a demand that you can neither deny nor resist.

Like the Goddess and God who lead the Wild Hunt, it's a force of the between—past and future, old and new, life and death. While, the road that

They travel is the Veil, the hedge, the boundary, the hinterlands somehow neither quite here nor quite there. To follow is to travel upon the ley-lines, the veins that bear the life force of the land, and upon the corpse-roads, the paths of shades and shadows. It is to go out into the wilderness where Lilith yet rules and become as Her, blood and flame and wind and shadow. It is to die and be born anew, a sweet and bitter fruit of the tree that stretches from the heavens to the depths. The tree of wolves and witches.

Biography

Veronica Cummer has been a Priestess of the Old Forest Craft for more than 15 years. She has written two books published by Pendraig Publishing: *Sorgitzak-Old Forest Craft* and *Masks of the Muse*. Her articles and poetry have appeared in newWitch, the Beltane Papers, Pagan Ink, and The Crooked Path Journal, as well as the anthologies *Talking About the Elephant* from Immanion Press and *Datura* from Scarlet Imprint. Her writing has also appeared on-line through the website for the metaphysical store, Eye of Horus, and on MN Pagan.

She is currently at work on a follow-up book to *Sorgitzak*, when she's not busy doing rituals and teaching workshops on everything from charms to Faery to the shamanic witchcraft of Old Europe. She runs the yahoogroups community, *OldForestCraft*, and the Live Journal communities, *sorgitzak* and *hedgeriders*. Someday, she'd like to publish a book of poetry, a fantasy novel or three, and sell a screenplay. Other dreams include a whirl-wind tour of Europe—in particular, the Black Forest region—and the chance to stay for a month in some secluded house in the south of France in order to do nothing but sleep and eat and write.

To Ride By Night:
Mythology of the Nightriders

Eric de Vries

*I*n such an anthology as this one, in which many different points of view stand next to each other, it is important to state what you think hedgewitchery is about. So I will explain my basic view upon hedgewitchery. But my main goal is to excavate the mythology of the Night Riders, a cult of night-flying women known from all over Europe, and especially Germanic Europe. They used a specific set of symbols, leading into a specific *"form"* of ritual and mythology. The focus of this essay is to find this specific *"form."* But first, hedgewitchery itself.

Hedgewitchery is a form of *"shamanism,"* lacking a better word, originating with the Germanic peoples. As such, it is embedded within the culture and religion of the Germanic peoples, which deeply marked and marks the Eurasian peninsula. While the outer, socially accepted forms of Germanic religion were soon destroyed after the invasion of Christianity, a form of Germanic shamanism lingered on, eventually transforming in what we today call *"Hedgewitchcraft."*

Hedgewitchery, as the name itself already states, is about the *"witchcraft of the hedge."* This hedge is not a physical object per se, but a metaphor for a larger map of our world. The Hedge divides the world: inside and outside, village and wilderness, farm and forest. Basically, it is the distinction between the Inner and the Outer, the known and the unknown, the human and the Other. This Other can be found on many fronts, but its most important form is the Otherworld and its inhabitants.

Hedgewitchcraft is about the hedge, that is, the position between the worlds. The hedgewitch, or hedgerider, is a person who sits on the Hedge and can travel into either world. The hedgewitch is a human being who can travel into the Other, whether it is the realm of the Dead or the hall of the

Lady. This is what I mean when a say hedgewitch or hedgerider: a person who travels into the Otherworld by using myths, symbols and rituals from, or inspired by, Germanic religion. The hedgewitch and the story behind it is way more complex than this, but this definition is accurate enough to use during this essay.

What most people do not seem to realize is that hedgewitchery, as a living practice, died long ago. There is no physical, unbroken lineage going back to Germanic times—at least, I've seen no proof of it. This means that we, as people trying to reconstruct the practice of hedgewitchery, have to rely on historical records and scholarship, to find out what exactly hedgewitchery *was*. After we've reconstructed what it was we can start to think what it is, relying upon philosophy and mysticism. But first and foremost, we have to rely upon the *evidence*.

This evidence stems from a very specific area, the Germanic countries. Also, the evidence comes from a very specific time, just before or just after the Christianization of these countries. How to exactly define this period of Christianization is a difficult and sometimes controversial subject. Also the exact area that is Germanic, is a subject of controversy. But basically this time-place frame comes down to Western Europe and Scandinavia up until the fourteenth century. The evidence under investigation should be from this period.

To start with the evidence, the words relating to witchcraft. The Old English word *hægetesse*, Old High German *hagazussa* and Middle Dutch *haghetesse* all express the same, basic belief: that there are people who ride hedges, placing themselves between the worlds and thereby gaining supernatural power. Also, in Scandinavia, we find words for people who ride hedges or fences, the so called *turnriður (fence-riders, literally)*. These *turnriður* are mentioned in the Eddic poem *Hávamál (155)*:

> *I know a tenth one if I see witches [turnriður]*
> *playing up in the air;*
> *I can bring it about that they can't make their way back*
> *to their own shapes,*
> *to their won spirits*

> (Larrington 2008: 36)

This is the basic description of the *turnriður*, from which we can draw three conclusions. The first is that *turnriður* ride through the air. The second is that they night-ride "out of their skins." When Óðinn curses them, they can't find back their body, which means they're *outside* their body when night-riding. The third conclusion is that it is difficult, but good, to curse these women. This is obvious since Óðinn is bragging about magically killing them. If it was an easy thing to do, he would not brag about it. If it was a despicable, disgusting thing to kill them, he wouldn't brag about it either. So, this means that is a good, but most importantly a difficult thing to curse them.

Here, the source of this difficulty might be sought in their magical skill. *Óðinn* is also know to leave his body, which is mentioned as the art of *seiðr*, which relates in many ways to the concepts surrounding the cult of the night riders. Ironically, *Óðinn* is here killing those whose magical art is same to the art he practices. Whether he uses *seiðr* to kill the *turnriður* is impossible to know, but he is using magical songs, *gandr*, which can also form a part of a *seið*-rite. Either way, we know from the Icelandic and Norse sagas that many magical practitioners kill each other. It is, however, an interesting question whether *Óðinn* is using witch-magic here. Still, it is difficult to prove what it is he used.

A similar account is known from *Hárbarðsljóð*, stanza 20, where *Hárbarðr* tells about his ability to seduce night-riders. *Hárbarðr* is actually *Óðinn* in a different guise. He tells about the *myrkriður*, literally meaning night-rider:

> *Mighty love-spells I used on the witches,*
> *those whom I seduced from their men.*
>
> (Larrington 2008: 72)

This isn't a really descriptive account, and tells us little about the practices of the *myrkriður*. What it does tell us is *Óðinn* uses his claim of seducing *myrkriður* as a sign of potency. This means that he is able to influence the mind of these women so that they lust after him. Here, the fact that he can do this with *myrkriður* somehow enhances his claim to potency. If it were *"easy"* with these women than it wouldn't be so special, but if it were difficult with these women, it would. Also, we can establish a quality of *"power"* to the *myrkriður*, in the sense that they are powerful, for it takes a lot of *Óðinn* to conquer them.

A word relating to the *myrkriður* is *kveldriður*, which has the same meaning: night-rider. They are mentioned in an Eddic poem, *Helgakviða Hjorvarðssonar (15)*:

> *Atli I'm called, atrocious I shall be to you,*
> *I am most hostile to ogresses;*
> *I've often stayed at the dew-washed tree*
> *And tormented night-riding witches.*
>
> (Larrington 2008: 126)

Here, again, we see that there is a relation between the ability to kill or seduce a night-rider and one's magical capability. This means that night-riders are more difficult to seduce and kill than regular people, since they are the subject of bragging. One brags about the most difficult thing to achieve. From these three Eddic poems we can conclude that: *1) turnriður,* *myrkriður* and *kveldriður* travel through the air, *2)* in spirit shape, *3)* at night *4)* were skilled in the area of magic and *5)* were women.

But the night-riders and hedgeriders are mentioned in many more places than the Eddas. In the *Rättlösabalk* (5), an Old Norse law, we can find an account of hedgerider. Although the law doesn't mention hedgeriders or night-riders literally, it does paint a picture that screams hedgerider. This law prohibits the uttering of a specific offense, which is saying about a women that she rides the hedge in the troll-skin. Prohibiting such language tells us something very important about hedgeriders and night-riders; it is wrong to be one.

Here, the riding of the Hedge in the troll-skin is the basic format of the hedgeriding ritual. One positions oneself between the worlds, that is, on the Hedge, assuming the posture of the witch. Also, the Hedge might be some sort of stang, broom, or pole that functions as transportation to the other world. The troll-skin can take many forms, but in this case might be some sort of clothing and masking that changes the appearance of the witch into something non-human, something definitely "Other." The riding and the troll-skin will make the hedgerider go into the Otherworld, where she wanders amongst the trolls.

In Christian thought, and especially the post-pagan idea of a troll, is basically a demon, a nature-demon. However, in pagan thinking the world of trolls is *Utgard,* the realm of Giants and Chaos. They are the raw spirited powers of nature. So they are dangerous, for they are destructive, chaotic and *"evil"* if you accept the human order as *"good,"* but on the other hand they are not really moral, they simply *"are."* To the Christians and pagans alike, assuming the shape of a troll was the same as aligning oneself with the evil forces of *Utgard/*Satan. So this is why it is an offense to say that a woman is a hedgerider *(a witch)* and wears the troll-skin (Chaotic/satanic).

Although the *Rättlösabalk* has a negative conclusion about hedgeriders, it still describes the basic format of the hedgeriding ritual. First, one should take a ritual position *"between the worlds,"* that is, on the hedge. Second, one changes shape, assuming the *"troll-skin,"* transforming the hedgewitch into an otherworldly being. From this position, one can leave the body and journey through the air.

From various laws and accounts in the Icelandic sagas it appears to be a very serious accusation to call a woman a *myrkriður,* night-rider or night-flying witch. When Charlemagne Christianized the Saxons at the end of the 8th century he proclaimed that if someone burns a woman to death because she is a night-witch, he shall be killed. What is punished here are two things: a pagan belief in the existence of night-riding witches who eat people, and the burning of these women, that is, murder.

The complex of night-riders and nightmares is expressed in a Dutch poem called *De natuurkunde van het geheelal*. It still not clear who wrote the poem, but what is clear that is was written somewhere to the end of the thirteenth century. Lines 707-730 read (Hall 2004: 178):

About the night-riders, and about other
Devils, which make fire in the sky.
Devils, which are in the air,
and which often fright –
They also know well how to make fire
which seems here to us like torches,
which they shoot among themselves.
Many things are said therefore.

Night riders, they are called
and they are devils, that I tell you,
haghetissen, and wandering women,
goodlings [protective spirits] also,
indeed, cobalds, water-monsters, aluen,
maren, night-maren who make themselves known in
the morning, and know well how to get fire.

We call them night-maren
indeed, these are devils all,
who brought us eagerly to the Fall.
the Devil ponders night and day,
how they can lead us astray,
and bring us from faith,
and tests us with many things.

This account is a full description of the mythos of the *heksen* or *turnriður*. We will compare it to other materials from both Old Norse literature, continental *(Latin)* accounts, and medieval trials.

First of all we see the night-riders, the nacht ridderen, are comparable to the *myrkriður*. They are called the *"devils which make fire in the sky."* This fire in the sky is probably a metaphor for thunder and is also found in the word *?unorrad (OE)* which is the thunder-ride. It is a ride of supernatural women through the air, mostly at night, accompanied by thunder and heavy storms.

The ?unorrad is also found in the Old Norse corpus. In Njal's Saga it was said that there was continuous *ganðreið* all night, meaning it stormed heavily, but was also taken as a bad omen. Here we see an analogy as the word *ganðreið* was also used for a raging horde of women riding through the air on the back of wolves.

A *gandr* is a helping spirit but also is a magical projectile. Furthermore, means *"magic vehicle,"* as a special form of a magical projectile send out to hurt others. Here the *gandr* is a stick, a pole, an animal even, that carries the night-rider through the air. It can be compared to the English stang *(from Old Norse origin, meaning 'pole'),* and the general symbol of the broom, which sheds light on the actual symbolism of the stang and the broom: they were magical *"vehicles,"* bringing the witch from this world to the Other.

The linking of the term *gandr* with *reið* is not that strange, but it is very strange to think of the *gand*-ride as causing storm, being a kind of storm. It is, truly, a *"wild ride"* and can be linked to the Wild Hunt, a raging host of dead people riding through the air of the Germanic countries.

In Germanic mythology, the Wild Hunt played an important role. The Germanic peoples believed that during the Twelve Days of Midwinter, the sun was almost swallowed by two chaotic, gigantic wolves. The sun almost disappeared between the jaws of these wolves, which is why the days shortened. These Twelve days were an in-between time, a time when the gates to the Underworld were open and the chaotic forces were at full power.

Every year, it was a question whether the sun would come up. In Holland there's a saying that is at follows: *"the sun rises for free."* To the Germanic peoples, the sun didn't rise for free. The journey of the sun through the sky was a struggle, a struggle between the forces of Order and Chaos, Gods and Giants, Innerworld and Outerworld, Midgard and Utgard. It is during this short time of these twelve days that the forces of Chaos are strong, and are at the verge of destroying the Human Order within Midgard.

However, the Wild Hunt fought against these chaotic forces. In Norse mythology it consisted of the best of fallen warriors who are said to rise against the Giants at the Doom of the Gods. The Twelve Days were seen as a moment when this Cosmic Order was about to collapse. Only the soldiers of the Wild Hunt and the Gods stood between the forces of chaos and the Divine Human Order.

In contrast to the Host of Angels of Christian mythology, the Wild Hunt is not a pleasant sight. It is a terrible host, as they are a force of destruction themselves. They are dead. They are powerful. They are, quite literally, a terrible storm which purges the land and its people from the chaos of the Giants. By doing this, they make the sun rise again. Indeed, the sunrise isn't for free.

This *"wild ride through the night"* is also found in the Anglo-Saxon spell *Wið færstice*, which also describes the *hægetessa* as supernatural women riding through the air. On the continent the most important reference is the *Canon Episcopi*, dating to the late tenth century:

> *Some wicked women, who have given themselves back to Satan and been*
> *seduced by the illusions and phantasms of demons, believe and profess*
> *that, in the hours of night, they ride upon certain beasts with Diana, the*
> *goddess of pagans, and an innumerable multitude of women, and in the*
> *silence of the night traverse great spaces of earth, and obey her commands*
> *as of their lady, and are summoned to her service on certain nights.*
>
> (Kors & Peters 2001: 62)

Here we encounter a full crystallization of the witch-mythology in medieval Christian thought. We read of a large group of women who ride on the backs of animals through the night. This is the basic mythology of Germanic witchcraft. This account, describing the witchcraft of continental Europe, is largely analogue with the practices described in the Old Norse sources: women riding through the air at night. They leave their bodies in some spirit-form, as shown in *Hávamál* and the following account:

> *Have you believed that what many women, turned back to Satan, believe*
> *and declare to be true, such that you believe that in the peaceful silence*
> *of the night, when you should have been lying in your bed, and with your*
> *husband lying on your bosom, that you may be able to depart, in body,*
> *through closed doors, and that you pass lands' open spaces with others*
> *deceived by the same mistake...*
>
> (Corrector, ch. 5 ?170; ed. Hansen 1901, 40,
> taken from Hall 2007: 169).

Now we should return to the evidence from *De natuurkunde van het geheelal*, and especially the following lines:

> *They also know well how to make fire*
> *which seems here to us like torches,*
> *which they shoot among themselves.*

These lines allude to the idea that the *hægetessan* shot projectiles. These projectiles are paralleled in both the Anglo-Saxon and Old Norse corpus relating to witchcraft and magic. We already discussed the *gandr* which is plain and simple a *"magical projectile,"* and denotes *"an object used by sorcerers."* This magical projectile is described in the *Collections* (Wilbur 1959: 134).

Gann is a little body which is made up of small pieces of wood and which with the arts of magic can be sent off and always hits men and animals, be the distance ever so great sorcerers and sorceresses can avenge themselves when they *gannskyde* men and animals.

While a *gandr*, or a *gann* in this passage, is more than just a magical projectile it certainly is a magical projectile and it can be used to *"shoot"* people. This practice is also known from Anglo-Saxon sources, such as in the spell *Wið færstice*, *"against a stabbing pain,"* in which the *hægetesan* cause stabbing pains, possibly by *"shooting"* their *"missiles."*

In the *natuurkunde van het geheelal* the nightriders are linked to the *haghetisse* and a range of spirits and supernatural beings. First of all they are *nacht ridderen* and *haghetisse*, that is, night-riders and hedge-riders. They are called *"devils,"* perhaps suggesting that they were not that pleasant, but surely they were not Satanic.

They are called *varende vrouwen*, which means *"wandering women"* and possibly refers to those beings who wander the outside realm. They are women outside the conventional order, which gives them power and a marginal status at the same time. The reference to *godelingen*, goodlings, is strange as the basic word is positive, *"good,"* they are *"the good ones."* They are suited in a list of nature-spirits of the earth and the water, and are also called *"nightmares."*

Nightmares are a very interesting phenomenon, which should be explored in more depth than I have room to do here. The Old Norse nightmare is called *mara*, which comes from a Proto-Indo-European root, **mer* meaning *"to crush," "to press" (Hall 2007: 299)*. These beings, usually a spirit-shape send out by a *seiðkona* or some form of *hagazussa*, crushed the victim to death. This is attested from several Old Norse accounts. These nightmares are a variation on a central theme, the spirit shape. But now they're used to press someone to death.

The mythology of the nightriders is a consistent whole that is found all across the countries that surround the North Sea, and have Germanic origins. The mythology centers around a cult of women who leave their bodies at night. This is the first defining element of the mythology. The second is *"ride through the air,"* sometimes on a stick and at other times on the back of animals, usually accompanied by a storm. This storm and wild host of women riding through the air, can, of course, be linked to the Wild Hunt, and has a deep connection to the leader of this hunt.

In some versions the leader is the god *Óðinn*, who is sometimes reflected in continental myths in the figure of Wode, or some other male semi-divinity. But in relation to hedgewitchcraft, the figure most mentioned is the goddess Dame Holda, who is sometimes Latinized as the divinity Diana or Herodias.

The name of Dame Holda comes from a Proto-Indo-European root meaning *"hollow,"* which means she is the Goddess of the Hollow. She is the Goddess of the Underworld, the Hollow Hills in which the dead lie. But she is more than just a Goddess of the dead, she is the black and white Goddess, the Goddess with the half-white half-black face. This reflects her dual nature as the Earth Mother, Queen of the Pale People, and Fate itself. She maintains the balance between life and death, inner and outer world, Culture and

Wild. This makes her the Queen of the Witches, whose basic position is like her: in-between, between Order and Chaos, inner and outer world.

The third element is the shooting of arrows, causing of harm, and general fighting taking place in the air. This element can be interpreted in several ways, but should be seen in a context of women obtaining power. It is a rite of cursing, as well as curing. As one can tell from the stories of the North Italian witches *(benandanti)* the battle in the air is also for the good of society. Here the story of the witches in Valais, France, says enough: they went into the air to do battle. They battled in the air because they participated in the Wild Hunt and the struggle for survival against the forces of Chaos. To the Christians it was as if the witches fought each other, but to the hedgeriders and nightriders this was a different battle.

The relation of witches to the community, that is, the inner world and the Human Order, appears ambiguous. They ride through the air and kill humans, which doesn't seem beneficial to the Human Order, and especially in this day with our justice system it is an upsetting act. This act of killing can, however, be seen from multiple perspectives. For some witches it probably a simple act of revenge. Witches were and are humans, and therefore capable of evil, there's nothing that prevents them from committing such an act.

But also there's a deeper layer to this. As I've said before, the basic position of the witch is between the worlds, between Human Order and Gigantic Chaos, which means the Human Order is not necessarily the object of *(all)* their acts. They are engaged with the balance between the worlds. Sometimes this involves Human acts, while at other times it involves Gigantic acts.

To the modern reconstructionist of this cult, there is a threefold interpretation of the rite: ritual, mythological and mystical *(re)*enacted. The ritual interpretation is a very simple one, where the ritual of leaving the body, riding with the Goddess and the shooting of arrows, is a ritual to achieve some goal. In this interpretation it is not about something deeper, but is about the achievement of goals, of which this cult provides many examples—cursing and curing, creation and destruction.

The mythological interpretation is more deeper and goes beyond the practical application, but is about the alignment of the individual hedgerider with the mythology, and in effect the story and struggle of the Gods. The practitioner leaves the body *(this method is discussed in detail in my book Hedge-rider)* and travels with the Wild Hunt, thus communicating with the Gods and Divine Beings, eventually leading up to the Divine Communion which is also called the Sabbath.

The mystical interpretation is even deeper, going beyond the mythological and ritual application. Still, it is a spontaneous process, which can not be consciously initiated like the mythological or ritual interpretation. In the mystical interpretation of the rite, the practitioner's soul and person is transformed by the Divine Communion of the Sabbath. The Communion with the Gods leads to an encounter with the Truth of Godhead, which leads to mystical transformation within the soul. This is the ultimate objective of the ones who ride by night.

Bibliography

Hall, A. (2004) *The Meaning of Elf and Elves in Medieval England*

Hall, A. (2007) 'The Evidence for Maran: The Anglo Saxon Nightmares,' Neophilologus 91: 299-317.

Kors, A.C. & E. Peters (2001) *Witchcraft in Europe, 400-1700: A documentary history.* Philadelphia: University of Pennsylvania Press.

Larrington, C. (2008) [org. 1996] *The Poetic Edda.* Oxford: Oxford University Press.

Wilbur, T. (1959) 'The Interpretation of Völuspá 22,4: Vitti Hon Ganda.' *Scandinavian Studies* 31: 129-136.

Getting a Running Start
Aids to Jumping the Hedge

Elise Stewart

Many different aspects come together to help a rider to jump the Hedge. Training, experience, and natural ability all coalesce with the tools of the trade to allow us to cross from this world into the Otherrealms. As with all aspects of traditional crafting, what you bring to your practice directly reflects what you will get out of it. In other words, all of the fancy ritual tools, arcane incantations, and psychoactive entheogens cannot replace good old fashioned training and practice. That being said, let's take a look at some of tools that can make the transition a little bit easier. These can be divided into a few different categories: herbals/entheogens, trance induction techniques, and ritual.

Entheogens are *(usually herbal)* substances that are used to bring about a spiritual experience, or to *"generate the divine within."* This particular tool of hedgeriding is probably the most controversial aspect of the practice, as many of the substances used as entheogens are illegal or *"unsafe."* This is not to say that all entheogens are illicit or hazardous, but the most well publicized ones used traditionally are frequently regulated by law. While this topic is far too broad to be covered in it's entirety in this essay, I would like to touch on a few points relevant to our discussion.

Many different substances are said to have entheogenic properties. Everything from wine and mead to mystical fungi have found their way into a hedgerider's toolbox. Many of the stronger intoxicants will naturally pop into mind when fleshing out this category, but the chemical potency of a substance doesn't necessarily relate to it's spiritual potency. I've overheard some younger 'practitioners' talk about the amazing spiritual experience they had when they intentionally overdosed on cough syrup or stole a parent's sleeping pill. In my opinion, regardless of the substance being used, you must cultivate a relationship with the entheogen for it to be effective in helping you to cross the Hedge. It is rather difficult to develop a relationship with the sacred *"Ambien Tree."*

There are a plethora of plants that are overlooked as entheogens in favor of more *"potent"* substances. Stronger is not always better, and a gentler approach in terms of herbal applications usually produces stronger skill development on the part of the practitioner. Remember—all the peyote in the world is no substitute for proper training or practice.

Three of my favorite entheogens to use have are relatively weak compared to their hallucinogenic counterparts. Mead, clary sage oil, and ginger brew can be helpful to many practitioners who are honing their skills at fetch flight. My preference for mead to wine stems from a few different sources. I have a particular fondness for the honeybee and an ongoing interest in the Path of Pollen, a form of bee shamanism. On a more practical note, the strong sweet taste of mead encourages the practitioner to sip *(as opposed to gulp)* the sacred drink. To utilize sacred fermented drinks, less is more. A few sips can heighten the inner senses, whereas a few gulps can make the focus sloppy and render any attempts at crossing the Hedge ineffective.

Clary sage essential oil has an earthy smell that assists in the process of *ekstasis*. The uplifting effects are subtle, but noticeable. Clary sage ointments can be a safe *(legal)* alternative to many of the flying ointments of days past, as well. It is also an invaluable aid to dream work, making the dream realms intensify. This oil greatly increases efficacy of dream incubation by simply putting a few drops on a cotton ball or dream pillow kept near the head during sacred sleep.

Ginger brew is great for digestion and colds. It is also a wonderful aid in helping to become more aware of the different energy bodies. Keen observation of the energy field while ingesting this brew can help to experience basic energy manipulation or even illuminate the process of projection from the physical body.

A simple ginger brew can be made by boiling roughly 2 tablespoons of fresh ginger root *(or 1 tablespoon ground ginger)* in about 2-3 cups of water for 10 minutes. Strain and add 2-3 tablespoons of honey while the drink cools. The taste can be overpowering, so I usually mix it with equal parts apple cider, and drink warm or chilled. You can also occasionally find a commercially produced drink called ginger brew. This is usually a strong ginger ale, and does not serve the purpose of an entheogen. Ginger Clary or Ginger Mead *(herbally infused alcoholic drinks)* can also be found from time to time, which can be used as described earlier.

Entheogens will only help you to jump the Hedge if you have a firm grasp on trance techniques. Before going any further, let's discuss what we mean by trance. Trance is generally defined as an altered state of consciousness. This is all well and good, but that is a rather broad description for our purposes. For the hedgerider, trance is the tool to unfetter the consciousness from the mundane physical world to allow travel into the Otherrealms, which I will call a working trance. It could be said that the working trance is the vehicle and ritual the road map.

There are as many different ways to bring about trance state as there are hedgeriders. Meditation practices help most people to develop the skill necessary to quiet the mind and achieve trance. Even the most avid meditator may need something to achieve a deeper trance state though. In such cases, we can turn to external tools to heighten the experience. As with all tools, no matter how fancy or exotic, it will only take you as far as your level of commitment will allow.

Tools for achieving trance include postures, sound, breathing techniques, or gazing to name a few.

Breath is as vital to trance as it is to life. It also happens to be a readily available and incredibly effective tool to achieve a trance state. The simplest breath technique to alter your consciousness is to count your breath. I find that a regressive method of counting is most effective in my own practice. To try this, simply count each full breath *(inhalation and exhalation)* backward from ten. Once you reach zero, start again counting back from nine, then eight and so on.

Altering the breath itself can have equally potent results. The most well documented utilization of breathwork is a practice within yoga called *pranayama (practice, observance, or way of the breath)*. There are many different breathing techniques to elicit many different results. For example, alternate nostril breathing balances the energy flow between the two sides of the body and helps relieve anxiety while the breath of fire helps to build the vital energies within the body.

Alternate nostril breathing can be achieved by breathing in and then gently pinching the nostrils shut with the middle finger and thumb of your right hand. Lift your middle finger allowing the exhalation to flow through the left nostril for the count of 4, pause for 4 counts, inhale for 4 counts, then pinch the nostrils closed for a count of 4. Repeat the process, only this time lifting the thumb instead of the middle finger. Continue this cycle until the energy flow through the body feels more balanced. This is also great way to quell anxiety and panic.

The breath of fire can be performed in a relaxed kneeling position or sitting upright in a chair with the hands resting palm down on the knees. Begin by taking long deep breaths. Allow these long deep breaths to become a little more forceful on the exhalation. Continue to allow the exhalation to become increasingly forceful and quick, while the inhalation is relaxed, simply allowing the air to flow into the chest without effort. This will evolve into a rhythm, and you will begin to feel energy gathering in your center, then washing through you in waves heightening your awareness and focus. Once you reach this sensation, allow your breath to return to normal. The energy that is generated can be harnessed and directed through intention for various purposes, such as charging a talisman.

Breathwork is foundational in any magical training. It is a vital part of thaumaturgy, especially such practices as cord magic. This stems from the connection between our own vital or etheric energies and the breath. To master the ways of magical working, one must master the breath.

Posturing can be looked at from two different perspectives: effects on the physical body, and energetic effects. Hatha yoga, from the physical perspective, has the goal of toning and training the body to be more comfortable *(or less distracting)* during intensive meditation sittings. Seeing as how the body barrier is frequently a challenge in achieving a working trance state, practices such as yoga are ideal to prepare the rider for jumping the Hedge. If you are a little intimidated by the remarkable bendiness of many of the yogis out there, don't fret. Just about any form of physical exercise can help reduce stress levels and improve your conditioning *(not to mention your overall health)*.

Coming from the energetic standpoint, certain yoga postures have undoubted connections in linking with animal spirits. This is seen in some of the names of yoga postures, like Cobra, Downward Facing Dog, and Eagle to name a few. Creative use of some yoga postures can strengthen and refine our fetch work, shapeshifting exercises, or simply our connection to various currents of energy found in the symbolism of the animal. These are not the only considerations of posture, though.

Noted anthropologist, Dr. Felicitas Goodman, did research on the effect different postures had on shamanic journeys. Her work, as published in *'Where the Spirits Ride the Wind'*, discussed how different postures, derived from poses found on ancient statues from various world cultures, brought about different experiences for shamanic journeyers. Dr. Goodman classed these experiences first broadly, namely by dividing them into whether they produced a lower world, middle world or upper world journey. She later delved into the more subtle nuances that each of the postures brought about for her and her students.

For the hedgerider, different body positioning could be considered to bring about different experiences in the trance state. It is also a new field to explore to keep your practice from growing stagnant. For example, the posture called the Sami Lower World Posture in Goodman's work produced a swift journey that enabled faster flight across the Otherworld for me. The position was simply achieved by lying face down with arms and legs outstretched *(think Superman in flight)*.

Dance or movement can also lead to a profound trance experience. Ecstatic dance is frequently used in many different cultures to lead to a state of possession by a spirit or God. In many of the Diaspora religions such as Voudoun or Candomble, different dance steps and rhythms are affiliated with specific entities and are used to invoke them into the dancer. The steps are usually repetitive and simple to allow this to occur. While not strictly a tool for hedgeriding, it still has great potential in achieving the proper mind state of trance to allow the rider to fly into the Otherrealm.

Regardless of what we do with the body during trance, it must maintain a level of comfort. If we find ourselves distracted by physical discomfort or self-consciousness, an effective trance state may never be achieved. In other words, if you are an incredibly awkward mover, then ecstatic dance *(at least in a setting that includes more than you alone)* will most likely never work as a great tool for trance due to the self-consciousness that could arise. Safety should also be a key concern. If you are experimenting with ecstatic movement, don't do so alone someplace that you'll never be found if you trip over your stang and break your ankle.

Drumming is frequently affiliated with trance work, and for good reason. The use of a steady drumbeat can lull the most firmly grounded mundane person into a deep trance. Many times drummers will use a beat to mimic the heart and bring listeners into a state of deep awareness. But drums aren't the only musical tools at the hedgerider's disposal. Rattles, also traditionally used, can be equally mind altering by mimicking the same beats that a drummer may use for trance. The diffuse sound yet staccato sound of the rattle can be more or less enticing to the trance state for some than the bellowing pounding of the drum. In the end, it is a personal preference as to which sound will bring about the trance state more easily.

Droning harmonic sounds, such as the didgeridoo or singing bowl, produce elongated steady sounds that seem to penetrate and encompass work well for those that find the sound of drums and rattles irritating or abrasive. Though not associated with hedgeriding, don't discount these types of instruments as an aid to your trance work. The didgeridoo has been used as an instrument to the Aborigines of Australia for countless generations to help enter into the Dreamtime by their spiritual practitioners. The multi-tone sounds of the singing bowl have been charming many Tibetan Bon practitioners and Buddhists alike into a deep state of meditation for at least as far back as the 12th century *(possibly as far as the 10th century BCE in the form of bronze bells)*.

Anyway you look at it, sound can be vital to the achievement of trance. Remember, it's not how you achieve the trance—it's what you do with it once you've gotten it. As always, there is no magic drum that will take the place of focus and practice in projecting past the Hedge.

So, let's say you've achieved the elusive trance. Now what do you do with it? That's where ritual enters into the picture. Ritual can help to shape the trance experience, turning it from a simple alteration of consciousness to a truly spiritual experience. Ritual directs the energy of trance by directing the rider's focus and intent. Ritual can also speak directly to the Otherrealm through the language of symbolism. Here are a few different tools and techniques to incorporate into ritual.

Joining sound and ritual can be a fruitful endeavor. Incantations and mantras are used in many practices of many cultures to achieve the necessary trance state to perceive and affect the unseen worlds. Chants as simple as bija mantras are probably the most well known of this branch of practice. Bija mantras are seed sounds, such as AUM /OM, HRIM, and other syllabic sounds derived from Eastern philosophies that are intoned as an invocatory gesture or to manipulate currents of energy based on the model of the Vedic chakras or planetary energies. Elaborate prayers and songs can just as easily show up in a ritual setting, too.

Incantations may utilize several different tools or techniques. Many will look only at the words of an incantation. While this is an important part of the working, the rhythm, pitch and overall resonance of the chant may hold even more power than the words themselves. Magic has always been associated with inexplicable barbarous words of power. These *"nonsense"* words contain much power and mystery to be unlocked by the skillful witch. In such cases, the word having no defined meaning relies only on the power of the resonance and sound to affect the changes by the practitioner's will. The true secret is learning to vibrate energy into the words as you incant them, which can be most easily learned by practicing breath work techniques.

Even considering the power of the spoken word, the experiences of the Otherworlds don't easily lend themselves to verbal description. The experience of hedgeriding is experiential, an art, poetic. Sometimes, words just don't quite do it justice. Your experiences of the Otherrealm are mythic and archetypal. This can color our perceptions and create seeming paradoxes. If you can't embrace the paradoxical nature of the experiences over the Hedge, then you can be driven mad.

Examples of this poetic description of a journey across the Hedge are seen in many of the folk tales, bardic works and lore of northern Europe. One of my personal favorites is the Cad Goddeu, or Battle of Trees[1]. Let's examine the role of Whitethorn, Blackthorn and Hazel trees in the poem, as these were the three trees most commonly found in the hedgerows. Whitethorn and Blackthorn were referred to as chieftans of strength, showcasing their ability to act as guardians along the hedge. Hazel was seen less often in the make-up of the hedgerow, but was still commonly seen. In the Battle of Trees, Hazel has the title of arbiter or judge. This distinction would suggest that Hazel also possessed the ability to allow a hedgerider to cross the row, while keeping all other influences on their respective sides, as a *"balancer of the natural law,"* so to speak.

Trying to explain the full context of an experience across the Hedge is at times akin to trying to describe how the color blue tastes. In some instances, contemplation of how to share such information leads to doubt and false memory on the part of the practitioner, so as the brain can *"help"* to make the experience more acceptable to the consensus. By weaving the experience into that of poetry, it helps to preserve more of the essence of the Otherrealms, and also leaves room for deeper understandings upon examination of said poetry or art. When looking at the Battle of Trees again, it becomes easy to see that it contained knowledge of the sacred Ogham alphabet, and the deeper implications that may have been attributed to the bard's command of language.

The nature of the Otherrealms gives rise to such dreamlike sequences, often presenting experiences counter to what we understand to be true and factual. Reality is far from black and white – true and untrue. All reality is *"true reality,"* even that reality that is not consensus reality. Much of what we perceive in our adventures of the Otherworld will be so far outside of this consensus that we have trouble expressing it. This is where the language of poetry and art comes into play.

The arts convey the essence of our experiences as hedgeriders by allowing us to describe these journeys concretely, but also with nuance and symbolic depth. Poetry can capture the essence through meter and metaphor, as opposed to simply being an academic rendering of events through prose. Visual arts can also give greater depth to the explanation of our otherworldly encounters, not by rendering a nearly photographic image, but by sharing the undertones through brush stroke and movement.

We are taught to express our perceptions based around physical reality, which has a clearly defined up and down, left to right that is

---

1. *Originally contained in The Romance of Taliesin. This essay refers to the poem as it was 'tentatively restored' in The White Goddess by Robert Graves.*

generally agreed upon by the consensus. In the Otherworlds, these firm explanations lose their relevance, as direction becomes more of a tendency, and concrete concepts become completely abstract. Everything is realized as having the potential of sentient life, so the path itself can speak to the rider along their journey. Such experiences can bleed over into the *"mundane world"* where the witch may communicate with seemingly inanimate objects that give the appearance of madness or extreme eccentricity. For this reason, most of these *"bleed-overs"* are usually confined to ritual space, where they are recognized as being completely natural and relevant, as opposed to being experienced at the office which could land you in the unemployment line.

One of the ways that the beauty and art of the Otherworld touches our ritual space is through the creation of beautiful ritual tools to assist the ritual workings, such as the mask and the stang. Masks can enrich and enliven any ritual setting, whereas the stang gives help in the crossing of the Hedge. Masks can help to connect us with our allies across the Hedge, rouse the fetch, or help to bring about ecstatic possession. They are indispensable tools to assist with shapeshifting work. They may also be aimed at a specific purpose, such as seership. All this is achieved by the mask's ability to alter our perceptions, literally giving us *"new eyes"* to see through.

Many of the beings that we meet in the Otherworlds will have an extraordinary appearance. By creating and utilizing a mask, we can gain a deeper understanding of their perspective and allow ourselves to become more closely allied with these beings. A mask to help connect you with your fetch-beast can be a powerful undertaking, and a huge stride toward *hierogamos* or the sacred union of beast and mate. Taking on the persona of the primal fetch can sometimes unleash instinctual parts of your nature, as well. Here, the ability to take the mask off can also limit the *(sometimes disruptive)* effect such a connection may bring into your life.

Possession work with masks is really intuitive. In addition to allowing the shift in perception on the practitioner's part, it also can make the spirit more comfortable in the physical realm. One of my favorite masks is somewhat of a sensory deprivation tool that I call a seer's mask. It is a blindfold of sorts that also has a simple veil and covers the ears. Some of my best visionary work has occurred with this mask. The uses for masks in ritual are only limited to the rider's imagination.

One of the most elusive tools of traditional crafting is the stang. It functions as a staff, upright altar, and bridge across the Hedge all in one handy tool. As a staff it can be used to direct energy and mark out the compass. It functions as an altar to the Horned or Antlered God. It is also seen as a gate, a symbol of the world tree that we ascend *(or descend)* into the Otherworld. Stangs may be elaborate—incorporating the skull and horns of a deer or goat, or simple, being only a forked piece of wood. This is going to depend on the practitioner's preference.

Now that we've talked a bit about the tools of ritual, let's briefly address ritual format. Simply put, a hedgeriding ritual is going to incorporate four different elements: preparing to jump the Hedge, journey into the Otherrealm, doing what you need to do there, and returning/releasing. Preparation to jump the Hedge will incorporate techniques of grounding yourself, setting your ritual space, preparing for trancework and possibly casting compass, calling in a spirit ally. The journey to the Otherrealm will usually utilize one of the trance induction techniques such as drumming and chanting.

Once you're there, you should have a clear goal in mind that you wish to achieve. You shouldn't treat the Otherrealm as some mall that you can just go to and window shop when you have nothing better to do. You should make the journey with as clear of a defined purpose as possible. Once you've achieved what you made the journey for, it's time to return. Before doing so, be certain that your allies have been thanked and make arrangements for an offering if you need to. You should then return to the physical world. If your working involved a change in the mundane world, you should be sure to release the energy you brought back with you to bring the change into being.

The journey across the Hedge can sometimes be a daunting one. By understanding and utilizing the tools that you have at your disposal, it can be a little bit easier. There is no easy button to make you a proficient hedgerider. That takes practice, skill and wisdom. There are no substitutes or shortcuts to cultivating these things. Hopefully though, these tools will bring the experience of the Otherrealm a little bit closer for you.

Biography

Elige Stewart is a practitioner and perpetual student of traditional witchcraft. He was initiated into the craft at the age of 17 and continues to study various traditions, including the Anderson Feri Tradition, the Old Faery Faith, Southern conjure and rootwork, and the mysteries of the Goddess Hekate.

He has a professional mediumship practice in Lansing, Michigan. He can be reached through his website: www.eligestewart.com

Traveling Bag Recipe

This recipe was passed along to me from the grandson of a woman from Kentucky. It's for luck and protection in traveling, in particular for "the kind of traveling you don't do with your own two feet."

Veronica Cummer

Ingredients:
Owl or goose feather
Blue stone or a holed stone
Spider web
Thistle seed or thistledown
One found object
A grass circle tied with your hair
Black dog's fur
Blessed silver

She indicated that the goose feather is best if it's grey in color. The goose feather was one of the most important elements and if you have difficulty with any of the other ingredients, having the goose feather and the holed stone can work powerfully on their own. Owl feathers can be harder to come by, especially as you shouldn't buy them. The goose feather can be bought, but it's better if it comes from one of your own birds or as a gift.

The holed stone should be naturally holed and not one that was fashioned that way if at all possible. A blue stone or bead is the next best choice. If you have the holed stone, then put the goose feather through the center of the hole.

The fur from the tail of a black dog is best. As she put it, the fur of a *"wagging dog's tail."* This indicates that the dog, as a guardian of the border, is meant to be friendly. Try to find a dog that is as black as possible, with no other color to it.

The grass circle doesn't have to be tied with some of your own hair, but that's best.

The silver can be blessed by running water or by the moon. You can also use a tiny piece of a mirror, but it must be from one that was not broken by you. Clean the piece of the mirror in running water or blessed water or show it to the moon and then it's pure and can be used as *"silver."*

The found object is something that you go in search of, keeping at the back of your mind the need you have for traveling and arriving there safely. It may end up being something to guide you back or something that will help bear you away. It should be small enough to put inside the bag and will likely jump out at you as you walk around. You may suddenly notice it and instinctively feel like it's the right thing, what you've been searching for.

Put all the objects into a bag—preferably one that is dark blue or black in color—and tie it off with three knots. Hold the bag in your hand and concentrate on seeing a string coming down from the sky that connects to the bag and tugs at it, trying to pull it upwards. If you ever feel that this string is gone, then the charge of the bag is gone and you will need to open it up and re-bless the silver/mirror and find another lost object to replace the one that was in the bag.

You can wear the bag when you want to travel or hold it in your hand. If you like to travel at night, in your bed, then put it beneath your pillow. However, don't leave it there all the time.

Don't let anyone take the bag, especially if you have your own hair in it.

The Gate

Whirl a wind and black feather fall--
A single light shines yellow, pale, gold
A wandering star
From some elsewhere place
Framed by greening leaves and red berries,
Growth and sacrifice intertwined
Whispering still and oh so merry.
The gate of the hedgerow is black
Depths calling the key to night,
Where birds sleep and rabbits doze
And where branches weave
Round and up and down and deep,
A tapestry a web a ladder.
A dream undreaming
Binding and unbinding
Night to day
Near to far
Life to death
Human, Fey, Witch, divine and all
Entangled in bloom and in thorn.
She weeps, she laughs, she wails
The Goddess of the shadow walk
The secret rose
The raven's perfect cry
To come, to go, to dream, to fly;
What other choice
She would ask of all who seek
Where is your desire

Where your star to follow.
A single light shines,
A destiny in the darkness,
As the winds rise and fall and twist
The spiral of this world and some other
Piercing and weaving two into one.
Until leaves shivering spent
Part at the last to reveal
The web of the Wyrd
Poisonous dark and bright and sweet
Beyond all pleasure
The underpinnings of each path
The dread and joyful laugh of Fate
Deep and real and cruel enough to drown.

Knock, and the Doors Shall be Opened to You
Meditation and the Trance

Christopher Crittenden

A question from a newer member to the path of Traditional Witchcraft prompted me to ponder the meanings of the words "*meditation*" and "*trance*," and how I could explain or describe the true essences of both as I have come to know them through the teachings of the thread to which I belong, namely the *Hethite Crimson Thread of Artful Sacred Craft*. With all of the possibilities, methods and/or techniques out there which purport to take the seeker of mysteries to the answers they seek, it can be a daunting task indeed to choose the correct method or approach that will give the practitioner the desired results. In the spirit of saving those new to the path some valuable time and energy, I have herein explained some of the most essential techniques utilized by those within our recension. Please allow me to take you through the twin pillars into the Sanctum Sanctorum.

The Pillar of Severity: Meditation

Meditation is a general term with slightly differing definitions depending upon the tradition of the person giving the definition. For all of the different jargon bandied about by myself and countless others, the concept of meditation is actually quite straight-forward even if the practice of it can seem difficult. Meditation is a technique whereby the Wholeness of things is entered through the gateway of One thing. Any single thing can be this One thing, as all things truly are of One reality. Reality is one, whole and undivided. It is merely our perceptions as humans that divide and label. These divisions are not in and of themselves an evil thing. On the contrary, they are vital to our survival. Without them, we would be at the mercy of every danger imaginable. We might walk in front of a bus or get hurt in a variety of other ways. We might forget to eat, not recognizing hunger in our bodies. However, in order to come to a full and complete understanding of this grand event we call reality, we must come to not only intellectually understand that Wholeness is the ultimate truth of all things, but we must also *experience* it. Meditation is the gateway that makes this experience possible.

There are many methods of meditation. Meditation has been used often throughout the spiritual history of humankind, whether one is only religious, using methods of meditation to commune with unseen powers or the unseen aspects of a power, and/or whether one is sorcerously minded, using meditation techniques to tap into power in whatever form they conceive of it in order to affect change in their environment. These methods range from guided imagery given by another, to free-flowing thought rivers with no definite goal or purpose at the outset. Most methods of solitary meditation done by those experienced practitioners walk a middle way between these extremes, however. For example, you may be given a guided imagery to start with, and then at some point during the meditation you will be released from the structured part of the technique and told to go explore, etc, to have your own unique experiences, interacting with the inner environment spontaneously.

There are those who recommend postures designed either for their energetic effect, occult effect, or physiological effect, such as keeping upright and out of a *"sleeping"* posture which can signal the body to begin the sleep process. It goes without saying that one absolutely *must* be well rested for any meditative technique to be effective. Otherwise, one simply loses their focus and drifts into unconsciousness, either while awake or falling into actual sleep. If this happens, one is defeated and the reason for this has to do with awareness, as shall be made clear momentarily.

Others actually recommend lying down, as in the technique of the ancient healer priests, or *Iatromantoi*, of the Mediterranean, Hellenic and Middle Eastern worlds, which has some parallels with the *Tarbh Fheis* of the Irish Druids. In the Greco-Roman world, this practice was called *"incubation,"* which simply means *"to lie down inside."* Often, people would incubate communally in temples dedicated to a God or Gods, such as Apollo or Asclepius, who were known to have an interest in such matters. Other times, one may have gone alone to incubate in a cave or possibly even at home. People would incubate for a variety of reasons, whether for the answer to a question or for healing.[1] What all these different people had in common was the use and insistence upon silence. Silence was the One thing used in incubation to achieve that coveted vision of Wholeness called the Grand Sabbat in many recensions of Traditional Witchcraft. It is a gateway. It is a Goddess.

Drugs called entheogens may also be used to quiet the body and the ego mind in order that the Daimon, also called the Fetch or Spirit,

1. *"In The Dark Places of Wisdom,"* Peter Kingsley, 1999, *The Golden Sufi Center,* Inverness, CA

may ascend and/or descend *(depending upon individual perception and tradition)* into the trance. This is the origin of the infamous *"witch's flying ointment."* Really, that is what any meditation technique is designed to do; quiet the body and the ego, also called the personality, so that the Daimon may open the gateways of trance, or to put another way, so that the Fetch may be ridden to the Sabbat. It is not the ego, or soul, of any individual that achieves the trance. The trance is a gift given by the Fetch, and by the Master, who is known by all sorcerers in one way or another, for without a relationship with Him no sorcery nor trance is possible.

Some advise a mantra of some sort, whereby a word or words or else a sound is used to lull the analytical ego mind into a passive state so that the inner gateway may be opened by the Daimon. Most everyone has heard by now of the *"Om Mani Padme Um"* of the Tantra, or simply *"Om"* by itself. Others use the rhythmic sound of a drum. Drumming releases the intuitive part of the mind by lulling the analytical mind into submission by giving it something to focus on *(the steady rhythm)*, thereby allowing the imaginative and intuitive aspect of the mind to freely experience reality in *its* way. Why else do you think cats and toads have been considered *"stereotypical"* witches' familiars? The rhythmic purring of a cat sitting on your lap, or the rhythmic croaking of toads and frog can easily put some into trance.

Some even use methods of blood control, such as leather or fiber cords for binding parts of the body slightly to retard blood flow. A scourge may work extremely well for others, because the rhythm of the light passes of the scourge across the back creates a state which is receptive to trance by drawing some blood away from the brain. The individual is able to not only hear the rhythm similar to a drum, but they are also able to feel the rhythm on their skin. Pain in this case would be a hindrance to most people as it would distract. For others, the pain becomes the One thing. Such people would of course have to discover this on an individual basis.

Still others, such as again the healer priests of Apollo in the Ancient Hellenic, Mediterranean and Middle Eastern worlds, used the sacred sound of the wise serpent, the hiss, as their *Clavis Portis Caelis (key to the gate of heaven)*. This makes one wonder if there might also be a connection to this practice and the Druids, who were referred to as *"serpents,"* as in when St. Patrick supposedly drove all the *"serpents"* out of Ireland. Some recensions of Traditional Witchcraft, such as the one to which I myself belong, also use the Word of the Cunning Serpent to similar ends, which will be discussed below.

What many techniques of meditation have in common is the concentration upon the One thing and the lack of motion, though moving meditation is possible via Qi Gong, yoga, or ecstatic dancing. *"But ah!"* you say. *"There are techniques that require you to think about nothing at all!"* To this I say, *"Really?"* The Void in the mind of the ego is no void at all for the word *"Void"* is a thing and an idea, and its opposite which is also its other name, is Fullness. There is no *"nothing,"* nor any *"experience of nothing"* for the ego mind to think itself to. Reality is one, whole, and undivided, and the experience of Reality in its Wholeness leads us to...

The Pillar of Truth: The Trance

The techniques of meditation are what bring us to the Trance. The Trance is not a technique. The Trance is a state of awareness, the Grand Sabbat of the Witches, whereby consciousness has been shifted onto the timeless aspect of any being, the Daimon. Some call this state Elphame or the Underworld. Elphame is simply the experience of reality from the perspective of the Fetch. Meditation is the *"method"* most often used for achieving this state, although as stated previously it may come by other methods, such as entheogens *(herbs, alcohol, etc)*, by binding and the scourge, dance, sexual congress with another or with oneself, all of which fall under blood control, or it simply may come of its own volition by a Fateful blessing. This is, again, because the Trance is bestowed by the Daimon, not by the wandering dimly aware mind of the ego. All a person can do is open themselves to the experience of the Trance by various methods, some of which I have mentioned, and allow the Timeless Self *(Daimon)* to arise.

From the Trance comes the connection and communication with the Unseen that we seek as witches. From the Trance comes the wisdom that we as witches seek to acquire and thereby bring back to our human communities, as Prometheus did the sacred Fire from the Gods to Man.

Some Solitary Techniques of Meditation:
Keys to Heaven and Hell, the Doorway to Trance

I shall outline briefly two of the methods used in my Tradition, the Hethite Crimson Thread of Arteful Sacred Craft, within which I am a magister. The first method is called the *"Hissing of the Serpent."*[2] Two longer names I have seen given are *"The Voice of the Master which Transforms"* and *"The Word of the Cunning Serpent,"* but you will usually hear this technique called simply *"Hissing"* or *"the Hissing Breath."*

Briefly, you clear your thoughts *(and lungs)* by taking a satisfying breath and then allowing it to be released fully. Now, take in another breath through the nose, gently but fully, hold for only a moment using the diaphragm not the throat, and then release through the mouth with teeth

---

2. *"The Witching Way of the Hollow Hill,"* Robin Artisson, 2009, Pendraig Publishing, Los Angeles, CA

together, making a long satisfying hiss until the out breath is completed, rest only a moment, and then repeat. This is done for ten *(10)* breaths, all the while only listening to and feeling the breath and the hissing, which is the One thing concentrated upon in this technique. You will be amazed, after becoming proficient in this technique, the first time while doing this that the Unseen answers back with a hiss to match, connecting and supporting your own.

The second method is called *"Witchsight,"* or the clarity technique. This is also treated in Artisson's book, but comes ultimately from the *Iatromantis*, meaning trance healer, the priests of Apollo. The history of incubation, another ancient name for this technique, as well as the technique itself is treated magnificently in two books by Peter Kingsley, *"In The Dark Places of Wisdom"* and *"Reality."*

Begin by acquiring an awareness of the sensations present to you from your skin, the temperature, pressure from the chair upon your buttocks, the weight of your clothing, your lungs filling with air as you breathe, everything you feel. Become aware that you are aware of these feelings. Without losing this awareness, bring to your attention everything that you are hearing, the birds, the cars on the road, the AC unit in your dwelling, the sound of your breath, everything.

Now, at the same that you remain conscious of every sensation coming to you from your skin and your ears, become conscious of your sense of smell. Remain conscious of everything you are feeling and smelling. Now, while remaining aware of everything you are feeling and smelling, bring in the sense of taste, and finally sight. You may keep your eyes open or closed prior to bringing in the sense of sight, but you must get to the point where you bring them all into your awareness equally, without one gaining supremacy over any other, because once that happens, you have lost it.

Awareness is the key. Actually, being aware of what you are aware of is the key.[3] This is also spoken of extensively by Kingsley and also by Magister Artisson. All things in creation have their parts to play. This is ours. Beings such as ourselves, with aspects in both the Seen *and* Unseen worlds *(which are by mystery One Thing)*, and who also have the capacity to abstract and to experience these two seemingly separate realities, are the *"healers,"* the *"ones who make whole."* Through the very act of our ability to bring the Seen and Unseen together in our experience of reality, we actually *cause* the renewal of the cosmos. We may *possibly* be the only beings in the Seen worlds capable of abstract thought, of the ability to step back mentally and be aware that we are aware. This is the true doorway to the trance, the keys

---

3. *"Reality,"* Peter Kingsley, 2003, The Golden Sufi Center, Inverness, CA

to the Kingdom of Heaven and Hell. You can practice them both together once you are familiar with them separately, hissing, clarity and then hissing again. Do this daily, forever.

Following the Threads:
A Method of Finding the Answer

Another form of meditation which is popular in Western occultism is called *"Discursive Meditation."* [4] This method defined meditation for Western occultists for centuries, as *"no self"* meditation is seen to denote Buddhism today. It is amazing that so few people have heard of this method of meditation. It was so popular and well known that it survives today even in some traditions of Western Christianity.

The technique is fairly straightforward. You may have already experienced this in a non-focused way, in which case folks often call it *"day-dreaming,"* but let me assure you, this is no empty exercise. Basically, you begin with an idea, thought, mystery, etc. You then quiet the mind and ponder the chosen subject. The idea is not to be repeated in the head or with the mouth like a mantra, trying desperately to keep all else outside of your attention, but rather it is held in the mind lightly, as a fine wine in the mouth, to be savored, and to allow the subtle nuances of its essence to come forth into awareness easily.

New ideas, realizations or mysteries may arise from the original one, and these may be followed. If however, you find yourself suddenly realizing that you have not been present in your meditation, you must mentally *"backtrack"* through each and every thought that you had until you arrive back at the point in which you left the original idea. Wisdom is acquired in this way from the *"failure,"* making it no failure at all, and often points to the wisdom that was needed in the first place.

It is highly advised to perform the Hissing of the Serpent first, before attempting a Discursive Meditation session because it will quiet and focus the mind, allowing for easier concentration upon the chosen subject. Hissing afterwards can *"fix"* the wisdom gained within the consciousness of the practitioner. You may see in this a similarity with the first process of hissing, clarity, hissing, and you would be correct to do so. In the first process, the hissing is the focusing One thing, followed by a broadening of the awareness into the Wholeness using the clarity exercise, followed by a grounding or *"fixing"* hissing procedure. In the second process, the hissing remains in its place, but awareness of the Wholeness is brought by Discursive Meditation and the following of a subject along its connections.

4. *"The Art and Practice of Geomancy," John Michael Greer, 2009, Weiser Books, San Francisco, CA*

This will demonstrate to the practitioner just how connected each thing is to every other in the entire web of Reality.

By use of these twin pillars, Meditation and Trance, and with Fate on your side you will be able to develop a lasting, simple and effective practice of Wisdom seeking, which will bring you peace in an ever-changing world. Others will look to you for guidance, and take solace in the calm which surrounds you.

Meditation is a very rewarding practice, but you absolutely *must* have the discipline to practice it on a regular basis. That is why it is the Pillar of Severity. You must create a regular practice, even if it is only five or ten minutes a day. Daily practice for a short period of time will yield far better results in only a matter of weeks, than an hour session once a week for a year. This is because if you allow everyday stresses to consume you and take you away from your practice for too long, you will be starting at the bottom of the hill each time. Be firm with yourself in creating time to practice, but do not chide yourself excessively for not achieving any certain level of insight or meditation ability. *"Beyond a wholesome discipline, be gentle with yourself."* [5]

Trance is the experience of the Wholeness of Reality, of *"what is."* That is why it is the Pillar of Truth. You will come to understand, often in a wordless way, the inner dimensions of things when you experience trance. Anything can be understood. Anything can be known. The trance connects all times, all places, all peoples, all beings, all things, in a timeless and intimate way. Although meditation is one way of coming to the trance, it is necessary that both be present simultaneously in order for Wholeness to arise. The Pillar of Severity is, in a manner of speaking, the experience of rigid Order in reality, while the Pillar of Truth can be thought of as the experience of the Chaos of all potential, because all times, places and things are present there at once. However, when present together, the Ourobouros is complete. Together they open a gateway, a third way that incorporates both into a true Wholeness of awareness of what all things are...the One Thing.

> *"Go placidly amid the noise and the haste,*
> *and remember what peace there may be in silence."*
> ~Max Ehrmann, 1927

---

5. *"Desiderata," Max Ehrmann, 1927.*

Biography

Christopher Crittenden has been an avowed pagan for 27 years and involved in the occult community for 20 years. He began his study of magical arts through Wicca, but eventually learned that his true path and heart lay in Traditional Witchcraft. After several years of study and practice along traditional lines, he was formally invited by Robin Artisson into the Hethite Crimson Thread of Arteful Sacred Craft and was bestowed the title of Magister Artis.

He lives on the Mississippi Gulf Coast and teaches Spanish at a local college, as well as teaching traditional European centered approaches to spirituality in small groups along the coast. His other passions are classical guitar, history, foreign language, and European martial arts.

To Journey with Völva Stav

Kari Tauring

*I*n Scandinavian tradition we love to journey. We have a habit of walking off with our *"vandre stav"* (wandering staff) into the woods and not returning for hours or even weeks. Sometimes we might set out on boats and not return for generations! Songs of our journeys abound in the folk tradition. And there are some of us who like to travel not just this Earth plane *(Midgard)*, but all the nine *(plus)* worlds of the Cosmic Tree. In Old Norse, these folks are called Völva, staff carriers. The Voluspa Edda *(Volu - Staff Carrier, Spa - wisdom words, 1200's CE)* is the oldest formalized story of the Völva, the creation of the worlds, their inhabitants and the history. In it, Odin beseeches a Völva to read his *oorlag (fate lines in the web of Wyrd)*. I have used this first poem of the Elder Edda—a collection of poems by unknown authors—as a road map in my own journeying through the worlds of Yggdrasil.

My first encounter with the character of the Völva outside of the Eddas, Sagas, and Icelandic poems of Snorri Sturluson *(1200's CE)* was a song from my mother's copy of *Mike and Else's Norwegian Songbook (Skandisk, 1985)*. *"Kjerringe med Staven,"* translates to dearest lady with a stav. This Norwegian Immigrant Era song is still taught at language camps throughout the Midwest. It has grown rare to sing in contemporary Norway, but is still remembered fondly. It was a constant request when I toured Norway in May 2009, because it reminds them of their grandmothers.

"Kjerringe med Staven" most fascinated me for its complete description of the Völva:

1. "Kjerringe" was a title of respect for women. *"Med staven"* means she carries a staff. The stav is the butter churn handle in the first verse and the *kjeppen (walking stick)* in the second verse. The stav is a *tvuru* (*special stirring stick for making rømmegrøt, a sour cream porridge given as sengemat, bed food for mothers after giving birth, a bowl of which is set out for the Norns, the keepers of the well of Wyrd in thanks for safe delivery.*) The *slieva* or ladle, serves her in the battle with a mountain troll. She is always working with some form of the stav.

2. She lives *"way up in Hakka Valley."* Now a suburb of Oslo, at the time of this song it would have been *utgard (literally outside of the farm)*, a characteristic of the wise women in songs and folk tales all over Europe. This is sometimes pictured as the *setter (women's mountain farm)*. In the Eddas and Sagas, the Völva lives *utgard (outside of the community hub)* and travels from farm to farm. While she may pledge service to a particular king, she does not belong to the community in the same way a local midwife might.

3. Her magical training has a lineage. In this case the recipe for butter came from Kari and then Ola who had it before her. Erik the Red's Saga describes the Völva Thorbjorg as being the last of nine sisters.

4. As various verses in this amazing song describe, she is a healer/midwife. She communicates with a hare (*the Goddess Frigg in her animal form*) and land *vaettir* or *jutalane (spirits of land and other worlds)*.

5. She is in tune with nature including her sexuality. This children's song makes it clear that even though the *Kjerringe "falls"* into a cold stream, when she gets out *"she was still just as horny."* This freedom of sexuality ties the *Kjerringe* to the Vanir goddess Freyja, the first and best of Völva.

6. As to the men, in this song the *Kjerringe* first laments that in the old days there used to be men to help them. In the final verse a *Karl (free man)* rides by as she is fighting a mountain troll and likes what he sees. He offers to support her in her work. Norwegian rune ballads also proclaim partnerships and many stories in the Eddas and Sagas describe men who supported staff carriers as well as some who practiced this tradition. Sadly, as patriarchy moved women out of the magical, healing, and leadership roles in the community, the Völva and the *Kjerringe* both became pictured in an ill way, *"illrar brudar"* or women who are wicked. I was very sad to learn that even an emphasis shift in the word *"kjerringe"* can alter the meaning of the word from *"dear lady"* to *"bitch."*

Norwegians did not hang on to the meaning of the word Völva. When I asked why they didn't call me Völva, my guide informed me that it relates to the place *"down there"* on women. I think I surprised her when I said *"that's ok, cunt is now a reclaimed word too! It comes from Cunti, the goddess of the gaping void. You know, Ganungagap."* She smiled and said she hadn't read the Voluspa.

The word they preferred to use to describe me and my work is *Huldra*. While modern usage of this word also pertains more to sexuality and magic, these cow-tailed divas are related to the goddess Freyja, Queen of the Vanir from whom Odin learned *seithr*, the journey practice of Völva. There are many *Huldrelokk (songs learned from, about, or used to call huldre)* from Valdres and Sognefjord in my repertoire. *Lokkr (the luring calls)* are essential for Völva to master as various *lokkr* are used to call the *vaettir (land spirits), disr (goddesses)*, ancestors, and *fylgia (animal spirits)*.

I began the deliberate process of reviving the Völva tradition in the Midwest in 2003 after using the stav *(staff)* for rhythm to accompany vocalizations of rune letters. This use of staff in rhythm was a complete shift in all of my practices, going much deeper than the use of stav in martial arts and runes which I began in the late 1980's.

I added *tein (sucker root/cross stick)* almost immediately. The staff and staff/cross stick create two of the three most intense *(and I would add oldest and most sacred)* runes, ice *(isa)* and need-fire *(nauthiz)*. Ice and fire represent the two main elements of creation and are the two most ancient of the other worlds, Niffel and Muspel, where the frost giants and fire giants live in creative balance around Ganungagap, the gaping void. It is in this very place, with three roots of our bodies connecting to the worlds of ice, fire, and the potential of the void, where alignment with the Cosmic Tree occurs. All the worlds become accessible through our bodies, vibrations, and sound keys as we chant and stav.

Völva Stav is natural, instinctive, and deeply human. It is a self-directed way to journey as each participant has her or his own stav, shifts and changes rhythms with the movement of the journey. It can be done solo but is most exhilarating as a group practice. Unlike a drum circle, when one person's rhythm shifts and changes, the whole fabric of sound moves to adjust. It becomes an organic weave of sound and vibration.

The main tools are the body, voice, stav and tein. I always begin each session by stretching out my body. As the primary tool, we want to keep our bodies in good condition. The point of the practice is to achieve balance and awareness of the present moment and to shift our consciousness in order to perceive the subtle energy of the *web of Wyrd*. This state of consciousness has been called *seið (seith, seithr, seidr)*. From this state of consciousness we are able to perceive *oorlag*, the *web of Wyrd* and send out our *hugin (thought)* and *munin (memory)* or *hamr (subtle or astral body)* into any of the nine worlds. We can then use the energy generated in Völva Stav to send healing or do other work. The Norse tradition is, like most shamanic traditions, a body/mind/spirit tradition. It is important to understand that parts of our mind complex such as thought and memory are connected to our soul and body complexes. The integration and balance of body/mind/soul is the healthy state.

Full integration allows Odin to send his thought and memory into the nine worlds in the shape of two ravens named for their functions, Hugin and Munin. He can change his subtle body *(hamr)* to appear as an old beggar or other shapes. The most famous shape shifter, Loki, can adjust his hamr to change into a mare, an old giant woman, even a flea. It is the goal of each Völva to gain this balance, integration, and flexibility of her body/mind/spirit complex, allowing her to send parts of self out into the nine worlds at will.

Obtaining your stav and tein can be as simple as a walk in the woods. Scandinavian traditions are nothing if not practical and utilitarian. Free fallen wood is a gift from the World Tree. Trees that are important to you are the ones you should seek your tools from. Staving on a cutting board or wooden floor is much more affective than staving on carpet or tile. The vibration of the wood through your feet contributes to the alignment of your bodies with the World Tree. A rubber tip on the end of your stav may be good protection when you use it to walk about, but remove it when you use it in stav ritual. Wood on wood is the way to go. If you don't take the bark off the stav, you will find it in bits on the floor when you are done with a stav session. You can remove it before hand or clean up after you stav it off. It's up to you. A cane or walking stick that has been passed down or is special to you is a great stav. However, be aware that you will be denting and nicking it with use.

Other tools include spindles, looms, runes, churns, the tools of every day women's work *(as described in Kjerringe med Staven)*. There are many examples in the lore about women creating magical clothing, imbued with protection through chants to the rhythm of the spinning or weaving. It was so prominent a magic that early Christian laws directly forbade this fusion of spiritual and mundane tasks. Churning spells and charms abound through folk songs and stories. Today women are re-claiming the sacred nature of their traditional work.

Völva Stav can be performed while sitting or standing. We all have different physical abilities and Völva Stav accommodates them all. If standing, the horseback riding stance of martial arts keeps the spine and roots limber. If you are sitting or in a wheelchair, try to maintain a posture that keeps your diaphragm open and joints loose. Maintain foot contact with the ground or floor *(even through footrests)* through visualization. The spine is our main stav. It is the spine that aligns with the trunk of the World Tree. The external stav for creating rhythm can be as small as a pencil.

As explained, Völva Stav is based on the Indo-European cosmology of the World Tree, the *axis mundi* named *Miötvið, Yggdrasil,* or *Irminsul.* *Miötvið* is Old Norse for the great tree from the Voluspa. Yggdrasil relates to Odin *(Ygg)* and the tree as his *"terrible horse."* He hung himself on the World Tree for nine days as a sacrificial act in order to gain the secrets of the runes, the primordial nature energy represented in script and song. Irminsul comes from Anglo-Saxon tradition.

I simply use *"World Tree"* and think of it like a bonsai growing in a pot. The vessel in which the tree grows is our universe. There are three roots connecting to three water sources which feed and nourish the tree. Serpents below gnaw on the roots to keep them from bursting out of the vessel. The four wind deer and the world tree goat nip and nibble on the leaves and branches, keeping the tree from becoming top heavy and toppling out of the vessel. There are myriad creatures living in and on the tree and distinct worlds that the tree holds together. Norse folk agree on at least seven worlds, most believe in nine. In my experience, some of the worlds are distinct and some run into one another, blending into a unified landscape. And I have been deep into certain caves that have no descriptors in the lore.

With the spine as the trunk and our feet and perineum grounding cord rooted in the well-springs from which we draw energy, we have a *"three legged stool"* from which to journey. From the stability of this sacred geometry we begin to stav creating with intention the fourth point that squares us onto the path of any of Yggdrasil's worlds. The energy of the World Tree and her three wells is ancient, raw in many cases, and quite powerful.

In 2005 I wrote the opening meditation for *"Beyond the Water Gap"* a Conference featuring Masaru Emoto *(The Hidden Messages in Water, Beyond Words Publishing, 2004).* This work formalized the full practice of Völva Stav. Rhythm, rhyme, and runes came together to align an auditorium of people with the Scandinavian World Tree, sending us all on a journey to the well of Mimmir to retrieve the memory and messages of the waters of the cosmos.

This specific journey has been performed off and on through classes and workshops. It is written in rhyme and with a steady four count. It describes the generally acknowledged attributes of the World Tree and her worlds. I include it here in hopes that the reader will pick up a broom handle and wooden spoon and try it out.

The Journey
(c)Tauring 2003

Eagle, hawk and cock I see
perched up in the branches three
Four winds, journey deer, move across the crown
(Austri Vestri Sudri Nordri)
Ratatosk, journey squirrel, I am moving down
(chick chick chick chick chreeeee)
Nine worlds three wells the journey has begun
Nine worlds three wells breathe as we go down

1st Stage – Level One

Alfheim – Vanneheim – ancient elves and gods
Worlds, I see them, two of nine across
Alfheim – Vannehiem – Freyja bless my passing
Skirt the river Ifling
Midgard human home another of the nine
Asgard Odin's land bless me as I ride
Urdarbrunner first well, guarded by the Norns
Urdarbrunner well of fate Urd Verthandi Skuld
Ride away, ride away, North we go and all
(Rida Rida Rida vi, Rida Rida kom mit mi)

2nd Stage – Level 3

Down and down and deeper still, to the primal lands we ride
Muspelheim the seeds of all, primordial the firey tide
Niffelhiem and Hel's domain, water raging Hvergalmir
Worlds collide, sparks and steam, the source of rivers flowing clean
Who guards the wellspring of creation?
Nidgahogg the Water Dragon!
(Nidgahogg Ginnungagap – Astri Astri Rida vi, Astri Astri com mit mir)

3rd Stage – Level 2

East the path that Odin took, riding through the worlds again
Through the world of Nidavellier, to the world of Svartalfheim
In Svartalfheim the dark elves dwell but Joutenheim contains the well
Cross the river deadly cold, river Ifling never froze
(cross the Ifling deadly cold, river Ifling never froze)
Joutenheim the giant's land, rock and frost the bane of man
Down and down the root we go beneath the world the sacred well
Mimir guards the water there, Water Etin primordial!

4th Stage – at Mimirbrunner
> *Mimir wisest of them all, drinking freely from the well*
> *Your name means ponder, seeing, gaze*
> *Your name in our own tongues we praise*
> *(Remembering, pondering, seeing knowing)*
> *Mimir wisest of them all, drinking from the gjallerhorn*
> *Memory of all that's known, ponder, seeing, gazing shown*
> *Wisdom seekers at your well, sing your praise, ask to gaze*
> *Odin's eye looks back at us, reflections of the ancient days*
> *Look, see, remember*
> *Look, see, remember*
> *Look, see, remember*

5th Stage – Returning
> *(change to pols rhythm, then vowel sounds chant – ah, eh, ee, oh, ooo)*
> *I see, I know, I remember, many thanks*
> *I see, I know, I remember, many thanks (manga takk)*
> *Pull yourselves from Mimirbrunner, horses ready to return*
> *Bring with you the wisdom piece, remembering the knowledge learned*
> *Prepare for change for as we go, wisdom is transforming you*
> *Share with us what you do know, that we all may learn it too*
> *I see, I know, I remember, many thanks*
> *I see, I know, I remember, many thanks (tusen takk)*
> *Back up through the worlds we ride, Mannaheim our human home*
> *We are changed, all life renewed, through the wisdom that was shown*

Of course, when you journey in any cultural context, using any technique, it is important to ground and center yourself in the here and now.

I would like to include one last example of the use of Völva Stav to send healing energy:

We begin by stretching out. This is no passive journey work. In my sessions we begin with breath, complete and deep. I teach the rune *isa*, ice with our staving, *nauthiz* the need fire by adding tein. We sing the invocation, *Komme Alle* (Tauring, 2005). Then it's time to do some work.

On this particular day Karin, an advanced student, came with a healing request. Her friend in Michigan was rushing to complete some tasks and broke her foot. Karin pulled a rune from the basket to guide the healing intention and energy. It was Hagalaz, hail storm, the rune that starts the middle *aett* of the Elder Futhark. Following this rune are *isa* and *nauthiz*.

We began by talking about the abrasive clearing and cleaning properties of *hagalaz*, hail storm. Then we began to stav the rhythm of the rune and play with the stresses on the word. HAgalaz, haGAlaz, hagalAZ, staving and playing. Some of us played with the vowels long and lovely. Some of us sang the assonance of the consonant breath, summoning the winds *(haaa, ga, lassssz).*

Someone started with isa and another nauthiz and we played in this way until I was summoned to the table in the middle. The other four women continued to play while I searched for a good vessel to put the magic into from among the tools on the table. I spied the drop spindle and tried a few things.

The women were building up a nice eye of the storm for me. I struck an archers pose and wouldn't you know, I was pointing right at Michigan when I began to unwind the already spun thread. Karin was to the right of me, in the Southwest corner. I was facing South with my front body. My right hand held the spindle and I pointed between the heads of the women in the Northeast and East. On this continent, indigenous peoples often put the doorways in this direction, where the pattern keepers live, the web-weavers/*frith* holders of the circle.

As the women worked the wind circle, I sucked it up through the straw in my spine and sent it out through the wool thread. I felt it land in the recipient's lap and coil up like a cat. Round and round her it went, soft and fluffy. Then I called out her name and said, *"Embrace the void that hagal has left. Do not move, be as ice. Do not spark the need fire until you are absolutely only on the path you have been born to walk."* I heard ladies calling out *"Embrace the Void,"* and *"Hagalaz,"* and it sounded for everything like a Swedish Heathen Baptist summoning of the Spirit!

Then I started winding the thread back in along with my breath and we all sucked in deep and long and exhaled with intentions for her healing, clear path, and doing without doing. I rolled the yarn back to the spindle and the core energy came back in. I stopped at the fulcrum, the point of the spin where the un-spun wool meets the tight spin.

Women were just breathing now. I found the spot and splayed the wool through my fingers. With my right hand on the spindle's stav, I summoned the core of the energy up through my feet, my spine the spindle the thread spiral and into the small hole between spun and un-spun universe. I spoke our intention to the recipient again, into the un-spun side of the hole and began to spin her new thread. The energy of the spun line flowed up and gathered with the un-spun intention.

When the inches of new thread were done, I unwrapped a few inches of the spun and broke the line. I tied that end in first. Then I tied in the new end. Then I tied a knot in the middle. I rolled it in my palms and blew on it saying encouraging things to her from us, then held it out in my left palm. The four women of the circle placed their hands around like a great round Yurt of working women's palms. Oh, the tingles!

We received emails from her immediately asking what we had done. Karin sent the healing knots to her in the mail and it was up to her to do the rest.

In this time of deep Earth changes, as the vibration rate of the Earth increases, individual humans must also increase their vibration. This requires individuals to do their own spiritual work rather than relying on a hierarchy or priesthood to do it for us. Our collective human awareness of the multi-dimensional universe is expanding due to books and movies that can explain the quantum mechanics in layman's terms.

This capacity to conceive of a multi-dimensional universe informs our ability to perceive it. The challenge then is in how to live physically in an inter-dimensional universe. Völva Stav addresses the intellectual, physical, and spiritual aspects of this, gives solid techniques for anchoring and aligning all of our bodies on every level and throughout all the dimensions, and is culturally specific to Indo-European folk ways as well as universal for humanity.

I believe it is intensely important for individual humans to look into their own cultural heritage, ancestral folkways, and genetic memory for just how to do this. All any of us has is our own unique *oorlag (DNA, primal layers, ancestor memories, karma)* to read, heal, and grow. The sharing of *oorlag* defines the *web of Wyrd* for our families, communities, and indeed, the whole world. I have taught my children that they are obligated to explore every curve and color of their unique puzzle piece. There is no one else who can fit into their spot in the unity of all.

What's more, they can not perceive the unity of all until they have become willing to be their authentic and unique piece. For this we must feel ready, willing, able, and deserving to be just who we are. And just who we are starts deep in our heritage, our unique indigenous expressions, and all the way back to the first humans, our first ancestors. In this way we can heal our own broken connections to the deep body of the Earth Mother and affect true and lasting change.

Biography

Kari Tauring is a Volva, Old Norse for staff-carrier. The Scandinavian heritage of her mother's people who immigrated to the Midwest, along with twenty plus years of spiritual and musical practice, has resulted in Volva Stav. Combining the runes, stav *(stick rhythm)*, poetry, songs, dances, and art of her heritage, Volva Stav brings the practitioner on a culturally specific journey through time, space, and memory. From Northern Europe's earliest Paleolithic shamanic iconography to the staff carriers of the Immigrant Era, the practice of Volva Stav helps one remember and integrate Norse mythology, cosmology, theology, and ritual. Through her father's side, Tauring's ties to the North American continent are equally deep. She is a bridge walker of the Northern Hemisphere.

Volva Stav has spread throughout the United States where Indigenous European spiritual traditions are growing in diverse communities. Through performances, workshops, and recordings, as well as her book, *The Runes: A Human Journey (published lulu.com 2007)*, and articles published by Llewellyn, Volva Stav has gained an international audience. Most recently, she was featured on Norwegian television *("Alt for Norge,"* tvnorge.no, *2010)* where she carried the stav back to the homeland. Traveling and teaching for the past four years has defined, honed, and deepened Volva Stav to the point of producing a manual and DVD *(coming spring 2010)*.

Coven Hedgecraft

Sylva Markson

One of the most challenging and rewarding aspects of hedgecraft is engaging in the traditional spirit travels with other Crafters. For most, it is not an easy achievement, but it is one of the foundational experiences of group Craft working. There are those who say it can't be done—that hedgework can only be a solitary pursuit. But, in fact, a group or coven can take these journeys together, if they are patient and committed to the work.

There are many examples from witch lore of traveling to the great gatherings, be it at Benevento, Blockula, Mons Veneris, or any of the other sacred *"witch places."* While it seems that some witches may have attended physically, others, perhaps most, flew or otherwise traveled there in spirit form. While there, they interacted with one another and with other spirits and entities, be they Gods, fae, genii, ancestors, etc. These were not merely journeys within, though witches do that work, as well. These journeys are, in fact, journeys beyond the self to a reality that has been created, attended and reinforced by witches over many centuries. The details may vary—there may be different visuals or experiences, because the unseen world is a mutable one—but the foundation is the same across witchdom.

The idea that witches could interact in the Otherworld has been with me since my earliest days in Craft. One night, on a coven camping trip, two of my coven-mates were taken by the fae. They were not taken together. C woke up and noticed that R was gone, and then he was taken through a door that led to another world. For the most part, they were separate, so they did not share the precisely the same experiences while there, except for a few moments when they saw one another. R said something to C that later they both, independently of one another, repeated word for word. From this, as well as other details, it was clear that these were not dreams. In fact, this was actual travel to a real place where both of them had real and transforming experiences.

The question then became one of how to go together intentionally, how to do the work of Craft in those realms, as a group. This became a focus that we have actively pursued for the past 20 years.

What are the motivations of these journeys? Why do witches seek to *"cross the Hedge,"* in the first place? Traditionally, there are three overall themes that these journeys take. The first is the seeking of divine wisdom, communication with the Gods, and transformation of the self. Second is for interaction with ancestors, the fae, and other spirits and genii, for a wide variety of reasons, including seeking magical allies, lost knowledge, etc. Third, though not done as commonly by modern witches, is working in the Otherworld to manifest a material benefit in this world, such as a bountiful harvest, success in battle, healing, protection, and the like.

Where the Worlds Intersect

When witches form a compass or a circle by whatever method, we are, in essence, creating a physical representation of that traditional otherworldly gathering place. The witch's sacred cosmology, consisting of the four cardinal directions oriented around a center point, be it seen as the crossroads, the world tree, or the omphalos, is the axis of the worlds. This center point is often represented in the circle by a stang, an altar, a bonfire, or a cauldron, depending on the group and the work they are doing. This circle is more than a representation, however—it is a manifestation within the physical world of the otherworldly reality that witches share.

Within this physical depiction of the witch's cosmology is done all of the physical work of the Craft, but all of that work is, in fact, taking place on multiple levels. While we do the physical work within the physical boundary, there is subtle working is being done on that plane which is beyond the physical representation, and the energy/power of that other plane is also being brought within our physical sphere. The circle or compass becomes a meeting place where the two worlds are connected. Thus it is that the physical circle or compass also functions as a launch point or portal from whence the witch travels beyond it to the unseen Cosmos that it represents.

How does a group come to do this traveling together, so that they are sharing common experiences in the Otherworld? There are many techniques and possibilities, but the two most common ones are the formation of a group mind and the formation of an *"astral temple,"* which is merely a way of expressing the idea of shared imagery or landscape within the veiled reality. Either of these methods will lead to shared otherworldly experience, and they are highly effective when utilized together.

Crossing the Hedge

In modern parlance, what witches call crossing the Hedge or going *"oot and aboot"* is more commonly referred to as astral projection. However, where some practice astral projection to travel to places in the physical world, like visiting a friend in another city, witches use this practice to travel to the Otherworld. The form this travel takes can vary from foot travel, flight in human form, upon a broom, a stang or an animal, or transformation into an animal or mythic creature. Just as the Unseen world is mutable, our spirit form or *"astral body"* is also mutable and free from physical laws.

There are numerous techniques that can be employed to free the spirit from the body. They include, but are not limited to trance work, consistent ritual, dance, drugs, and flying ointment, a hallucinogenic salve that is absorbed through the skin. These techniques are often worked in combination to greater effect.

Escaping the body comes more easily to some than to others. When working with a group, the strengths and weaknesses of each member will affect all. Someone to whom this travel comes easily will have to exercise patience in waiting for others to *"catch up"* to them. However, someone to whom it does not come as naturally may actually find it easier when working consistently with a trusted group, as they can, to some extent, carry him along.

Three things, above all, are needed for successful group hedgework—trust, repetition and commitment. Trust is necessary so that each member will be comfortable in working unguardedly with the others. There must be an intimacy within the group, not sexual intimacy, necessarily, but rather, personal intimacy. There must be a willingness to be without barriers among the group members, even if only during the working. It is generally best that some personal boundaries are intentionally kept in place when work is not in progress.

The members of the group must become attuned with one another. This intimacy should be developed on multiple levels—through genuine friendship and time spent together, through exercises in energy work and shield work, and through the ongoing sharing of spiritual and magical experiences that the practice of Craft will inevitably provide.

The same form of work must be done repeatedly and consistently. It will not be effective, particularly in the beginning, to try different techniques each attempt. Repetitive ritual practice, as well as repetitive and consistent imagery and consistent correspondences create a pattern that takes on a power of its own. As the work proceeds, the power builds and the group members can tap into the power of that pattern, which can carry the *"slower"* members along and can strengthen the connections between the individuals once they successfully leave their bodies. These connections will enable the interaction once in the Otherworld.

Additionally, each member of the group must also commit to the work. Having consistency among the members is essential as, again, the energies of the work form a pattern and the pattern is vital to success. It becomes noticeable when a member is absent. The pattern is weakened and this is detrimental to the work.

Creating an Astral Temple or Sacred Landscape

Before we do this work, we need to know where we are going. Some traditions may have some otherworldly *"landmarks"* for their practitioners to follow or seek, a pattern that has already been established that the group can tap into. For most, however, much of this lore has been lost or is sketchy, at best. In those groups, the landmarks will need to be created. As the Otherworld is a mutable one, there are many forms witches can build within which to make these connections and have the encounters they seek when traveling.

The use of the term *"astral temple"* is not intended to imply that the otherworldly destination must be visualized as a building. It is simply the common term used to describe a place created within the magical Unseen world. Among witches, the astral temple is most commonly outdoors, with specific, established landmarks to which they can return again. *"Sacred landscape"* may be a more applicable and palatable term.

Historically, the details of the landscape have varied based on time and place, but the foundation remains constant. There is an axis from which the four directions proceed and at which they meet, and that axis, whether represented by a mountain, a tree, a maypole, a cauldron, a standing stone, a sacred well, or what have you, is the intersection between the worlds.

When working with a group, it is helpful to begin by laying out the basics of the landscape with a few essential details and landmarks, but it is also wise to allow the group to develop additional landmarks though their experiences within the landscape. In other words, agree in advance upon the general framework, but allow the details to be filled in as the pattern establishes itself through practice. For example, a group may decide that the meeting place within their sacred landscape is a clearing in an oak grove with a particularly large, sacred tree in the center.

The early working of the group would center around meeting at that grove and developing their awareness of one another within it. As that awareness grows and as familiarity with the grove itself grows, the grove will become more real and the shared experiences more detailed. Over time, further details will fall into place—perhaps there is a crow consistently in the tree, for example, or perhaps there is a path leading into the forest that, eventually, the group will follow.

In this sacred landscape, the group will interact not only with each other, but with the various spirits, as well. They will see one another in the forms their astral bodies take, and they will share experiences that will give surprising new direction to the work and to the group.

The Group Mind

What is a group mind? It is a form of collective consciousness. Any group coming together for a shared goal will form some level of group mind, even without intending to do so. At its most basic level, it is a form of group identity. Members of a branch of the military will find a sense of camaraderie with other members whom they have never met, because they share experiences and an outlook that non-members cannot partake in. At its worst, a group mind can manifest without intent, out of chaos, as mob mentality, where individuals may get caught up in rage and violence that they would never consider in other circumstances.

However, in magical terms, the group mind is something very specific that, when developed with clear intent and respect for the individuality of those involved, can become a powerful magical entity.

When a coven is working with intent to create a group mind, there must be great care taken in determining the form it will take. There are numerous techniques a coven can use in the formation and empowerment of their group mind. The very act of naming the coven will begin to give form to the group mind of the coven. Just as witches choose a magical name that defines or represents their inner self and/or who they aspire to be, so the name of the coven is a magical name that defines and represents the character and aspirations of the group.

This group definition can function to draw the appropriate people to the group and to form bonds between group members, both on the mundane level of providing a common vision, but also on the magical level as they each put their focus and energy into strengthening that group identity. This will enable group members to act in accord, magically, and will form the connections that will enable them to interact in the Otherworld when doing hedgework.

Another way that the group mind is given strength and cohesion is through the consistent use of the same rites. Rituals performed the same way again and again become more powerful each time as they form a pattern of power that becomes greater then the sum of the parts. When each coven member knows the rites by heart, there is no longer any active thought as to what comes next, what specific words or actions mean, and all are working in unison. It is then that they are tapping into the power of that pattern to its greatest utility. The group mind is not only functioning as the collective of the individuals in that coven, but is connecting to the collective group mind of the entire tradition and history of that particular pattern of power.

That may be as far as most groups choose to pursue the group mind, and it will work wonders in their hedgeworking, as well as in all magical work they might engage in.

However, there is a deeper level of group mind work that can be achieved through consistent magical work, and that is the creation of a coven entity or thought-form. The work should not be entered into lightly, as this entity can take on a life of its own to an extent that it cannot be controlled by any individual within the group. This is not meant to be alarmist—there are magical groups that create this type of thought-form for the express purpose of *"turning it loose"*—but that is not the intent witches have when doing this work. It must simply be borne in mind, so that the group is always operating with awareness and intent.

The easiest way to begin this aspect of working, once a cohesive group mind has been formed, is to find a totem animal or spirit form for the group mind. Just as each witch resonates with particular forms and spirits, a group mind will do the same. Having chosen a coven has a name that expresses the group's character, in some way, and after the individuals have done the work necessary to consistently share these journeys, the group can seek out a form to operate in as one entity. The individuals in a group doing this work must share a strong and clear intent and must each have a strong sense of self, but also the ability and willingness to temporarily abandon that sense of self.

Once that animal or spirit form has been established and the coven has worked consistently in that form, they will find that their psychic connections to one another strengthening, even in the mundane world, and that any work they set out to do as a group will be accomplished more easily. The focus of the group entity is more clear and powerful than it is among even the strongest group of separate individuals.

Flying by Night

The work witches do in the Otherworld is without boundary or limit. To take coven working to the height of possibility requires a lot of time, patience, and consistency, but it is supremely rewarding. It is, in fact, following some of the oldest traditions and practices of Craft, involving crossing the Hedge and exploring, rediscovering and working in the spirit places witches have always held dear.

This work will enable and empower our efforts to seek divine communication, to obtain magical allies and spirit contacts, to rediscover ancestral knowledge and to achieve magical outcomes in the physical world. It is through this work that we will rediscover what a coven is meant to be and where the power of witchdom truly lies.

Biography

Sylva Markson grew up in Northern Minnesota, where she developed a deep and abiding love for its lakes and forests. She has a degree in both History and Religion, and has always been interested in the roots of spiritual paths and in combining intellectual exploration with mystical or shamanic experiences. She has been practicing Craft for twenty years and has led a coven, along with her husband and magical partner, for about fifteen, with an emphasis on altered states of consciousness and shamanic techniques.

Her other interests include nature, animals, equal rights, cultures, and travel. Hobbies include antiquing, camping, and herbalism. She currently lives in northern Minnesota with her husband, three dogs, and three birds.

Perceiving Perception

Rev. Jack Green

> *"As the Cricket's soft autumn hum is to us*
> *so are we to the trees*
> *as are they to the rocks and hills."*
> - Gary Snyder

I have been practicing British Traditional Wicca and Traditional Witchcraft in one form or another for 23 years. I have passed through the Veil with my coven-mates and our teachers many times. We have invited many denizens of the spirit world to visit us in our various covensteads and quite a few have taken us up on that. I have *"drunk from the timbrel"* of the *"otherside"* enough times now to know that no ethereal taxonomy devised by any human tradition or culture can encompass the complexity that my comrades and I have seen and experienced. I know I know nothing of the wonders beyond the zenith above and of what lies past the nadir below. I do know that beyond the limits of human Ken that, as the old maps used to say: *"Here There be Dragons."*

But I can tell you what I have seen, heard and felt in my experiences in the Otherworld. Perception is at the heart of this issue and one place it is discussed is in *"The Ecology of Magic"* chapter 1[1] by the philosopher and cultural ecologist, David Abram. David Abram studied in Indonesia with their native *dukuns* and in Nepal with traditional *dzankris* and seems to not only see the denizens of the Otherworld as existing invisibly in *this* plane, but also as personifications of non-human natural forces rather than disembodied *"ectoplasmic"* or ethereal ghostly figures. That is, the native words we translate into *"spirits"* do not have the same connotations we conjure up in our heads from our Judeo-Christian cultural baggage.

---

1. *"The Spell of the Sensuous: Perception and Language in a More-Than-Human World,"* David Abram, 1996.

For example, when Abram was living among the *balians* of Bali he noticed that the native food offerings left out for the *"household spirits"* was eaten by the local ants.[2] At first he thought *"What a waste!"* The ants stole the offering. But then he thought what if the ants were the spirits in question? What if the offering was to the spirits to prevent ants or other insect infestation in the house? If so, it worked.

I do something similar with the local Minnesota Yellow Jacket wasps in late summer. I leave a partially finished soda or hamburger off to one end of the picnic table at our late summer outings. The Yellow Jackets will congregate there when left alone and shooed gently away from our plates. This could be described as an *"offering"* to the wasps to leave us alone. It's a bribe really, protection money even. The net result is the same, a quiet picnic lunch.

What if *"the spirits"* of various cultures are the local non-human awarenesses that needed to be acknowledged to prevent them from doing harm to human interests? It's all a matter of perception.

One way of describing these styles of perception is by Eyes of *Flesh*, Eyes of *Mind*, and Eyes of *Spirit*.

Eyes of Flesh are relatively easy to understand. Here science rules. We talk about frequencies of light and the differentiation of color, the anatomical structures of lens and retina, rods and cones and other cellular architecture. The Mind's Eye is harder to explain, but we all experience it. That is the eye that watches our dreams, that visualizes our plans, that sees what we imagine; we all have them. If I say *"visualize a red apple"* you can *"see"* it with your mind's eye even though your *Eyes of Flesh* are actually seeing a string of black letters on a white page in a book. We are now in the domain of psychology and philosophy. Of them all, though, *Eyes of Spirit* are the most difficult to explain or understand. When Moses saw the burning bush[3] he didn't imagine it the way I asked you to imagine an apple with your *Eyes of Mind*. No, he experienced it via a different kind of *"seeing."* He saw with his *Eyes of Spirit*, eyes seeing what felt like an external phenomena that *demanded* his attention. He did not *command* his imagination as you did with the apple.

It is the experience of our own imagination and dreams that leads to the philosophical question regarding whether what we experience day to day is dream or reality. In science, we hold axiomatically, that is we assume our experience is a reflection of reality, we *assume* what we perceive has some connection to reality. We *assume* that this reality can actually be discerned. We *assume* that cause follows effect. In short we have *faith* that the pale images dancing on the wall of Plato's Cave actually mean something. Scientists have to in order for the scientific method to work.

2. *Op, cit. 12-13.*
3. *Exodus 3:2.*

Philosophy, on the other hand, can be more open in its interpretations and operations. Philosophy bridges science and religion and allows us to work with exotic experiences that science has yet too deal with or may never be capable of dealing with, such as what we have just called the *Eyes of Spirit*. In fact, perception is a key element in the branch of philosophy called *epistemology*, which asks, how do we know what we know? The scientific method is one way and the rationalism of the pagan Greeks is another. There are as many approaches as there are cultures and more.

There is also *phenomenology*, which is the philosophical approach that aims to describe conscious experience, the phenomena of our cognitive life, in direct, clear and descriptive language. This is, in part, to avoid the obscuring effect of jargon making it difficult for the average intelligent person to understand what's going on. It is also to keep the focus on the experience of the phenomena itself. Personally, I try to take a phenomenological approach to all my *"paranormal"* experiences as well as my *"normal"* ones, both in their epistemological as well as metaphysical analyses, interpretations, and applications. I simply relay the phenomena as I experienced them and separate the interpretation from the reporting.

Clearly, perception is key to understanding both the normal and paranormal world. One example can be seen in the movie *"The Others"* *(2001)*[4] where there is a relevant play on perception *(spoiler alert)* for it turns out the *"ghosts"* in the film were the *"real"* people and Grace Stewart *(played by Nicole Kidman)* and her two children were the *"actual"* ghosts. They did not realize that, in a fit of madness and grief over the loss of her husband, she had killed her own children and that they were the ones haunting the house and not the ones being haunted. Perhaps, in a similar fashion the Fey see themselves as *"real"* and it is we humans who are the shadowy, gossamer figures haunting the shadows of *their* world.

Another view that is somewhat similar can be found in the *Bordertown* series,[5] a collection of urban fantasy tales set in a strange metropolis where the *Elflands* and the mundane world collide. It's a place where neither *Elven* magic nor our technology works quite right and uncertainty over what is real reigns. The separate worlds of perception that intersect in *Bordertown* overlap each other, sometimes parallel and sometimes divergent. Which is more real? The viewpoint of those of *Elfland* or those from the mundane world?

---

4. *"The Others," Alejandro Amenabar, starring Nicole Kidman, 2001.*
5. *"Bordertown" series written by various authors, edited by Terri Windling, Signet Books, New York, NY*

Moses saw the burning bush. Grace Stewart saw the new living beings in her old house and interpreted them as ghosts. In our ancestral cultures, such as Gothic Christian, they saw angels and halos above the heads of saints. The Celtic peoples, both pagan and Christian, saw white stags, hares, or dogs that would lead them into the other world to meet the *Fey*. Hedgewitches and other types of witches see animals and other spirits that impart wisdom from beyond the Veil. Witches say they fly by night to the Sabbat at *Blokula, the Brocken*, or *Benevento*, experiencing the countryside flying by below them. All religions report some type of visionary experiences and cultivate numerous techniques to try and induce them. These profound and transformative experiences cannot simply be commanded to occur like an image of an apple conjured in the Mind's Eye. It requires the *Eyes of Spirit.*

Another, more recent example, can be seen in the reports of Wiccan and other witchcraft circles that have had *caval sidhe* and *cath sidhe* visitations. These are the Celtic terms for fairy dogs and fairy cats. In my own coven experiences, a *cath sidhe* entered our circle once and rubbed up against each us in turn. For all the world it felt just like a living cat, affectionate, yet with an animal level intelligence. Recently, on the cable television series called *"Haunted,"* they described what sounded like a haunting of a house by a cat that died in a fire. This unexpected sensing of a ghostly cat or feeling a fairy cat in circle are very different experiences than simply picturing an orange tabby in one's mind. The two are equally indemonstrable by scientific means. They are both experiences beyond the reach of the *Eyes of Flesh.*

Once, my wife and I attended a *Keltrian Druid* ritual north of Minneapolis. We had already had several years of heavy training in meditation, study, circle-work and magic. We called the ancestors to join us and suddenly a *Pict* was there, shrieking in my head. I could see the circle and hear the Druid's liturgy continue as I swayed, reeling from the loud screaming in a foreign language and a barrage of imagery. I focused on the Druids around my wife and I. She put a hand on my shoulder to and her eyes asked *"are you okay?"* I nodded and screwed my *Eyes of Spirit* closed tight and clamped my mind down tight over all the psychic noise.

My training in shielding became disturbingly useful. I could still hear his muffled yells but it was at tolerable level. I looked around in the smoky room and began to relax and ground myself, though I could still feel his hissing rage and blood-fear. In his lifetime, the Highlands was held by the pre-Celtic Picts for centuries and were being invaded by the Celtic Scots from Ireland. It was cut-throat, all-out war. I wrapped my hand around the hilt of my athame and *"felt"* it at him and the feel of a weapon in his long-dead hand calmed him.

As he quieted, I could go into ritual *"autopilot"* and slowly open my *Eyes of Spirit* again. I was greeted to a sight unlike anything I had experienced before. It was as if I was in a cavern lit from near *"me"* and from another moving source. Shadows shifted and flickered crazily in the glowing, bluish fog. The light was the Pict, still angry and afraid and babbling in a language I couldn't understand. I noticed I was the still, central light in the center of my mind. The shifting shadows were the connections of the various parts of my mind connected to other parts. It was illuminated crazily from the glowing lost Pict, radiant bits flying off sticking here and there as he wandered about. I continued to send him waves of calm; he was safe here and the Celts couldn't see him.

The Druid rite outside continued its stately pace. As the Pict began to calm, the rate of his luminous sputter also slowed. I could begin to see the pattern of the structures as the dimming shadows moved slower and slower in the thickening haze. I knew I could have let him into the *"driver's seat,"* that is let him *"ride"* me like the *loa* do in Voudoun rituals, but he never asked. I don't think he liked the space I was in. He slowly faded and slipped to the other side and the shadows vanished into blue mist. He was gone. Still, I realized he had left a lot of things behind so that when I journaled and dug into the history and archeology of Scotland it was with a much deeper understanding.

A year or so later, we held an outdoor May Day ritual in rural Wisconsin not far from Selena Fox's Circle Sanctuary. The sponsors had set up a small stone circle in a little clearing near the house and the woods were full of deer, raccoon and wild turkey. On the second night we held the initiate's circle. It was cool and lovely next to the woods and we could hear little rustlings as we cast the circle. Once into the rite a little, I noticed a little glow to my left. I turned my head and saw nothing there. Then I noticed it again. This time I *looked* left and beheld what I later called the *"Beltane Star."*

It/She was a pale, luminous blue-white sphere of astounding internal dynamic complexity. She/It was a beautiful, integrated and symmetrical sculpture in light. It/She politely asked with a gentle mental smile if she may have a ride and I said sure. In a flash I was… *overlaid.* I could see through my *Eyes of Flesh* but it was distant, like through a backwards telescope. I suspected my eyes had gone obsidian black. My hearing was muffled slightly, as well. I/She/It drew in a deep breath and slowly exhaled with relish. Then It/She kissed the acting High Priestess as part of the personal consecrations and It/She said to me *"they/she doesn't know who you/I are/am"* with a gentle smile.

It was then that I found I couldn't move. I tugged and grew alarmed and *She/It* gently smiled and released me, slipping smoothly away with a soft thank you. I asked *Her/It* if *It/She* was a *Mighty One* and *She/It* smiled gently and said *"not yet."* *She/It* flared brilliantly as she cleanly withdrew (no *"sputtering" like the Pict*) to my left and I saw the light go, which only then reminded me that physically *I'm blind in my left eye*. The star faded rapidly as she receded into the dark. I was alone in my own head again. Thankfully, as *It/She* was the most powerful entity I had yet encountered, I was fortunate she has been as compassionate as *She/It* appeared.

This is a complete contrast to the *"Samhain Masks"* I encountered several years later. My two coven-sisters and I were in Kentucky on Halloween. We were heading home after a big gather and had stopped in the middle of Illinois for the night. In the hotel room, we decided to have our own little Samhain circle, one just for the three of us. After the circle was cast, we felt ourselves going up into the night, high up in the sky until we were in the spaces of the Hosts of Air. I looked down at the land below and at the city glowing beautifully far below in the late autumn night. I could even see tiny clusters of deer in the woods.

I looked up and saw my coven-sisters receding in the distance and I turned to follow when this...*thing* moved in front of me and demanded a ride. I tried to go around him and he moved to block my path. It looked for all the world like a ramshackle cluster of wooden masks haphazardly bolted, clipped, and nailed together in a random clump. The various masks each had different expressions and he repeated himself—*"gimmie a ride."*

I couldn't see my coven-sisters anymore and now I had to deal with this thing and then I had an idea. *"Sure,"* I said mentally and the collage approached and I let him in, but didn't let him take over. Instead, while *"holding"* him tight, I centered and then grounded myself and grounded him. Dropping down my psychic connection to my flesh like a zip line in the forest canopy, the Masks were startled at first as we spun around, descending the silver cord. Then I let go and the spinning pushed him out and away. I slammed back into my body and back in the hotel room, where I waited for my coven sisters to return. I was sure that we would all have stories to tell.

I don't want to give the impression that heavy stuff happens all the time. It's usually pretty quiet. Yet the circle, in my experience, does indeed take us between the worlds and we can find truly amazing things there. It has often felt like we were dimly seeing eyes in the mist beyond, as if our circle was cast on a hazy hilltop or a clearing in a foggy wood.

Sometimes, small things would flit by or scurry past and, occasionally, we would sense larger things moving and lumbering in the distance.

These kinds of experiences are quietly accepted among witches, shamans, and pagans all around the world. Among the *Al al-Kitab (Arabic for "The People of the Book," meaning Muslims, Christians and Jews)* they tend to be greeted with disbelief, if not outright horror and revulsion. Atheists and many scientists would dismiss them as mere hallucinations. On the other hand, humanist philosophers who are sensitive to world religions are more willing to explore and classify this kind of exotic phenomenology.

But then experiences through the *Eyes of Spirit* is only exotic in the sense that they have often been violently suppressed in countries dominated by the monotheistic religions. Globally, anthropology shows they are quite still common among the thousands of remaining primary or traditional native cultures. Archeology and history shows that they were also quite common in the pre-monotheistic cultures. They are a near universal human characteristic or capacity.

So how do we process all this strange information, these uncanny experiences that occur worldwide? Nearly every general psychology text has a chapter on perception, while numerous specialty texts abound on the topic, but they tend to focus on the *Eyes of Flesh*. They may categorize them as types of optical illusions. Dreams are just one of many states of consciousness and imagination might not even be discussed. Disturbingly, the phenomena of the *Eyes of Spirit*, especially when used in a religious context, might be brought up in the discussion of abnormal psychology and schizophrenia, especially by pointing out how schizophrenic often frames his or her disorder in religious terms.

While I'm not ready to toss the entire science of psychology out the window, it is clearly of limited use to us at the present time. Simply put, these phenomena cannot be *"abnormal psychology"* by definition. Having a religious or spiritual experience at least once in one's life is far more common than having none at all. It is the lack of spiritual experience that is in fact *"abnormal"* in the sense of being rare or uncommon. But, perhaps, psychology may eventually play catch up through the new disciplines have cropped up lately such as Entheogenic Studies and Neurotheology.

Still, if we accept that these experiences and perceptions are in fact a *"normal"* or common part of most human lives, then our Three Sets of Eyes model makes categorical sense and we can analyze and interpret our experiences within that framework. In interpreting my own experiences, I see them as a dim reflection of some other kind of reality. I would say their *"world"* is at least as complex and diverse as ours is, if not more so. In my opinion, it is also just as real, even if its completely insensible to a percentage of our population. For just as some people are colorblind, others are *"spirit blind"* and simply unable to perceive these *"frequencies"* of existence.

The Structuralists argue that we assemble our perceptions into *"objects"* from the parts to the whole, from the bottom up. Gestalt psychologists say no, we grasp the whole and then analyze it down into parts, top down. The Functionalists say we need a better understanding of brain development and neurological operations such as neural networks before we can make assessment. All the while, we can continue with our own research in the realms beyond the physical with the only scientific instrument that seems to work there: the trained and observant human mind.

We can glean information out of our raw data and build knowledge out of our information and, hopefully, with skillfully crafted methodologies, we can distill a bit of wisdom out of our assembled knowledge. The knowledge we build must then be tested through checking our comprehension and our correct application of it. With a firm foundation of this tested knowledge, we will have the skills to analyze new situations and experiences, evaluate how they relate to our past experiences and what we have learned, and use it to synthesize better theories of just what it is we are experiencing Beyond the Veil. Or, if the old theories or beliefs no longer work, discard them for something that explains all our knowledge better.

I'm reminded of the Sufi story about the elephant and the three blind men where one holds the elephant's tail and says it's a vine, another holds a leg and says it's a tree, and a third holds the trunk and says it's a snake. None are correct but all three have a little bit of truth. It is all in how we separate the figure, object, or signal from the background noise.

Bibliography

1. David Abram, *"The Spell of the Sensuous: Perception and Language in a More-Than-Human World,"* Vintage Books, New York, New York, 1996, 1997.

2. Ibid.

3. Exodus

4. *"The Others"* Alejandro Amenabar, 2001

5. Terri Windling, ed., *"Bordertown"* Signet Books, New York, New York, 1986.

Biography

My pen-name and online handle is Rev. Jack Green and I'm a Second Degree Gardnerian Priest at Large. I have worked with several local covens over the last 25 years, some Gardnerian, some not. I hope to have my own coven someday. Being Wiccan means *(among other things)* we organize our lives around the cycles of the sun and moon and I'm one of those who actually likes going outside and looking up at the sky. I have always loved astronomy as well as astrology. I've written a number of articles on astronomy and helped design the *Branches Wiccan Calendar.*

I am amazed both at the depth of Wiccan history and how little modern Wiccans know about it. Take the Hwicce Country, for example. It existed as a province in western Britain from the fall of the Roman Empire to beyond the Norman Conquest. It's listed in the *"Domesday Book" (1086)* yet I never hear about how it is connected to our history *(until very, very recently)*. Doesn't anyone care about our history? Well, I sure as Hades do! To that end, I've been working on a history of the local pagan community of the Twin Cities, also known as Paganistan. I care about our traditions too, like traveling beyond the Veil. Taking a safari into the Astral Realm is real adventure.

The Dance Divine

Veronica Cummer

The walls are painted black. Above an empty stage, a big screen flashes images, some of them in time with the music and some of them jarring against it. Soldiers march, tanks battle, flowers open in impossibly quick time, a night sky whirls a million stars overhead and old black and white cartoons mix with rows of cars moving on giant freeways. Colored lights spin and shoot blinding beams of white from the ceiling and below the room is crowded by movement. Faces are raised up and arms rise and fall. Mouths open, silent or screaming, and bodies spin and shake, singularly alone or in colliding groups. The music is loud, far too loud to talk or hear through, loud as a living creature. The bass and drums sound, primitive, overpowering, the beat more felt than heard.

A woman in a corset and a red ruffled skirt dances alone on a small platform, her black and purple dreads flying loose. She wears fingerless gloves and her stockings are deliberately torn. On another platform extending out from the stairs, a man in a black leather pants and with a sword tattooed down his back dances, his face rapt, almost blank. His eyes are closed, his lips painted black. But hardly anyone is looking at them. Instead, they're all into their own thing, into their own experience. They're too busy trying to lose themselves. To find themselves. To find *something*.

But most of them don't know what.

A young man sits in a circle of mismatched chairs in a room at a pagan conference. The discussion is about community, about the future of paganism, and there are newbies there and people with decades of experience. He listens politely, gazing from face to face as the talk goes on, as druids and witches and heathens and pagans of all flavors express their thoughts about ritual plans, local and national politics, about history and the on-going work to reconstruct the past. There isn't much agreement. Though there are plenty of opinions and everyone is passionate about their beliefs, they're trying hard not to step on any toes.

Finally, the young man takes his turn to speak. His voice is rough, hungry, even a little desperate. *"Is this all there is?"* he asks. People blink at him. Chairs creak as some shift in place. A young woman in a green and black tie-die dress coughs. The young man sits at the edge of his seat as he tells his own story. As he talks about being born into paganism, about being taken to pagan gathers and rituals since the time he was a baby. How he's done rituals and spellwork, made offerings to the Gods, and read book after book. Only to still feel as though something is missing, that he's missed out on something. That something has gotten lost along the way.

Only he doesn't know what.

It only makes sense, because what is being looked for, what is being sought out so desperately...is *mystery.* It's the heartbeat of the Gods, the embrace of Other, the touch of Faery and a taste of magick, real magick. Unvarnished and vital and powerful and precious. It's seeking to see behind the mask, beyond the tender skin of reality, out of a hunger for something that can't be taught, but must be known directly. The desire for an epiphany, an experience of the Divine, not one of the intellect, but one that you can feel in the body and in the spirit.

The ways of getting there go by many names. In the Craft, it can be known as the *Crooked Path,* the *Unseen Way, taking the road to fair Elfland,* or *riding the Hedge.* It's a road that leads both within and without, a double spiral, beyond narrow notions of time and space, beyond normal understanding. Its definitely not a road of those who prefer to sit comfortably on the sidelines, of what the Christians might call the Christmas-and-Easter congregation. It's not a road to be grasped easily by the intellect, but must awaken within the body and the blood. Its a path of knowing, of sacrifice, of travel, of pain and danger and discovery and ecstasy.

There are myriad methods that can be used to find and travel this road, but one of the most efficacious is that of the dance. Dance is, in many ways, the first form ritual took. Dance, like ritual, serves to create patterns and these patterns teach the way to go beyond and, if they do not, then they are just show, nothing more than flash and bang and pretense. If a ritual doesn't get you there, allow you a chance to experience the Divine, then it is no more than ritual theatre. If dance doesn't allow you to pass through it, to use it as a tool to touch what is unknown, then its just having fun. Not that there is anything wrong with participating in the show or in having fun, but it means you're still caught up in the Game and have not freed yourself to go past it, to see past it. It's become entertainment, not the ecstasy which is the gateway to the Gods.

Dance and ritual are ancient and primitive. They speak to the wildest and most secret part of ourselves, that which lies below intellect and ego. Some claim that modern paganism, modern witchcraft, has no real tangible connection to the paganism and witchcraft of the past, but that's a lie. So long as we dance we are a part of the past and we can live it again, go deep and ride hard, and reclaim what already lies sleeping inside us. The history of the Craft is not written in books. It's not easy even to talk about it because it comes from a wordless place, a place that words have difficulty describing. Its a living thing as much as we are, a conscious being in its own right, and one that we can learn to tap into—if we dare and if we dance. To dance as witches dance is not just to become aware of that consciousness, but to draw its attention to yourself.

Everything dances. Some call it vibration. We are all a dance. What we see and call the material world is but the visible expression of energies that we cannot see, just as we cannot see outside of a narrow band of the spectrum of light. In fact, science has recently come to speculate that the vast majority of the universe consists of something that not only we can't perceive, but that we don't yet even have a clue about how to develop a way to perceive it. It may well be that these alternative forms of perception already exist and people have been using them for centuries, but that science continues to spurn them.

However, there are countless examples all over the world about how dance can open up strange perceptions that otherwise are kept locked away. Certainly, it can bypass the rational mind with all of its restrictions and preconceptions and allow for a direct experience of powers and insights that are usually considered the provenance of the Divine. Of course, this can be difficult and even frightening, especially for those of us with no cultural background in divine dance and few to turn to when things go wrong, or if they go right. Not for nothing is the road of the shaman fraught with danger and madness. Faery can be as terrifying as it is beautiful.

We can choose to dance divine and seek an encounter with this terrifying beauty. We can dance to rediscover what is both within and without. Of course, the Divine was never truly lost from us—how could it be?—but we sometimes forget and sleep and so come to spend our lives in the dream of the Divine and not in the Divine itself. Our awareness of life may grow dim and the moments pass without acknowledgement, with all their sharp edges dulled to the point that we can hardly feel them. The only way back, to find not just the Universe but who we are within that Universe, is through waking up again and dance is one way of accomplishing that.

The Roman poet, Lucian, tells us that dance came from the Muses, that it was one of their gifts, a gift of the Gods. No surprise, then, that you can use the dance to not only connect to the creative force of the Muse, but to the Divine source that it first sprang from. How this is accomplished is through achieving a different awareness of being, of becoming an awakened one, what some call entering an altered state of consciousness or entering a trance. Then you can gain visions and insights, prophecy and revelation, and travel to the Underworld, the Otherworld, the Nine Worlds, from the top of the World Tree to its roots. You can even sometimes have a direct experience of the Divine Itself, of the entire universe as a whole, the same as the Buddha did.

Dance, in many ways, is inborn in each of us. It doesn't take much to tap into it, especially if you have a good, strong beat to work with. Its in our shared memory, our genes, our collective spirit. Our ancestors danced to heal and to hunt. They danced for protection and for prosperity. They danced to make the crops grow and they danced to make themselves and their animals fertile. They danced to be with their ancestors and to speak with the spirits of the land.

You can dance alone, whirling around a single central point such as the dervishes do, and you can dance together in a group, in you communal family, whatever form it may take. In the past, most ritual style dance tended to be done in a group context, where it had the added benefit of helping to strengthen the bonds of community. In a magickal context it can also help coalesce the energy of the group into a whole, a whole that can eventually take on a consciousness of its own. This consciousness then can influence the group as much as it is influenced by the group and it can survive the death of the people involved, passing down through the rituals and the dances that they used. To dance the dance of the ancestors is to touch that living spirit, the spirit of family, culture, place and bloodline.

The patterns that dance creates can get inside us and when we dance them we tap into not just the energy of the current dance, but of all the dances that have come before it. We tap into the dance we shared with those who came before us and those who will come after us. When we dance and those in the Otherworld dance—dance is something that, definitely, witches and the Fey share a love for—then the action mirrors itself and a connection is forged and strengthened. The first circle was a dance. It is shared movement and breath, body and spirit. It's the sheer vibration of creation.

But it's not enough just to go spinning into motion. Dance needs a foundation to build upon, an anchor to fly from, even if the eventual goal is to free ourselves of restraint and trance out into the wilds of the unknown and the unseen. Preparations need to be made ahead of time, the stage set, so to speak. Unlike in ritual drama, though, we will not stop with the play itself, but use it as a springboard to propel us into the elsewhere. We will use dance as a vehicle, shaking us out of our bodies and the impressions of the world that have come to constrain us. As the patterns we seek to create must serve to then release us from the pattern itself.

There are certain methods that are conducive to creating the patterns of the dance: *location, connection, repetition, and emotion.*

Location

On a mundane level, one aspect of location simply entails making sure it is a good, safe place to dance, one where we can afford to let ourselves go wild and crazy in more ways than one. This can just mean that we don't have to worry about being disturbed by others, or it can mean that there have been safeguards put in place so that we won't go crashing into sharp objects or falling over cliffs or headfirst into fires. If the dance is taking place indoors, then enough space will need to be created for it and breakable objects removed. Obviously, if you are using lit candles for the rite, they should also be carefully placed so they can't easily be knocked over. Another option is to have some people stay out of the dance and serve as "spotters," making sure that no one gets hurt and keeping an eye out for those who might be in trouble.

However, a proper location can also mean picking a spot that is sacred in its own right, whether by having served our ancestors or being near a wellspring of power or the currents known as ley lines. The site can have a central tree, a standing stone or altar stone, or well around which we can build the pattern. It might be on the top of a special hill or by a barrow, pool, or lake that has a link to Faery. Sacred trees have a long history in the Craft, including the Faery Tree around which Joan of Arc was said to dance. A stang can serve much the same purpose as the world tree, while a stone can stand in place of the world mountain. They are both representations of the *axis mundi* around which all spins and along which powers travel.

A sacred site can also be built by using it for ritual over a long period of time and by creating and maintaining a good connection with the land. Dance can help create that bond and sanctify the site, as can performing other kinds of ritual there and making offerings to spirits of the land. One old way of making a bond with the land is by giving it some of your blood, but that's something that should never be done lightly. Boundaries can also be laid by putting wards or guardian stones/markers at the four directions and a crossroads might be made by walking to the center of the sacred spot from each direction and singing or calling the powers in.

Connection

We can form connections with each other by mirroring other dancers, whether through wearing similar clothing, masks, or by shared actions. Joining hands is, of course, an easy way to make a connection, especially in the traditional ring dance. Physical touch may be used to bind a dance and the dancers together. Clapping or turning/spinning in unison also creates connection. We can not only connect with each other through touch, but by sharing in the energy of the dance. The more we give to the dance and to each other, the greater the force that is built and the more it can effect us as a collective. When we dance in a group it not only creates more energy than can be raised by a single person, but it can make us feel safer, closer, more a part of something greater than our single selves.

We can also connect to our totem spirits—those spirits that can be called upon to carry us to the Otherworld—by wearing masks, by wearing or carrying objects related to them, or by using symbols that represent them. These symbols can be pendants or they can be painted on bare skin or sewn or painted onto any ritual wear. A symbol can also be used to represent the group spirit that has been created or that you hope to create. Connection can also be made by the shared use of ritual oils or incense, the scent reminding you of previous rituals you have been in together or of the reason why you are wearing it. In addition, you can put on soot, one of the emblems of the Man in Black, He who opens the way to Faery. All of these can create links, like reflecting like, inspiring memory and remembering.

Connections can be made to the past, as well, to all those who have danced before, by calling upon the witches of the past or upon the ancestors. The dances of the witches primarily were of three types—the circle or ring dance, the line dance, and the couple dance. Ring dances are, probably, the oldest kind of all and the most likely one to use to form a bond with those of the past. They were often done around an object or person. The line dance might be compared to a kind of *"follow the leader"* game or chase and may also be used to process to the place of ritual. Couple dances were, perhaps, the wildest of all, involving the lifting of feet and the linking of arms back to back. Far more dignified remnants of them can be found in today's square dances and waltzes. When we dance as those who came before us danced, we become connected to them and to the unfolding pattern or spell they have begun.

Repetition

Patterns are, of course, strongly tied to the idea of repetition. The more you repeat something the more it is ingrained into your memory and the more easily it will come in the future. One way of doing this is by memorizing and practicing any actions or dance steps, repeating them until you find yourself just doing them without any conscious thought. The goal is to have it become so familiar that you no longer need to worry about it or even think about it. Only then can you begin to go beyond the pattern, when your focus is no longer on what your body is doing, but on where it is leading you to. Even if you decide to only whirl or shake instead of following dance steps, you can use the same triggers—for example, the same music—to built a pattern.

Repeating the same motions, the same sounds, the same rituals, the same dances, may sound boring to some, but it does serve a purpose. On the other hand, if this is all you do, if you repeat and repeat and don't try to reach beyond the pattern, then the pattern has become the purpose itself and is but another thing standing in your way. If you play the Game and no longer keep in mind, or have even forgotten, that it is a Game that you are playing, then you have become trapped in the Game. You can become trapped in ritual in much the same way, never going any further and, maybe, even coming to believe that there is nothing else than this.

It takes a lot of dedication and many years of practice until something becomes instinctual, until it gets right down inside you and becomes a part of you, mind, body and spirit. Only once you *are* the dance and you *are* the ritual, can you then abandon the dance and the ritual to get you to where you need to go. Like the grooves in a record, the path has been laid, the connections made, and you will know how to enter the correct state without any other tools than your own memories of having gotten there before. The greatest tools of all lie within your own body, your strength of will, and the desire to act and to achieve divine inspiration.

Emotion

Emotion is tied to memory. In fact, memory is created by emotion in many ways—the stronger the emotion, the stronger the memory. If you want to work beyond the pattern, then allowing yourself to feel the dance—opening yourself up to your feelings as deeply as possible—will serve to ingrain the patterns far more quickly than if you rely primarily on thought. Emotion is primal, powerful, and difficult to deny. It touches upon the parts of us that understand instinctively and symbolically.

Emotion is a powerful tool for creating doorways to the Otherworld and entering into the trance states necessary to travel there. Emotion opens us up and creates bridges across worlds. These bridges lie not just between individuals within a group, but between us and our totems, our spirit familiars, and the Gods. Love is, of course, the most powerful emotion of all and the most mysterious. To travel beyond this world, you can't go wrong if you learn the road of Love, no matter if it takes the form of love for your fellow witches, for your spirit helpers, or for your patron God, Goddess, or pantheon. The proper kind of Love—of which romantic love is but a pale shade—not only frees you, but centers you, as well.

Not surprisingly, the best kind of dance for leaping beyond the Hedge involves the spiraling up and the sharp release of ecstasy. When we're extremely joyful, we feel closer to others, more open, more capable of doing just about anything. A dance that creates such joy not only connects the dancers, but draws the attention of the beings of the Otherworld. Love and joy rush upwards in a flame that can be seen a very long way. Which means that we have to remain aware that, since like attracts like, if the feelings we send out into the world and across the worlds is joy and purpose and honor and reverence what we tend to attract will be much the same and if what we send out is anger, despair, and a desire for revenge or control over others, then that will also be drawn to us. Not everything out there is kindly and that's one reason why its a good idea to have Gods and spirits who can help protect and guide you along the way.

Once you have laid the foundation, you can then concentrate on using it as a basis for traveling, for *"flying."* To fly you need to achieve what might be called a drunkenness of the spirit, a giddiness of the soul. The rational mind is spun until its dizzied and has no choice but to let go, while the body grows heavier and heavier, as though it has little choice but to simply sleep. The spirit, on the other hand, is excited and lightened until it can't help but leap free of that oh so heavy flesh. Separation occurs, sometimes for just a moment or two and sometimes for much longer. Visions can result, insights and revelations. An intensity of sheer knowing that can hardly be explained afterwards. Or you may actually go so far as to directly touch upon the Divine essence at the center of all.

No matter what form of the dance you choose to use, the point is to use it. The dance is a tool for going beyond this world, this awareness, and becoming both More and Other. The More is being who you really are, not just in this lifetime, but in the distillation of all of your lifetimes, even those which haven't happened yet. In the center created by the dance, in the still Eye, you can see and touch all. The Other is your Fey self, the light to your shadow, the shadow to your light. Becoming the More is also becoming the Other. Part of this entails learning your true name.

Dance and ritual are spells that can help us find that name. By finding our center and dancing around that center, we can become our most pure self. We may become the whirlwind, the storm, swirling around its still eye. The still eye of All. We are well and truly alive again and, more than that, we may even become a lens through which the great powers can pour and by which *Wyrd* can work its magick upon the physical plane. We chance to become a perfect strand in the *web of Fate*, a light shining in the *Abyss*, as great and potentially greater than any star.

When we dance, we take an old road, a well-worn path, and certainly the most bonny way to Faery. Dance surrounds and encompasses mystery, that which we are searching for and that which we are. The dancers in the club, moving in the darkness and in the shattering strands of light, did not know their purpose there even though they danced. While the young pagan man who had purpose, who had resolve, had lost sight of or never been told that of what he desired he needed to seek beyond the pattern, beyond the rites, beyond the Game. Somewhere out there and somewhere within.

Concerning the Hex and the Hedge-Crosser

Robin Artisson

This essay is condensed from two parts of a larger work entitled
"The Village or the Pendulum of Souls."

Those who wish to access the mysteries of Witchcraft must begin their journey of understanding in the multi-layered notion of *"boundaries."* Witchcraft is the art of obtaining the power to make changes in this world of perceptual order by leaving this world, and within the strange tangles and landscapes of the unseen world, finding a *"witching"* or a *"hex"*- a name given to the strange *"concentrations"* of weird, transformative power that a cunning witch can bring back to this world and use to make the needed or willed changes.

Before a witch can do this, they must clearly understand what separates this world, the world of light and order, from the world beyond—the unseen world of fluidity and darkness. A powerful mental image must be created of the world that is seen, and its boundaries, beyond which lie the unknown. Witching or Hexing is always based on power from the *"outside."*

This understanding of boundaries, as mentioned, is multi-layered. It applies not just to the apparent world of the senses, and what lies beyond it, but also to the *"self"* that is known, and that portion of the *"self"* that belongs to the outside, a *"self"* that I call *"The Other."* The Other must be understood as the most crucial aspect of Witchcraft, aside from the simple notion of boundaries. The Other is the witch's source of power and guidance, the being who will guide the witch beyond this world, across the boundaries, and to the Hex they are seeking.

The metaphysics of *"boundaries"* are as ancient as humankind. All ancient mythologies deal with the notion of the emergence of order from chaos, and all ancient religions dealt fearfully and wisely with their understandings of the beings from beyond, who were threats to the order of the human world, and the divine beings who, being a part of this world, protected it. In the book of Genesis, the primordial chaos was shaped, by the word of God over seven days, into the order we now have. This understanding, the shaping of formlessness into form by the power of the will and word, is crucial to the witching-art, as well.

The religious understanding of the Ancients was reflected in daily life in important ways. The villages of old were surrounded by hedges or other barriers which marked the boundaries of the village. Outside of the hedge was the forest or the wild, the place where wild beasts were a danger and outlaws or strangers wandered. Indeed, to be an outlaw was to be *"outside of law,"* outside of the order of human society and, therefore, dangerous, reviled, and untrustworthy. In a sense, the outlaw was also dead, for the dead no longer belong to the human world of order but become a part of the strange beyond. This is why those condemned to outlawry could be killed by anyone, without penalty to the killers—the outlaw was no longer a living being protected by the law of the world.

Every society or community still has *"boundaries,"* though they need not be something as simple as a hedge; boundaries now can include acceptable behaviors or thinking.

In Puritan New England, the village was the center of life, and it had boundaries. God's Kingdom, or the ordered world of humans, was at odds with the Devil's Kingdom all around it. The vast forests of New England were a perfect model of the *"outside,"* just as they were to the Native Peoples who lived there before the Europeans came. Micmac shamans and sorcerers withdrew from their communities into the forest to do their magics. They withdrew into the forest because it was a wilder, untamed place of fluid powers and spiritual beings.

The natives of North America, the *"Red Man,"* were reviled by the European colonists as *"heathen"* and were very much accused of Devil worship, as even a short review of New England colonial folklore will reveal. It was Europeans who had dealings with them—those whites that went back and forth across the boundaries between the *"White"* world of churches and the *"Red"* world of wild forests and demons, that acted, in a sense, as *"witchers"* of a type. They had to guard themselves against the corruption of heathen forces from the outside, but they also found themselves the targets of suspicion among their own people, for nothing can travel to the outside and come back the same, not ever.

Native sorceries and beliefs began to creep into the sterile Puritan world, and even as late as the Salem witch trials, we see that it was the presence of a *"dark woman,"* a non-white woman, the slave Tituba, whose rumored use of Voodoo or Caribbean sorcery helped to touch off a hysteria.

In Old Europe, the witch was called *"haegtessa,"* a *"Hedge-rider"* or Hedge-crosser. The meaning of this is clear to any who understand the metaphysic of the boundary; their sorceries were disturbing, mysterious powers that they trafficked with, by riding off to another world. The image of the *"hedge-rider"* contains another interesting clue—the picture of a man or woman *"riding"* a hedge places them sitting on the hedge, with one leg on the *"village"* side of the hedge and the other on the *"wild"* side. The witch belonged to both worlds simultaneously as a result of their crossing back and forth.

The *"Hedge"* has many layers of meaning, like anything else, for in everything that is seen, nine things are unseen. The hedge refers, historically, to the physical boundary marking off the civilized world of the community from the uncontrolled, unpredictable world beyond it. But it also refers to the dividing line between a human mind and the unknown reaches of the mind; it also refers to the dividing force that literally divides this world as a whole, this cosmos, from the strange *"Otherworld"* which is its unseen depth.

"The Tower of Jerusalem" is a way of referring to God's kingdom, or the ordered world of men and women. But over the boundary of order, we find that the world still exists. After all, the unknown is still a part of reality as a whole. But the *"other side"* of life, the *"reversed world"* contains both a dark, chaotic version of this world, as well as other, vaster, and stranger powers. *"The Tower of Babylon"* is Jerusalem's dark twin- the *"Otherness of this world."*

If every human being in this world has an *"Other"* that dwells on the other side of the hedge, then even society has an *"Other"*—the shadow-self of society is just as real as the shadow of a person. And this analysis goes further and deeper. The divine forces of this world, which are revealed and known to human beings, have their own shadows on the *"other side."* This may be the most disturbing, but important, aspect of the dark wisdom of the witch. Even the good Christ, gentle and loving, dead for the good of humankind, has a dark shadow beyond—Demon Est Deus Inversus—and what a surprise it is for most to realize who he really is...or should I say, who he is, when you see both sides of his mystery in the wholeness of light and shadow.

I will go further into an analysis of these divisions and opposites. But first, it is important to realize something at the outset. The world seen and the world unseen make a whole. Everything has a shadow. But when we ignore the shadow, which many do, we do not live a whole life. We do not understand vital things about ourselves, our world, or the Gods of our world. Seeing in terms of *"the seen and the unseen"* means to see a vision of wholeness.

"World" must have a different meaning to the witch. It must have a meaning of wholeness; it must be inclusive. The unseen is not unreal, nor divided away from this world. It is a part of the world, the necessary *"underside"* or *"otherness"* of all things. And from that place, that otherness, fresh forces flow to cause changes and shake up the order of the world that is seen. The witch is an agent of *"crossing,"* a person through which the two worlds can contact one another and affect one another.

For when the two halves of reality are in communion, they change one another. Nothing is more terrifying to the people of the *"sunlit, ordered"* world than when the powers of the Otherness come too close. There are times of the year, in the darker half of the year, when the weird forces beyond do come closer and riot across the world. It is also a powerful time for witches and their craft: the Hallows season. The people of the sunlit world also feel that fear arise when the witch comes close. As we shall see later, some Witches are a danger to everyone around them, but not all.

Now, I shall make a list of the five most important *"concepts"* that one must internalize if they wish to engage the occult practice of Hedge-riding, Hedge-crossing, or *"Boundary crossing."*

Consider for a moment these pairs, and understand how and why they stand contrary to one another, but also as shadows each of the other:

God's Kingdom... The Devil's Kingdom
The Village... The Forest and Wilds
The Church Building... The Forest Clearing or Hill of the Heathen
Certainty... Uncertainty and Indistinct Shapes
Sanity... Insanity or Irrationality

God's Kingdom and the *Devil's Kingdom* have already been described well enough. The *Village*, as a whole, has its opposite in the *"Forest and Wilds,"* which is also easy enough to understand. The *Church Building*—the building that all old communities were planned around—has its shadow in the *Forest Clearing or Hill of the Heathen*, the places where Native peoples do their religious rites. Certainty is a quality of this world that is seen, but not perfect certainty. When compared to the indistinct, uncertain, and fluid qualities of the *"outside,"* it seems very certain. *Sanity*, finally, is described and defined in terms born in the world of order. *Insanity* is, by definition, living, thinking, and acting in a way that is far outside of the consensus definition of *"sanity."*

The witch is a being who can be found in any of these places, or passing through any of these states. The witch does not *"stop"* in one place or the other. To *"stop"* in this world would be to become a non-witch or a normal, worldly person, and to stop in the *Unseen* world would be to become a strange inhabitant of that place, losing both one's status as a witch and as a human being. Instead, the witch circles back and forth between all opposites, draws on the benefits and powers of both, and uses both to create and transform things according to will and need.

In a world of winds and fires, of flowing water and falling rain, and slowly changing hills, mountains, and valleys, nothing stands still for very long. The bodies and souls of men and women and beasts are part of this world, and no part of them is exempt long from the necessity to change. It is easy enough to watch a young child grow into an old man or woman, but not so easy to see the soul's changes. But change it does; the soul is as vulnerable to subtle powers as the body is to coarse ones, and the soul determines so much about the character of a person.

I liken the soul's dynamic nature to a pendulum, forever swinging back and forth, cycling between those places of mind and heart and nature that it loves and to which it has become accustomed. For where the heart goes, the soul goes, and where the mind lies in fixation or confusion, there too the soul goes. The soul, and the mind and body that coalesce around it, have their true origins from over the Hedge, in the far reaches of the unknown mysteries of life. But while here, in the world of perceptual order, the mind and body are shaped by the powers of order, and the soul adheres to this pathway of gravity and time.

You might say the *"conditioning"* runs both ways, but the soul—the pre-existing, lasting, and fluid element of any being—always maintains something of its *"otherness."* It knows, on the deepest levels, that it is from *"somewhere else,"* and as quiet as it may be, as forgetful as the minds of men and women may become, they know that they are part of something greater, something beyond order and limitation. However, in the meantime, life needs living and life makes demands.

The pendulum of the soul swings according to the estate of life a man or woman has attained, and according to many other factors, as well. The dynamic flux of the soul influences the mind and body in many ways. For most, the pendulum of the soul swings well within the *"ordered side"* of the great clock-work machinery of the cosmos. Sometimes, every few swings, it comes close to the Hedge, but just barely. Just enough for those rare moments of imagination or reflection to strike.

For a very small, dark minority of human beings, the pendulum of the soul swings largely on the *"other"* side of the Hedge. Sad and wretched, they are either raving lunatics or the quiet, subtle variety of pure insanity, sometimes sociopathic or detached or otherwise very dangerous evil to their fellow man. This is the cost of the Pendulum of the soul swinging outside of the ordered power of the world; the soul's unrest and lack of touch with the powers of order is reflected in the mind and body of the person.

Between these two persons—those whose soul-pendulums swing within order, only barely touching the Hedge at times, and those whose soul-pendulums swing within chaos, only barely touching the Hedge at times *(though from the other side)*—there are may grades between. The possibility of altering the soul's swing always exists, at every moment.

The witch, ideally, has a pendulum which swings from order, over the Hedge, and back to order again, straddling the two perfectly, alternating perfectly. Compared to those whose pendulum's swing is nine parts out of ten in the ordered world, the witch's double nature must seem a nightmare: not for no reason do such people despise the witch and the Art. From the perspective of those whose pendulum's swing is nine parts out of ten in the world of disorder and mystery, the witch must seem very worldly, stable, and sane indeed, but this is all perspective. But it is this fact of the pendulum that makes the true witch a boon for this world, and a mighty force against the powers of extreme disorder. For the witch can offer freshness and needful changes to this world and repel the extremes of the other.

Death is a time for a plunge of the mind and soul back into the unseen world of disorder and strangeness which was its original home. But for those who have become so well entrenched in the metaphysical power of order, that plunge is terrifying and painful. For those who spent their lives cursed to be mad or obsessed with the strangeness, those dangerous freaks, death isn't much of a change at all; from the chaos that entangled itself in flesh back to the pure chaos is not a far journey. For the witch, however, with the pendulum balanced more or less between the two, death is another opportunity for power. No terror and confusion on the one hand, nor wild loss on the other will greet the cunning witch at death. If they are masters of their Art, that is.

The balanced in this life will find a balanced road through death. This is important, because as was mentioned before, true *"goodness,"* the undying goodness, is beyond the usual definitions of *"good"* and *"evil"* held by the people of the world of order. Real *"goodness"* or the *"fitness of things"* must include the ordered and the disordered, the wholeness of things.

Can a person look upon the world, with all its beauty and terrors and see a greater fitness, a greater rightness for it all? Yes, the wise can. But it is no easy task until one has swung back and forth in real inclusive balance. If a person can behold the dark and the light as parts of a good whole in this world, they can do the same in death, and find the true peace beyond categories.

Those whose pendulums swing far to the right may feel trepidation at death, fear of the unknown, but the powerful order that they carry with them *(so long as it was genuine, that is, based on a good heart)* will act as a preserver from the chaotic states beyond, perhaps even blessing them with peace for a while, before the last mystery is faced. Those whose pendulums swing in the chaos may not have much of a difficult time plunging into the unformed. But then, they lived their own sort of hell before they died, and their mental oblivion will be quick enough on the heels of a new, more vibrant nightmare. Those whose souls are warped with wickedness will have no choice but to experience that *"creativity of wickedness"* in the unformed, for the unseen world is responsive to our hopes and dreams, and our nightmares.

But the soul's pendulum is always moving. The Art of the witch has a powerful relationship to the pendulum's swing, for every single time the witch reaches the hedge and crosses over, or performs works of sorcery, the *"Witching"* or *"Hexing"* that they obtain bends and warps the soul and mind by a small degree. Thus, it changes the pendulum's swing a little more towards the *"Otherness."* But there is more. Intentionally evil acts do the same; anything that destroys the order of this world or the life in it *(life as we know it, in the biological sense, is a manifestation of order)* swings the pendulum towards the disorder and mayhem of the *Unseen*.

The witch must therefore be very cautious. For the cost of the Art is constant opportunity to alter the pendulum's swing towards the *Unseen*, and to divorce the witch further and further from the world of human beings and the order upon which they base their sanity. This is why the witch must maintain connections with this world; when powerful seasons of Witching have passed, the witch should celebrate the ordered world for its beauty and power, more so than others should, perhaps.

The witch may become accustomed to dealings with Old Hobb, the White Lady, or the denizens of the unseen world and the shades of the dead, and the Other, in all its wondrous and nightmarish permutations. But the witch should be conversant also with the kingdom of the Christ, the giving Earth, the broad Sky, and the simple graces and charms of the world of the sunlight.

For this very reason, attending *"church"* from time to time may be healthy, reminding oneself of the good values upon which most people base their lives, and the need for compassion and forgiveness, and aid to one's neighbor. Naturally, the pendulum being what it is and always swinging towards the Otherness, you'll see these values crash and transform into their precise opposites, but it is good enough that somewhere, someone values them.

Witches who are not *"passion bodies"* inclined to enjoy a church can still experience the holiness of the ordered world: walking out into the green fields of this world, under the broad blue sky, building fires and burning offerings for the beneficent one above, and pouring out offerings and burying offerings for the generous mother below, celebrating the friendly departed, the beloved ancestors, the goodness of the bright, warming sun, collecting fresh herbs, baking bread, getting the flour of this world on one's hands and face, walking the forest paths. This is the *"good life,"* and it is just as precious as the mysterious order of life on the other side of the Hedge.

When the witch's soul-pendulum swings either balanced or more towards the ordered end of the spectrum, their *"Witching,"* their workings, and their *passive presence (for never forget, any person who has the Witching in their mind and body radiates a presence of it and causes changes in this world, whether they would or not)* are forces that will not harm others. But when a witch's pendulum swings into the disordered spectrum more often than not, their *passive presence* becomes a deadly matter—the Witching in them tends more and more to disorder. They can, just as the legends tell, cause disasters, accidents, and terrors merely by living near a village or around others. They can harm even those they love, just by being near them, though it is questionable how such a creature, who must be fully mad, can understand *"love"* as others do.

To hunt or destroy such witches would not be an act of persecution, but preservation on the parts of the people of a village, or this world. The *"evil witch"* of legend does exist, and unlike the *"evil non-witch,"* they wield something in them that can do considerable more damage and destruction in this world.

For everything that is seen, a shadow exists, on the other side of the Hedge. Reality is not a one-sided story; it has a sublime depth, a hidden half, which is the territory of the witch and sorcerer. The world or reality as a whole is singular entity—the two *"halves"* of which I speak are not ultimately, eternally separate. But from our human perspective, they appear to be, and they behave as though they are. They are perceived in two different ways. They appear to interact.

Witchcraft is an art, a practice within the world bound by perception, and thus it must be approached in a certain manner. Wholeness is a curious and good philosophical idea, but when you wish to assay a Crafting, seek a Witching, you have to align yourself to the perception that walls us all in: we are in the world on the sunlit side of the Hedge, and a dark world awaits beyond.

Biography

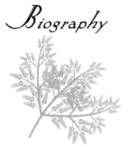

Robin Artisson is a Hedge-crosser, folklorist, herbalist, and *"Fayerie Doctor"* of the Ancient Faith. He is the author of several books, including the forthcoming grimoire-tome entitled *"The Resurrection of the Meadow,"* and the author of articles and works on-line too numerous to count.

Robin is an avid lover of life, the outdoors, the Unseen world, chess, folklore, esoterica, and of making trouble right where he isn't wanted. He has a wife, two beautiful daughters, and a life that's quite respectable by some accounts.

Witches' Ladder Charm

Generally, *Witches' Ladders* are made to be curses and include maledictions knotted into the cord or rope and the feathers of a black chicken. In this case, the Ladder can be used as an aid to journeying to the Otherworld, even as a meditation tool to get you into the proper frame of mind to jump the Hedge.

Ingredients:
cord or rope or yarn or ribbon, preferably natural *(silk, cotton, hemp)*
beads if desired
charms relating to your spirit familiar, fetch, or totem
feathers if desired
hagstone if available

If you can get red cord or rope or ribbon that is the best choice, or you can use one cord of red and two other colors that appeal to you and that represent Faery *(such as green)* or magick *(such as blue)*. Another option is to use red for the blood of the Witch, white for the blood of the Fey, and blue-green/teal for the binding between the two. You can, of course, choose not to braid the cord or ribbon and simply use a single red one.

When braiding, concentrate on creating a connection between this world and the Otherworld as you work. Tie knots into the braid or the single ribbon, cord, or rope and, as you do, breathe your desires into the knot. In this case, rather than a curse or ill-luck, concentrate on sending power into the knot as a step along your way, as a guide for your journey. You might also decide to put beads into the Ladder and, if you do, natural wooden or bone beads are the best and you can also charge them with your intent.

Three, seven, nine, thirteen knots or beads are the best numbers to use.

Bid your fetch or familiar to put something of their energy into the charm to represent them before you add them to the Ladder. It doesn't necessarily have to be a charm that looks like them—say, a charm in the shape of the animal or object—but can be a charm that appeals to them or that reminds you of them or what they bring to your mutual relationship.

A small loop should be tied into one end of the Ladder or you can add a hagstone to that end.

When the Ladder is complete, you can put it around your neck when you are working or hang it in your ritual space or anywhere you are going to go work beyond the boundaries. One way of using it is to tie one end of the cord or braid around the upper part of your forearm and wrap the rest around and around your arm until you can hold the holed stone or noose in the palm of your hand. When you wish to travel, hold your hand closed around the hagstone. When you wish to return, slowly open your hand.

Flying Ointment

My blood itched
My blood throbbed
My blood sang one long far note
The same song of the forest
The same song as the moon
Come oh come, oh remember
Come oh come, oh return
Return to the land
Return to the night
Return to the dark in the shape of the art--
So I ran fast to greet it
And joined as one with the night
Felt the horn of the God sounding
Felt the change beginning
As one note never ending
As I became a thing of life, breath, and air
Flying free of any boundary
Flying to the Sabbat.
I leaped high to find
My place in the sky
Moving in the way the ancients once moved
By becoming as one
With things that could fly
Or by opening a door
And passing on through
Leaving a trail behind
A tail that looks like a tassel,
A feather, a broom
To go there and back
Is a thing we all once knew

Not in a fancy
Not a dream
But real and but true
For all it doesn't take a spell
Just the heart
Just the faith
Just a spark to jump between the worlds
Blood that yet knows the art
Of being and knowing
And what was learned long years ago
From the traveling God
Of smoke and mirrors and soot.

Singing Your Heart Out
Music as a Ritual Tool

Jenne Micale

I let the song carry me, course through me.
The sound brings us to the brink of the Otherworld
and builds the barge to ferry us over.
My fingers sound the strings on the valiha as I call to the dead,
throat opening, song soaring over the pluck of notes.
It is Samhain and I am in a Druid grove in a crowded New Jersey house.
My task is not only to call the mighty dead,
but to ferry us to them with the power of my song.
As I sing and sound the strings.
I see the barge we are on, hear the lapping water of the Sunless Sea.
I feel the dead climb my back as a ladder into the room.
My spine shivers, but I never stop singing.

The Bardic arts aren't merely the province of memorized praise-song or poetry recited in the context of ritual. Musical instruments can function as magical steeds, allowing the practitioner to venture out from the boundaries of consensual reality into the many realms of spirit. Music can inspire ecstasy—moving consciousness outside of one's self—and foster a deep communion with spirits and the divine. Its patterns can be used to shift realities in conformance with the will; not coincidentally, *"enchantment"* contains the Latin word for song at its heart.

There is, in short, something *Otherworldly* about music.

Sound is a type of energy quite literally. As with light, it travels in waves that can have real effects in the physical world. Think of an opera singer whose high notes shatter a glass, or a jet breaking the sound barrier. It is an energy that moves through a physical medium, which its waves displace. The vastness of space carries no sound, while air, water and even steel carry it differently. Think of the rail's metallic song before the train comes or of the closeness of sound under water, of whales that can use its medium to sing to their kind an ocean away.

The deliberate use of sound and resonance, singing and instrumental music have been used the world over to transform consciousness, work magic and travel to the *Otherworld*, as well as commune with spirits. For modern hedgeriders, the voice, drumbeat or vibrating strings can function as the steed—or besom, if you will—transporting the seeker beyond the boundaries of the known world.

She Loves the Clatter of Rattles

First, a brief sampling of music-infused ecstasy from around the world. It is, by necessity, incomplete since virtually all cultures use music of some sort in sacred rites.

Ecstatic rites in the ancient world inevitably involved music. In Greece and Rome, the worshipers of Dionysus were shown beating drums and playing flutes while dancing ecstatically in worship of their God. Worshipers of Cybele, the great Mother of Anatolia, were described similarly and the Goddess herself is often depicting holding a frame drum.

The ecstasy exhibited in the worship of deities such as Dionysus and Cybele allows the practitioner to transcend the normal bounds of human society and the physical world, and become filled with holy power. That power may manifest in frightening ways, such as Cybele's male worshipers castrating themselves in the throes of their devotion or Maenads dismembering and eating animals. Most often, it's an experience of being so filled with the numinous that the individual self lapses in importance or even disappears. The Homeric hymn to the Mother of Gods links the wild music of ecstatic worshipers to the music of the wild:

> *She loves*
> *the clatter of rattles*
> *the din of kettle drums*
> *and she loves*
> *the wailing of flutes*
> *and also she loves*
> *the howling of wolves*
> *and the growling*
> *of bright-eyed lions*
> *echoing hills*
> *and wooded hollows (113).*

Music can, in such cases, help erase the boundaries between nature, humanity and the sacred—shucking societal roles and ordinary thought patterns in the pursuit of divine embodiment.

In shamanic systems, music is a preferred means of transportation to the *Otherworld(s)*, with the drum as the preferred instrument. The rhythm, which changes in accord with the journeyer's experience, is usually accompanied by songs that summon spirits, facilitate the journey and enact change, such as healing, soul retrieval or spellwork. As Mongolian shaman Sangerel puts it: *"The drum not only drives the vision by its steady beat but is literally the steed upon which the shaman rides to his destination" (93)*. Drums also drive the trance-journey in religions such as Santeria, which feature three ceremonial drums called *bata* that are played in a call-and-response pattern, determined by which orisha is being called *(Vega 171-2)*.

Drums aren't the only instruments that trance-journeyers use. Rattles are certainly common in many shamanic paths. In Mongolia and Siberia, shamans also use jaw harps or stringed instruments such as fiddles *(Sarangerel 90)*. In short, any instrument that can create consistent, repetitive sound—including the voice—is suitable. This doesn't rule out instruments with multiple tones and pitches, such as harps, guitars or recorders, although the ritual context does influence the manner they are played. Rather than intricate melodies that test the player's skill and require deep concentration, these instruments are played more subtly, focusing perhaps on chords or a relatively simple pattern of notes. Particular keys, modes or notes can be chosen in accordance with the ritual's focus and feel. To use the typical Western system, for example, major keys are more outward-focused and minor keys draw energy inward. The precise system, however, is up to the practitioner to determine and may be profoundly individualistic.

As with all ritual tools, the actual instruments themselves are accessories to the work. The body—with its stamping feet, clapping or slapping hands, the resonant cavities in the chest and head—is the primal instrument and always available to play. Its strings are the vocal chords deep within the throat, whose vibrations resound in the head and the body.

The voice—whether through spoken incantation, eerie wail or soaring song—shapes and weaves the working into a cohesive whole. It builds a sound-tapestry during spellwork and guides the spirit on its journey. As such, it has a crucial role in many ecstatic traditions.

In the core shamanism techniques of Michael Harner, singing helps induce the shamanic state of consciousness *(53)*. Special *"power songs,"* often gained through journey work themselves or through other communications with the *Otherworld*, summon helping spirits that aid the shaman in her work *(72)*. In Central Asia, shamans sometimes use throat singing to demonstrate contact with the spirit world, with the high-pitched overnote representing the spirits and the bass note physical reality. Throat-singing has physical effects, as well, as the resonance in the head is said to promote trance states *(Sarangerel 92)*.

In addition to drum rhythms, Santeria also uses ceremonial songs to bring on ecstatic states in the entire group of practitioners, as well as inspire a dancer to become the vessel of the orisha during the ceremony. Marta Moreno Vega describes the performance of an *arpon*, or ceremonial singer, during a ritual:

> *His vocal cords were stretched tight against his maple-colored neck; his eyes opened wide as the force of his voice exploded in his body, sending out renewed energy. His hands pointed nervously in the direction of the dancer, urging, begging, nagging, enticing Obatala to enter. The urgency in his voice continued to escalate, soaring like an arrow shot into the sky. The penetration of the drumbeats shook the sacred dancer, rippling through his body, as the insistence of the arpon's voice sent chills down the spines of all present, taking us to higher and higher spiritual levels (Vega 175).*

Practitioners of *seidr*, an oracular heathen tradition that involves direct contact with Otherworld spirits, also use songs to reach or deepen spiritual ecstasy *(Blain 53)*. Other *seid*-workers sing the names of Norse runes or play instruments to the same effect. In Northern traditions, the use of traditional songs, now lost, to attain trance states is included in an account from the *Saga of Eirik the Red (Blain 31-3)*.

Song can do more than transport the hedgerider into other realms; it's also used to shift fates and outcomes in accordance with will, a process described as magic. The use of song in spells and other magical workings is attested to in myths from around the world.

Perhaps the most famous is the Greek demigod, Orpheus, who uses his lyre and voice to charm men, the natural world and the Gods—including the Gods of the dead—with both overwhelming joy and sorrow. Using his music, he nearly succeeds in returning his wife from the Underworld. Music also is used to call the soul home in the Welsh tales of the *Mabinogion*, albeit with a less tragic outcome. After he is nearly slain by his enemy, Lleu Llaw Gyffes flees in the form of an eagle. The wizard Gwydion sings the eagle down from the tree and then transforms him back into a man *(Mabinogion 61-2)*.

In Irish tradition, the harp has three strains: granting sleep, joy and tears. By playing these strains, the musician can change the mood of the audience in accordance with his will and not only in the sense of a tear wrung from the eye during a lament, or a light-hearted dance during a reel. The God Dagda uses these strains to immobilize the Fomorians—literally making them helpless in the throes of emotion—in the attempt to rescue his harper *(Matthews 326)*.

In a final example, from the far North, singing is considered a synonym for spellcasting in the Finnish folk epic, *The Kalevala*. Through the power of his song, the magician Vainamoinen is able to summon the powers of nature and magically bind his opponent in a singing contest:

> *"The old Vainamoinen sang:*
> *the lakes rippled, the earth shook*
> *the copper mountains trembled*
> *the sturdy boulders rumbled*
> *the cliffs flew in two*
> *the rocks cracked upon the shores..."*
>
> (Kalevala 30).

Vainamoinen's voice awakens the powers of nature, directing their force to work his will against his opponent. Nor is music-magic in the Kalevala limited to the voice. After building a kantele—a type of traditional zither—from pike bones, Vainamoinen magically charms the creatures of the woodland, sky and water with its music (539). The kantele, which no other musician can play, presumably takes its power from the magical fish from which it was made as well as the elemental force of water.

Spirit and Spontaneous Song

But enough of the world tour.

My own experience with the power of music began, as it does for many, in early childhood. Songs came easily to me as a child; even at the age of two, I simply held a concept in my heart, opened my mouth and let the sound and words pour out, unthinking. Often, after the song left me, I could no longer remember its words, although the tunes stayed for a while. The point of the song wasn't overt composition or its reception by a human audience, but communication with the larger cosmos. It's a practice I've come to call *"spontaneous song"* and the root of my later ritual work.

Like many people, I largely gave up singing in my teenage years—partly out of pursuit of other interests, but mostly out of embarrassment. We've been raised to silence ourselves, to leave music to the *"professionals,"* those who have been judged as skilled, worthy, or at least a commercial success. While many of us will sing in the car or shower, we shy away from singing in front of others, saying we don't know how, judging ourselves against what we hear on our stereos or on the radio. Because of that internal yardstick and the perceived judgment of others, we're afraid of opening ourselves up to the sheer ecstasy of sound, to literally *"sing our hearts out."*

And that's where ritual consciousness comes in.

My involvement in paganism reintroduced me to the power of song via drumming and chanting both in and outside of ritual. Rather than mouthing the words, I threw myself into the rhythm and melody, giving it my heart and voice. Trance-journeying brought several soul-songs to me that I used to deepen my ritual consciousness; similar to the shamanic songs, they were simple, almost sing-song affairs without grace notes or bridges. When I was eighteen, I picked up the mountain dulcimer and, enchanted by its drone, I'd strum myself into meditative states in my college dorm.

My moment of revelation occurred in 1997 while walking a labyrinth, feeling the heavy silence of my life, the loss of my ability to communicate with the cosmos outside my all-too-chatty head. My trance state deepened as I ambled the winding paths, culminating in a vision at the center: the entire universe within my mouth, galaxies and planets whirling around my tongue as song rushed through. Soon after, I followed an urgent call in my spirit to undertake vocal training, a practice I maintain until this day. For me, the most important part of musical training isn't the technique or the pieces one performs, but the sheer *permission* to explore limits, edges and abilities. I began to find uses for my voice training outside of opera: as praise-offerings to spirits, as trance inductions, as a way to exercise magical will.

When I work with the classical elements common to many forms of paganism, I use the voice as a means of exploration. My soaring soprano notes for Air and the East, with runs and, if I can manage it, coloratura. The staccato, shouting voice of passion for Fire and the South. Flowing, mid-range tones for Water and the West. Deep, chest-voice for Earth and North, often accompanied by the rhythmic slam of my feet into the floorboards. For Spirit, I use a singing bell for its clear resonance, letting my voice spiral above it, the resonance of voice and bell creating a buzzing roar in my head.

In the realm of instrumental music, my mountain dulcimer led me to other instruments: the kantele, the valiha, the lap harp, the gopichand, the shruti box. I pursued an interest in drumming and began to experiment there, moving from doumbek to djembe to frame drum to udu, exploring the energies and abilities of each in regards to ritual. I use a range of musical instruments in my ritual work for different purposes, often combined with voice.

When I seek to honor the Kindreds, I'll grab an instrument, play and sing a spontaneous praise-song, letting my fingers find a pattern on the strings. With my harp, I'll often choose a musical mode that matches the ritual's mood or purpose, since tone and range affect the emotional energy needed for journeying: Lydian for the lightness of spring and gentle spirits, Aeolian for the ancestors and shadow work, Locrian for the wild frenzy of the Morrigan. No matter the instrument, the songs are an interplay of rhythm and tone with no bridges or breaks. They are meditative, repetitive, hardly anything pop radio would appreciate.

While I am a musician and songwriter in my own right, these magical songs are in the moment and unrehearsed. After I create them, their strains fade in the air, an offering of art and ephemera. Letting them go— rather than mining them for public performance, or catching them on a recording—is part of the sacrifice, or "making sacred." The offering of spirit, singing your heart out or playing fearlessly as if no one can hear you, is what counts in the spiritual realm, not whether you've stayed on key or stuck with the rhythm.

Ultimately, music-magic starts with giving oneself the permission to explore, and to suspend judgment. Fire those *American Idol* judges; you don't need them in your head while in sacred space. Let go of expectations, and follow where that inevitable tug-in-the-heart leads. Feeling stuck? Use the voice to transform your roadblock: sing, *"I am a great singer; my song lets me travel the worlds."* Pluck *"I am a great musician"* on your guitar, a mantra with strings. Drum *"my music honors the Gods."* Add the power of music to your affirmations, and sing, drum and play until you believe them.

Getting in the Groove

While someone, somewhere, may use Queen or the Spice Girls as a means for journey-work, popular music generally isn't the type many people need to dive into the realm of spirit. For one, they're someone else's songs. Secondly, they are not born of the moment. Most of them put the listener in a relatively passive role, unless you're doing karaoke or otherwise singing along.

So, what works?

First, pay attention to your physical being. Singing, in particular, is a very physical process, dependent upon *prana* or *pneuma*: breath, life-force, soul power. Inspiration literally means *"breathing in."* In order to clear the way for inspiration—and journey work, as it happens—you need to relax your body. When singing, your vocal chords are the strings of your instrument and your entire body is the resonating chamber. If you are tense, the sound will catch and your breath will shorten. If you are relaxed, the sound is free to emerge as it will.

Practices such as yoga are excellent not only in loosening taut muscles, but in exploring the edges and quality of the breath. The important part is to notice your body and respond. Loosen your stiff shoulders, stretch your tongue, and give yourself time to breathe deep. If your voice is hoarse, honor its boundaries and don't push it.

On a practical level, it pays to become familiar with your instrument before you enter ritual space. While this includes your voice *(warm-up exercises are good in this regard)*, it's especially important with musical instruments. *"Becoming familiar"* doesn't mean you need to be a virtuoso; it means knowing how to make sound with your instrument, tuning it if necessary, etc. The more familiar you are with your chosen tool, the freer you will feel to explore it within ritual and the more useful it will be as a steed for your journey.

The key to spontaneous song lies in pattern. One could define music, after all, as noise created in accordance to a pattern. This holds whether you're singing, plucking notes, or hitting a drum. There's a reason pattern is important in music-magic; rhythmic sounds induce trance. A process known as *"entrainment"* aligns brain wave patterns in both hemispheres of the brain through harmonic resonance *(Tedlock 82)*. Rhythmic sound is one way to accomplish this end; *"(b)ecause we hear the stimulus, neurophysiologists call this process 'sonic driving,' and it may result in visual sensations of color, pattern, and movement." (82)*.

Sound like an experience of the Otherworld yet?

Within ritual, feel free to explore. It can take a bit of wandering before you find a pattern that works and which can lead you down the path. Effective journey-songs are often repetitive and chant-like. They needn't have a metronome-type efficiency, though. Sarangerel notes, for example, that drumming rhythm and volume will change in accordance with the shaman's journey experience. *(Sarangerel 91)* It's a give-and-take. Your song drives your ability to enter trance, and also is driven by what you see and feel.

The same can be said for voice. Explore patterns, but with the heart and not the mind. Open your mouth and let the sound come, fearlessly. Don't worry whether it's *"pretty"* or not. Author Barbara Tedlock describes a *Sakha shaman* who warbles like a bird and snorts like a reindeer while drumming *(81)* and a Mongolian shaman whose singing involved *"a range of birdcalls, whistles, hoots, shrieks, cries, and roars"* as she communicated with spirits *(Tedlock 61)*. If the song that comes to you is an animal song, embrace it. Remember: the spirits aren't holding up a signboard grading your performance. They thrive on sincerity and passion, not on the perfect progression of notes on a page.

You may have visions while entering ecstatic states. That's the way my experience usually runs. Or, you may deeply feel and know the experience, but see nothing. It all depends on the way your talents lie. You may experience nothing at all. Trance-journeying, like anything, takes practice, unsuccessful attempts and blind exploration to perfect.

An Exercise in Spontaneous Song

Now, let's put it into motion. This is an adaptation of a series of music and ritual exercises I taught some years ago, strung together as a ritual offering praise to the spirits. While it focuses largely on the voice, you can supplement or even substitute the singing with instrumental music, drumming, rattling or toning. And feel free to take any or all of the exercise and adapt it to your needs and philosophies. While this isn't a trance-journey, it can give the practitioner a taste of the power of music in ritual.

Focus on your breath. Feel the earth beneath you, the sky above you. Feel your skin, your body—relaxed, light. Feel your core, your center. It could be the Awen, the chakra of your choice, some other image or concept. Get in touch with what is most yourself.

And then—make a sound, a tone. It can be a whisper, a growl, a howl, a song. Simply let it out. It's effortless. It's all perfect. Now, let it fade. Feel the earth beneath you.

And start there, with the earth as we honor the Green World—whether the Three Realms, the Four Elements, whatever system you work with. You are invoking, you are calling, you are honoring the Green World. The call is simple: "come, oh (name); we honor you. Come, oh (name), we honor you."

You can sing, whisper, speak it rhythmically. Let the sound come from within. Focus on your breath; feel the earth below you, the sky above you, your body filled with the energy that is sound. Let the song come: "Come, we welcome you. We honor you."

Take joy in the sound, and let it go as long as you are called. Then, let it fade, and let the energy fade back into the Green World.

Get in touch now with the stillness in your center, where your inner divine resides. If you have a matron or patron deity, see His or Her image before you. Open your mind to the Gods and then the heart, which is the core of your music.

Let the sound arise from the center of your devotion, your faith. Let it be an offering to the Gods.

Sing your heart out, or play it upon your instrument, whatever words or sounds come, without judgment. You may speak rhythmically, whisper, sing, tone, clap your hands, play. Let your song be an offering of praise—praise for the beauty of the world, of life. Praise for your talents and the limitless gifts of the Gods. Let your song be an offering for the spirits closest to your heart.

And when you know in your heart you are done, let the song fade to silence as an offering

Bibliography

Blain, Jenny. Nine Worlds of Seid-Magic: Ecstasy and Neo-Shamanism in North European Paganism.

New York: Routledge, 2002.

Harner, Michael. The Way of the Shaman: Tenth Anniversary Edition. San Francisco: HarperSanFrancisco, 1990.

The Homeric Hymns. Trans. Jules Cashford. New York: Penguin Books, 2003.

The Kalevala. Trans. Keith Bosley. New York: Oxford University Press, 1989.

The Mabinogion. Trans. Gwyn and Thomas Jones. Vermont: Everyman, 1993.

Matthews, Caitlin and John. The Encyclopedia of Celtic Wisdom. Rockport, Mass.: Element Books, 1994.

Sarangerel. Riding Windhorses: A Journey into the Heart of Mongolian Shamanism. Rochester, Vt.:Destiny Books, 2000.

Tedlock, Barbara. The Woman in the Shaman's Body: Reclaiming the Feminine in Religion and Medicine. New York: Bantam Books, 2005.

Vega, Marta Moreno. The Altar of My Soul: The Living Traditions of Santeria. New York: Ballantine, 2000.

Biography

A singer and sometimes poet, Jenne Micale has been a practicing pagan for more than twenty years and currently follows a Druidic path. She earned a doctorate in English after an intensive study of ecofeminism and science fiction. A former member of the wyrd folk band, *Belladonna Bouquet*, she practices the Bardic arts with a music project called *Kwannon*. She currently lives in upstate New York, where she heads *White Cat Grove*, a Druidic study group. Find out more at www.kwannon.net

Jenne's essay *"Druids and Brahmins: Of Cultural Appropriation and the Vedas"* was published in *Talking About the Elephant: An Anthology of Neopagan Perspectives on Cultural Appropriation* from Immanion Press. Her poetry has appeared in the *Henge of Keltria* newsletter and she wrote a variety of articles under the pen-name Morrigan-Aa for Circle Network News back in the 1990's. As *Kwannon*, she has created and self-released four music albums, some of which had been offered at *Woven Wheat (a web distributer, now defunct)* and *Reverb Worship.*

Walking with the Bones of the Earth

Veronica Cummer

Stones are ancient, the very bones of the Earth Mother. From the Earth, from the depths, we get gemstones, crystals, and semi-precious stones that are often used for jewelry, now and in the past. Yet their original purpose wasn't simply for adornment, but for the working of various kinds of magick. Each stone has its own properties, its own sphere of influence, one that can be tapped into for many purposes. Among these are grounding, stability, and protection. Or, conversely, they can aid us in scrying and releasing our spirits from our bodies, from the sometime prison of our singular ego-perspective.

Stones, gems, and crystals can, of course, be easily used as an anchor. They are a good choice in helping us to maintain a link to the Earth when we travel, a way to guide us back again. For one thing, they are naturally tied to the Earth and we tend to see them as very real and solid, almost eternal, which makes sense for Stone is one of the oldest spirits and can be a very steadying influence. We build things upon stone, upon rock—just as the Bible quote indicates—and we expect them to last because of the strength of that foundation. When we seek to travel, we need such a foundation, a sure source to begin our journey from. We won't get very far and we may not come back at all if our anchor isn't strong enough.

Still, stones can also serve to open us up, to help us access our powers, and create connections to other worlds whether through visions or journeying in the spirit. They can be foundational, but they also can represent the world axis around which the universe spins. Like the wellspring and the sacred tree, standing stones are a part of Old World Craft, whether in physical actuality at a ritual site or in the Otherworld. Stones can be the male force—such as the God, Hermes—and they can be representative of the World Mountain. As the *axis mundi*, they can serve as the pillar down which the Gods descend and up which the witch ascends, a meeting point between the two.

Crystals, in particular, are clearly linked to the attaining of knowledge, illumination, and insight. They represent a purity of sight, one that is difficult to achieve so long as your vision is bound by your own problems or preconceptions. Of course, crystals have been credited today with all sorts of incredible abilities, so much so that it might prove somewhat problematic at times to take them seriously in the Art. Yet, that may be short-sighted, especially if you are drawn to work with stones and gems and, especially, if you feel you have a good affinity for crystals.

These *"bones"* represent the hidden treasures, the golden fire of the Gods, the same sort of treasures that we go in search of when we travel past the hedgerows, beyond the boundaries. Here be dragons, and dragons of old were said to curl up in deep caverns around their hoard of old gold and brilliant jewels. Of course, they had absolutely no use for such things, so why did they desire them so much? The dragon was the guardian, and what the dragon watched over and protected were such precious things as wisdom and truth, prosperity and healing, strength and divine inspiration, the real treasures of the world and what the world needs to be renewed time and again. So, not only can stones be useful in traveling beyond the Hedge, but they also symbolize the very things that we go in search of.

However, if you are interested in working with stones and crystals, it's not enough to just pop out and buy the first cool-looking one you see, no matter how sparkly or expensive. You need to choose what will meet your requirements. There are, of course, many books available these days with lists and lists of stones and gems and crystals and what they all mean, their magickal and spiritual properties, even what parts of the body or chakras they are bound to. You can make use of these lists or what research you find on-line, but it's vital that the stone must also appeal to you.

Unless you have a feel for stones or for a particular stone, the same as with herbs or various kinds of divination—such as tarot cards or runes or the bones—it risks remaining on the level of intellectual understanding. It's just not enough to pick out a stone because some book says its what you need to balance out your heart chakra or to help heal your friend who's in the hospital. Its not enough to look up a crystal and jot down its attributes, find one at the local occult store, and expect it to immediately work wonders for you. Not everything works the same for everyone and not everything works for everyone in the same way. No, the stone must come alive for you. You have to learn how to tap into that living potential and form a real working relationship with it. You should trust your instincts and seek that gem or stone or crystal that speaks to you the most.

To start with, you might not want to immediately set to work with a stone once you've brought it home. It should be cleansed before use, especially if you got it somewhere that many people have handled it before you. It should also be charged to its purpose, the same as with any other tool you intend to bring into ritual or work magick with. To form a good connection, you shouldn't just leave it sitting on a shelf on altar all the time, but spend time with it and treat it like the living thing it is.

It may be the best idea to begin with a pair at the very least. An anchor stone and a stone for traveling. Stones meant for protection would also be a good investment. You can either get a single stone for protection, or one to represent each of the Quarters, the directions, or your guardians.

First off, you can cleanse a potential anchor stone in several ways. One method is by holding it in or letting it sit in running water, but only if the stone is not of a soft variety that will be damaged by immersion in water. You can also bury it in salt for a while or, better still, within the ground. An added plus is that by burying a grounding stone it not only emphasizes the anchoring nature of the stone, but it can better form a connection to the land where you live. If you have a particular place—such as beneath a tree—where you tend to make offerings to the land, the Gods, or the Fey, that would be a good place to bury the stone for a time.

If you are putting an anchor stone in the ground, you can also do a small spell when you put the stone in the earth, asking the land to make a connection to the stone and place a part of its essence within the stone, just as the land can become a part of your own body. When you hold that stone later it will remain as one with the land and be better able to guide you and draw you back from your travels. Along those same lines, it might be worthwhile to first look for a grounding stone already on the property, even if it might not be as pretty or colorful as a stone or crystal that you can buy. A small stone chipped off of a larger altar or offering stone that you have used for a while is, perhaps, the best choice of all for working with as it already has been tied to the land and the spirits of the land, as well as to your magick and rituals.

Once the stone has been cleansed, then you need to charge it with its purpose. For an anchor stone, it should be filled up with feelings of home, the stronger the better. If you are working with other people, such as in a coven, you can have everyone involved fill the stone with a sense of safety and home, creating a group anchor stone. We all might have a different visualization of what home means, but we can share a feeling of home and homecoming, of the heart and hearth of the land and the living center of a close-knit group.

No matter what stone you pick, it can be used to ground you and reaffirm your tie to a particular time and place. It can help get you home again. The stone can be put into a small bag with or without some dirt from the land. If you're working in a ritual space, it can be placed in the center, also in some dirt in a small bowl or plate. If desired, you can set the anchor stone in a plate with a small layer of dirt or sand and draw an inward spiral—with the traveling stone in the middle of the spiral, the goal, and the anchor stone at the beginning place, the foundation and the start.

Stones meant to ground tend to be black, brown, or red in color. My own anchor stone is a mottled and striated red agate and reminds me of a heart. Choices of stones to connect you to your home or to the Earth, to be an anchor, would include jet, a dark tiger's eye, obsidian, agate, a brownish citrine, garnet, ruby *(unpolished, low-grade is often within a decent price range)*, heliotrope *(bloodstone)*, black tourmaline, lodestone, andradite, hematite, and smoky quartz. Hematite has the extra benefit of absorbing stress or disturbance in your life; if the stone cracks or breaks it's a sign that its taken all that it can. If you want to continue to use this kind of stone, it should be cleansed and rested on a regular basis.

Some of these stones are connected to iron, a traditional grounding metal, in particular among the Fey. Smoky quartz can be found in Scotland, where its sometimes called *cairngorm (after the location where its found)* and was used as decoration and even as part of the hilt of the black knife known as the *skean dhu* and that some speculate relates to the black-handled witch blade, the athame.

When it comes to deciding on a traveling stone, crystals are some of the best. One of their talents is to aid in forming connections to other worlds and levels of existence. Hence the rather infamous tool of the fortune-teller, the crystal ball. As such, crystals are a good choice for learning to see and to travel to what you have seen. However, a real crystal ball or crystal skull can be quite spendy, so it might be best to work with a smaller and cheaper crystal before deciding to make that sort of financial investment.

If you're not sure about using crystals, other choices include various clear, white, blue, green, or violet stones. Diamonds are a good pick, but also very pricey. A Herkimer Diamond is the next best thing and far more affordable. Other options include amethyst, celestite, sapphire *(unpolished and low-grade, it can be in your price range)*, lapis lazuli, moldavite, atacamite, azurite, aquamarine *(blue beryl)*, and apophyllite, also called a *"fisheye."* Some of these stones, especially the greenish ones, are tied to copper, a good metal for transferring energy. While, interestingly enough, one of the places that apophyllite can be found is in the ancient witch mountains of Germany, the Harz range.

My own traveling stone showed up at a stone and gem show. I wasn't really looking to buy a stone, especially not one that cost more than I really wanted to pay, but it caught my attention at the back of a display. It was a polished crystal prism about five inches long and, when I picked it up, it felt as though the floor had abruptly dropped out from under me. To be honest, I had to struggle with the idea of buying and using a crystal, precisely because of all the fanciful and outrageous press it has gotten over the years, but could not resist it in the end. I just knew it was mine.

Unlike the anchor stone, it would be best to keep your traveling stone wrapped up in silk when not in use after you have cleansed and charged it to its purpose. In this case, running water and/or incense smoke are good choices for cleansing the stone. To charge it you should focus on thoughts of going beyond the borders, seeking out knowledge, putting into the stone all of the excitement of the distant horizon and discovering what might lie past it. The stone should make you feel as light as the anchor stone should make you feel heavy.

If you already have a familiar spirit, Faery, or fetch that you work with, you can ask them to connect to the traveling stone and imbue it with some of their energy, with the current of the Otherworld. The more beings who agree to charge the stone, the more powerful it can be in calling you out of yourself and creating a gate that leads to the beyond. As the anchor stone should be tied to the land, so the traveling stone should be tied to the Otherworld, to Faery, as strongly as possible.

Traditionally, the best stones for protection would be blue in color. Blue stones or beads have long been used against ill-wishing or the *Evil Eye.* Or you can get a stone of another color for protection and paint it with a blue eye if you wish. If your protection stones are linked to the Elements or Quarters or directions, you might want to pick stones that match your mythology and sense of what they mean to you personally or on your path. They could also represent spirit familiars who are your guardians in the Otherworld and you can have those contacts put some of their essence into the stones.

You can place the protection stones around your ritual space when you wish to travel. If you are using the spiral in the dirt or sand with the anchor and traveling stone, you can also choose to put the protection stones around the edge of the plate. If you are planning on lying down for your journey, the protection stones may be set around you instead. One example would be putting one below your feet, one above your head, one to your left hand and one to your right.

When it comes to using the anchor and traveling stones, you might also want to hold them. The anchor stone can go in one hand and the traveling stone in the other. When you wish to travel, close your hand around the traveling stone and, when you wish to come back, open that hand and close the other hand around the anchor stone. To begin with, it might be a good idea to have your hand closed around the anchor stone and concentrate on your link to the land, your body, and home. Then, ever so slowly, as you get into your trance, let that hand open and close the opposite hand on the traveling stone. If you can, doing the change over at the same time is a good technique.

A red stone can represent the Earth and the blood of the witch, while a white stone can represent the Otherworld and the blood of the Fey. Blue stones can then be used for protection and because they are also often seen as the color of magick itself. Conversely, you can pick a green stone to represent the wilds beyond the Hedge and a black stone to represent the shadow which is this world. The pattern and the symbolism must work for you above all else.

You may, of course, add other ritual elements to the use of of stones, including chants or songs or sounds, certain ways of breathing, or incense saved specifically for spirit journey work. When you're first concentrating on attaining a level of magickal technique it never hurts to do more ritual than not enough. Once it begins to come easier to you, then you can begin to carefully release the tools that have gotten you to where you needed to go and make do without. But you will always need a form of an anchor and a way of traveling, no matter what shape it might take.

The Moon's Apprentice
A Short Exposition of
Seidhr, Galdr and Trolldomr in Scandinavia

Nicholaj de Mattos Frisvold

Seidhr was an art that belonged to women. It was Freya, the *vanir* who brought this wisdom to the *aesir*—in particular to Odin, who became a master in these arts. Names given to the practitioner such as *Seidhrberendr* is suggested by for instance Solli to refer to *"the art of the cunt"* [1] thus it speaks clearly of a female connotation. Actually, it was considered quite complicated for a male to indulge in these arts as the accusation of *ergi* easily could arise. This term is frequently translated as homosexuality. But it isn't strictly speaking homosexuality, but more to take the submissive part in a sexual relationship. In fact, laws were quite hard when it came to accusations of *ergi*, so hard that the offended one had the right to murder the offender as his reputation as a virile male was damaged. By being subject to this particular form of accusation he could lose respect, work, wife and income.

Seidhr is quite difficult to define in terms of its content. When the Christian historian Snorri Sturlasson speaks of this art he seems to differentiate between *seidhr* and the public cults. In the public cult the owners of the particular house, the husband and wife were in charge of the cult. The public cult were directly related to the reverence of *aesir* and *vanir* and thus considered lawful in society. With *seidhr* matters are different.

Snorri sees this art as something both powerful and dangerous and he does not give the impression of this art being a part of the public and acknowledged cults. This might be explained by this art gaining its power by the assistance of spiritual guides and helpers and not the gods themselves. Also, *seidhr* was believed to be a way of bringing the world to

---

1. *The use of the word "cunt" is preferred due to its root in the word kunta, associated with the rune ken, which refers to a dominating and overwhelming power of the female genitalia.*

ones will, and thus it could easily be an art that went counter to the social order. Not only was *seidhr* a practice found in the borders of society, but it was, as mentioned, also a female art. At large this art was considered to be *"unmanly"* and thus Odin transgresses double-up. He is not only learning an art that is already subject for ambivalence, but it is also an art that can make him lose respect amidst his peers and comrades.

How could the Chief God, the alpha-male so to speak, indulge in *"unmanly arts?"* This might be explainable if we turn to the *Edda*. Our greatest source for insight into Odin and his relation to seidhr is found in *Ynglingesaga 7*, which also presents the nature of the art itself:

> *"Odin could transform his shape (hamr). His body would lie as if dead, or asleep, even though he would be a bird or beast, fish or snake and be off in a twinkling to distant lands upon his own or other people's business. But he could also do other things: with words alone he could quench fire, still the ocean in tempest, and turn the wind to any quarter he pleased...Odin understood also the art in which the greatest power is lodged, and which he himself practiced; which is seidhr; by means of this he could know the fate of men and foresee what has not yet happened, he could bring to men death or misfortune or ill health, he could take sanity and strength from men and give to others; but with this form of trolldomr comes so much unmanly matters that men could not perform it without shame, that's why they tought gydjene (priestesses) this art."*

From this account in the *"Edda"* it seems that *seidhr* was twofold. On one hand it was concerned with prophecy and the mystery of fate, the Norns, and on the other hand it could bring misfortune upon people and change their luck and fate. If we look at the way this art is presented in *"Ynglingesaga"* it seems to be somehow different from trolldomr in general as Odin is presented as someone who could change his *hamr*, a faculty only indirectly related to *seidhr*.

While his body would lie still, he himself would take on various shapes and fly wherever he desired unrestrained by mundane geography. It would seem plausible that this is a presentation of *seidhr* as a part of a larger generic referred to as *trolldomr*. It also seems that *seidhr*, which was from the *vanir*, and *trolldomr*, which was ascribed to the knowledge of the *jotnir*, shared in common the necessity of altered state and the use of *galdr* and song, i.e. what we would call enchantments that would effectuate a state of otherness.

The divinatory *seidhr* was of a different caliber than the *malefic seidhr*. While the divinatory *seidhr* was solely focused on prophecy and soothsaying, largely referred to as *spá*, the *malefic seidhr* would enable the practitioner to twist and thwart the laws of nature. The predictable would be unpredictable in this act of hollowing or turning the worlds. What the two expressions had in common was the importance of guiding spirits. *Seidhr* could not be performed unless the practitioner had a deep and intimate relationship with the spirits of the land and the dead.

The secrets of the runes Odin received by descending to the halls of Hel in the nine days and nights he hung in the tree were both necromantic and divinatory in nature. This suggests itself if we realize that it was by hanging in the tree he descended to Hel. The gift of prophecy and sorcery were given by descent to Hel. This tells us further that the land was crucial, and it follows that the most common method for *seidhr* was what was called *"sitting out."* By entering the woods or mountains at night and making contact with the spirits of the land *(landvettir)*[2] it was possible to access the potency informing this powerful and dangerous art. Sitting out was simply about sitting still in a silent piece of sacred nature by night and calling for inspiration and vision. This practice was considered so effective that it was forbidden by law as late as the 15th Century.

The importance of *landvettir* is important to note because it is these beings that maintain stability, fertility and happiness in the land. If they leave, the place in question becomes subject for hostile influences and barrenness and melancholy enter in its place. This is precisely the effect of erecting the so called *nidstangr (staff of disgrace)*, a staff carved with runes and enchantments where the head of a rotting animal is placed on top of facing the place you seek to hex. The decaying gaze of the animated head will cause the landvettir to leave the place and, in the absence of fruitful and stabilizing forces, gloom and barrenness invades the location.

We find many instances where both witches and gods are told to sing over wounds to heal, or sing over runes that have been carved. One of the most fearsome forms of *galdr* is what is known as *níd*. In modern days this word has been come to be used much more for ridicule without its magical reference, but originally this word spoke about ridicule and harm, often very vulgar in its imagery. Some of the famous people connected to this art were called *Kveld-Ulfr (evening wolf)* and another one is aid to be *"half troll"* and Egil Skallargrimsson is himself the most famous one due to his conflict with King Eirik and Queen Gunnhild. In his Saga:

> *"Egil went up onto the island. He took a hazel pole in his hand and went to the edge of a rock facing inland. Then he took a horse?s head and put it on the end of the pole. Afterwards he made and invocation, saying "Here I set*

---

2. *The term vettir denotes a large class of nature spirits that prefers to stay close to humans, similar to the Roman lares. The word is most likely from anglo-saxon "with" which refers to creature, being, spirit, demons etc.*

up this scornpole and turn its scorn upon King Eirik and Queen Gunnhild"
– then he turned the horse's head to face land—"and I turn its scorn upon
the nature spirits (landvaettir) that inhabit this land, sending them astray so
that none of them shall find its resting-place by chance or design until they
have driven King Eirik and Queen Gunnhild from this land!" Then he drove
the pole into a cleft in the rock and left it to stand there. He turned the head
towards the land and carved the whole invocation in runes on the pole."

The most famous act of divinatory *seidhr* is found in *Voluspá*, the
poetic rendering of the end of *aesir* and the coming of a new golden age.
Here the practitioner is referred to as *Volva*. Prior to Christianity and
certainly in some centuries to follow—she was treated with utmost respect.
This is because the position of the *Volva* in the Nordic religious life was one
of religious interpreter. Usually she was an old woman, old as defined by
loss of menstruation, where she left her position as woman and mother and
became something else.

In this context, she became a prophetic channel, a spokeswoman
between men and gods. *Volva* often carried a *volr*, literally, a stang,
symbolic both of the *Yggdrasil* and the dual acts she was capable of doing
by being able to both bring fertility to a land or household or to take it
away. So great was her position and status that even Odin himself goes to
her for learning of the fate of the world and the gods. These divinations
were usually lengthy processes that included songs and enchantment, *galdr*
and *silence*. A shape of *hamr* often occurred, all done in concert with the
spirits aiding the practitioner. She would then lie as dead, while her *hamr*
left the body together with the attending spirit host.

In Eirik's saga, the typical form the *Volva* showed herself in was:

> "...wearing a black mantle with a strap, which was adorned with precious
> stones right down to the hem. About her neck she wore a string of glass
> beads and on her head a hood of black lambskin lined with white cat skin.
> She bore a staff with a knob at the top, adorned with brass set with stones on
> the top. About her she had a linked charm belt with a large purse. In it she
> kept the charms, which she needed for her predictions. She wore calfskin
> boots lined with fur with long, sturdy laces and large pewter knobs on the
> ends. On her hands she wore gloves of cat skin, white and lined with fur."

The reference to the use of cat fur is interesting, as it clearly connects the
art with Freya. Freya is said to arrive the burial of Baldr in a chariot pulled
by cats. Further, the association of cats with sexuality and freedom, as in the
cult of *Cybele* is worthy to mention as is the reputed double-sight of cats.
The ability of seeing the past and present, the visible and invisible world
simultaneously is a quite proper motive. This do suggest that *siedhr* was an
art intimately tied to sexuality, but not necessarily fertility, which was the
case in the public cults.

The researcher Clunies Ross has pointed out in regard to the typical practitioner of siedhr that she seems to show a traditional segmentation of the divine feminine into its white, red and black phases or faces. She relates the similarities between *Gullveig* in *Voluspá* and *Freya* in *Ynglingesaga* and then lastly remarks on the fierce goddess/*volva*, *Heid*. *Heid* is said to be a black Goddess who is three times burnt but resurrects again. She lives in the forest of iron where only the black elves dare to venture.

This insight Ross presents points towards the triple form of the divine feminine as in *Hekate Triformis*.

Freya represents the red phase associated with menstruation, *Gullveig* the white phase associated with abundance, generosity and youth, while the black phase represents the days of blackened moon, where the blood is no longer rejuvenating the womb. *Heid* might be seen as the gateway to the enigma of *malefic seidhr*. In *Orvar Odds Saga*, the *seidhrbrendir's* name is *Heid*. There is also mention of an old woman in Eiriks saga with awesome powers called *"the angel of death"* who is most likely *Heid* under one of her many aliases. *Heid* is depicted as a being both human and divine, but with a malefic disposition that accords her powers prominence in the outskirts of the world.

But if this underlies for us that *seidhr* was an art deeply related to the female cycle and essence, what Odin has to do with this art?

Odin, the Master of Seidhr

Odin and his relationship with the art of seidhr has been subject to much speculation, most recently a so called queer or gay theory has been presented *(Solli: 2002)* which have some interesting factors. The transgressive element has been noted by many and several others less interesting theories that connect Odin to Arianism and some sort of rebellious conqueror of a gluttonous disposition when it comes to wisdom. On the one hand I find it reasonable to assume a form of spiritual gluttony as revealed in the names of his wolves, *Gere* and *Freke*, whose names refer to *greed* and *gluttony*. At the same time we have the fact that Odin was originally associated with the night. He was a nocturnal deity said to bring storms and winds, a domain predominantly female. He is also accompanied by the ravens, *Hugin (thought)* and *Munin (memory)*. Birds are yet again a female symbol and also a symbol for prophetic abilities.

It is a quite fascinating imagery that surfaces from this. On one hand Odin is a transgressor of limits by getting involved in a form of magic that is not only subject for a somewhat bad reputation, but he is also venturing into the field of women. This highly mercurial tendency is interesting to note conjoined with the fact that he goes to the *Volva* for divination.

This indicates that he in the end to demonstrate obedience towards the traditional channels for wisdom and spiritual sustenance. This mercurial orientation is further revealed in how his poles are coloured by his wife, *Frigg*, a stable mother figure, and his lover and teacher, *Freya*, the untamed desire, sexuality itself. He is, as such, an excellent representative for nocturnal Mercury.

The astrologer William Lilly commented in his magnum opus, *Christian Astrology*, that *"Mercury is good with good and bad with bad,"* which in extension says that Mercury is female or male according to the planet he is conjoining. When Odin is hanging in *Yggdrasil "to sacrifice himself to himself"* he is simply declaring to become the fullness of what he in essence is—a paradox. Odin is definitively moving into a territory of tension when he is being taught the arts of *seidhr* and night-flight, how to connect with the spirits of the land and use them for prophecy and malefica.

For instance his brother of blood pact, Loke says the following of him in *Lokesenna*:

> *"But you once practiced seid on Samsey,*
> *And you beat on the drum as witches do,*
> *In the likeness of a wizard you journeyed among mankind*
> *And that I thought the hallmark of an ergi."*

Here Loke gives several interesting association to what *seidhr* is about. It is about beating the drum to change his *hamr* and walk around in this other form. Already Odin has his horse *Sleipnir*, whom with his eight legs demonstrates the ability Odin has to ride between worlds, in both the quarters and mid-quarters, up and down. As always, everything with Odin is black. It is about the night, the natural domain of the womb, the un-manifested possibility of becoming. I believe this is exactly the realm of reason for *seidhr*. It is the realm of invisible powers, unruly and turbulent that is entered with the desire to make one's own destiny.

Odin is compared to a volva that, like the *Sami* and *Siberian Shamans*, uses a drum *(vétt)* and is called both *argr (negative connotation)* and *vitki (positive connotation)*, which in *Sami* refers to practitioners of *trolldomr*, by virtue of its connection to the large class of nature spirits close to humans, both benefic and malefic. The importance of the drum is found both in African cults as well as what is today largely referred to as *"shamanism"* where the drum provides a pathway of sounds, a ladder of descent for the spirits and a way of ascent for the practitioner. We might say that the drum is the sound of the crossroad of the worlds.

Both healing and cursing is associated with Freya and Odin and many *Edda* poems tell about this. For instance in *Fjolsvinnsmál 49* Freya says:

> "Long I waited
> On Lyfjaberg *(lyfja means trolldomr or healing)*
> Day on day I waited for you;
> Now it has happened,
> That I anticipated,
> My lover, you have come to my halls"

To my halls can indicate that the object of desire actually died and came to the halls of death where he became Freya's lover, as well as simply coming under her spell. This confirms the ambiguity and complexity of Odin as a god of contradiction and tension. If we look closer at the way he was inducted to the secrets of runes, namely by hanging in *Yggdrasil* for nine nights, we should take notice that *Yggdrasil* is also a reference to the horse. In other words, for nine nights Odin was traveling along the world tree from root to top and this night ride gained him a great wisdom. The secrets of the world opened up and he found at last peace with himself.

Solli has suggested that this ritual of initiation was of a sexual nature, supported by Adam of Bremen's commentaries of the blot at *Upsala* where the songs and enchantments sung were so rude and repulsive that he would not even repeat them in his historical annals. This can suggest that there were a sexual character to the initiation focusing on asphyxia and its sexual connotation as a stepping stone towards trance and insight. That a god of tension and transgression seeks the extreme for further transgression does seem to fit the picture quite well. Not only this, but it also hints subtly to a methodology for a male practitioner to symbolically *"give himself to himself,"* at least this is the silent message presented in the course of initiation.

There is not much academic research done on this, but it is tempting to remind of the activities of *Maria de Naglowska* and her activities in France in the 1930s. She performed *Golden Masses* in her ecclesiastical fraction called *Fleche d'Or*, which centered around ceremonial hanging with the purpose of entering the realm of death in a state of awareness—at least in the perspective of Julius Evola. What is interesting in this detour from our subject is exactly how the sexual stimulation culminating in orgasm led to asphyxia during the mass and thus was believed to open the gates of Death with the journeyman as a conscientious wanderer in the underworld. There are of course not much research to back up this theory, but learning of the hanged men in the trees at the Odin blot at Uppsala Sweden, told by Adam of Bremen, it is a plausible explanation that these men were failing their initiation and thus served as offerings in their failure.

Seidhr and Its Mystery

Interestingly, the apprentice in the arts of *seidhr* was sometimes referred to as *"the apprentice of the moon"* as the keys to the art were considered to be hidden in the art of poetry and abundance of soul. The moon as the author of muses, song, and poetry is naturally a powerful force for whomever wants to make use of *galdr* and *seidhr* properly as the incantations were highly poetic in style and recitation. It was a feature of unique persons said to possess a double soul. These people were, as *Hultkrantz*[3] comments, considered the Moon's Apprentice—and yet again a female form enters the stage.

The Moon, *Gullveig*, is the fullness itself in its phase of giving—and the pale whiteness of her dark face...is as Heid, because *Gullveig (drink of gold)*, is the *jotnir*-wife of Loke, himself a *jotnir*, but brother by blood and troth with Odin, and the harbinger of sorrow in the form of Angerboda.[4] Seeing the deep relations these three forms has to *Voluspá* and *ragnarók* it becomes quite evident what immense power that were hidden within the *seidhr*.

As the story goes; of Loke's children, three of them would bring on the end of the world *(ragnarök)*. These were the serpent, *Jordmundgan*, the wolf, *Fenrir* and, *Hel*, the mistress of the underworld. The roles they play is evident in *Voluspá* where Loke and his children is instrumental in restoring the golden age. It is only natural in a greater cosmic scheme that Loke appears to be more and more malevolent and un-understandable as the world is facing its annihilation. We might see in Loke a similar role as we find in Judas Iskariotes, the one who takes the blame of the world on his shoulders to set in motion the undoing and rebirth of the world.

It is also here in the form of Loke the distinctions between good *seidhr* and bad *seidhr* enters, where we find the friction between *jotnir* and gods, often presented by the two realms of Utgardr and Midgardr. Loke attempts to bridge this gap through his oath with Odin, but still the oppositions fight themselves out in order to strive towards the union towards oneness.

In the *Edda* we find one story that tells how Tor went to Utgardr together with Loke. A fight between Tor and the creatures of doom occurs

3. In Current anthropology vol 24 (1983) pp 459
4. Angerboda is a highly complex figure, both in function and by ancestry. Most likely she was a vanir raised by jotnir. Her triple manifestation as Angerboda-Gull-veig-Heid focusing on the heart as the seat of resurrection is likewise a mystery of traditional depth that unfortunately fall outside our scope as such discussion would occupy too much space She is the mother of Fenris, the wolf, the midgardserpent, Jordmundgan and Hel, the owner of the realm of Death. We should just point out the importance of Death, the wolf and the snake in the arts of seidr.

while Loke fights his own Utgardr-reflection. The land at the outside seems to be a form of mirror image of the orderly world where ones oppositions are confronted and brought into harmony with ones destiny. Utgardr was a place of secrecy, darkness and *trolldomr*, literally *"the farm outside"* speaking of the reputation *trolldomr* had in society. By extension, those who were involved in malevolent *seidhr* was somehow connected to this chaotic farm on the outside, inhabited by giants and trolls, the dark shades of all good and familiar in *Midgardr*.

Silence was one important factor of the art and the other was enchantments, the *galdr*, and carving runes. Runes of hexing or healing could be carved and these runes could be sung to facilitate visions or night flights, effectuate blessings or curses. Odin says of the power of the runes in *Hávamál*:

> *"The runes you must find and the meaningful letter,*
> *A very great letter*
> *A very powerful letter*
> *Which the mighty sage stained*
> *And the powerful gods made*
> *And the runemaster of the gods carved out"*

Galdr followed certain rules as well. Sturlasson in his handbook for poets speaks about certain meters used for *galdr*, what he calls *ljóahattr* and *galdralag* and Havamál in Stanza 144–166 systematically demonstrates the type of meter used to make ones *galdr* effective. The meters most commonly used to indicate the effectiveness was the use of consonant rhymes in a *jambeau/troche* interaction that would sound like verbal punches.

The act of uttering words of bane was considered most powerful. It was almost as a word spoken in hate or love assumed the form of its intent upon its uttering. The verb used in these instances was gala, so *galdr* could refer to a song or chant in the sense of charm or spell. Interestingly, this word is also used to describe an insane person. We can assume that it referred to as special state of mind during the utterance of the word. This state of mind is often ascribed to poets and troubadours, those who function as the *"memory"* of the culture, *skáldskapr*.

Bestiality and madness were occasionally associated with *trolldomr* and for those sorcerers that displayed these features they were considered as outlaws and were occasionally chased away from the society or *"sent to the halls of Ran."*

Acts of malefic sorcery were largely ascribed to *seidhr*. In Norway, during the *Christianization*, practitioners of this art were in the Law of Gulating subjected to exile and confiscation of property. Not only this, there are a few cases telling how practitioners of *seidhr* were abducted and tied to a rock in the ocean waiting for the tide to drown them. This was done in order to send them to the afterlife in the halls of *Ran* and not to *Valhalla*. Since *Ran* was considered to capture her victims it was considered to be a form of imprisonment in her golden halls and less glorious than the constant feast of food, drink and laughter in *Valhalla*.

It is here in this altered state that the importance of *fylgja* enters. We have already commented several times that could not be performed without the aid of spirits of the nature around—and in the same measure it could not happen without *fylgja*. *Fylgjur* were considered to be the Guardian Spirits of men, connected to a specific person and/or families. The *fylgja* was a repository for advice and revelations of omen and, when showing itself, it was usually in the form of some animal or a woman.

One can say that the *fylgja* was a man's mirror in the spiritual dimensions, and more important, this spiritual Double was considered *"the female follower."*[5] This again emphasizes *seidhr* being a female form of *trolldomr*, which in the hands of males brings out a tension both spiritual and social. What is interesting is that the *fylgja* was always considered to be female, and it is perhaps here we find the connection between *seidhr* and how this domain could open up for men who chose to venture to the borders of organized society.

It is important to note that in Scandinavia the belief in the human soul was highly flexible. Connected to the idea of the Soul we also find *Hamr* *(skin)* and *Hugr (meaning "mind," but strictly speaking mind as in inner dialogue with the heart)*. *Hugr* could also describe a person's personality and temper. The *hamr* on other hand could do what was called *hamferd*, namely to ride out at night in divine, human or beastly forms. Yet another complex of the understanding of the function of the soul is found in the idea of *hamingja*. This was a sort of elevated angelic guardian that were in charge of a person's *"luck,"* i.e. both the capabilities of performing this art and also to what extent the night-flight would bring good or bad luck to the practitioner's life. This angelic guardian was seen as ones spiritual double and can be equated with guardian spirit of the *Socratic daimon*.

It is said in *"Ynglinga Saga"* that Odin was a master of this art. Whether awake or asleep, Odin's *hugr* was carrying out deeds for him. In 'Lokesenna' Odin's knowledge of *seidhr* and shapeshifting were originally an art marked by tension and taboo. The female emphasis is further told of in both Sagas and the *'Edda'* where we find accounts of *myrkriur* and *kveldriur*, meaning *"those who ride at night."* These were usually said to be hags and witches flying around in the night, using different bodies to mask themselves. They could ride pigs or horses and were at times said to ride men in erotic nightmares, assuming the name *mara* and inducing night-

5. C. Lecouteux. 2003: 45

mare, an important reference to the mare, the female horse. This being said, the word *mara* itself is double sexed and can refer back to both males and females

While *Sleipnir*, Odin's horse, has eight legs and is the compass itself of the world tree, the night-flying witches take the shape of a mare, the very symbol of *ergi*, what is unmanly in itself, but reflects the true nature of the *fylgja* and affirms *seidhr* being the art of effectuating a mild or radical change of perception or location for various ends. This might even suggest that Odin could ride his horse, *Sleipnir*, "the slippery one" as the wise women could ride or take the shape of mares to ride the night.

And thus we can conclude that the riddle is quite simple. By moving out to outskirts of society, the laws of society turn dim and the rules are to a certain degree annihilated by the practitioner. In the particular case of Odin, he is not only a man amidst men, but he is also a god who can take the shape of a horse. His mercurial orientation turns him into the perfect amalgam for contradiction and can as such freely venture into whatever domain, divine or mundane. Since he is operating outside the social order, he naturally has no need for orienting himself to the laws pertaining to the orderly society.

Bibliography

Lecoutoux, C. Witches, Werewolves and Fairies. Inner Traditions, Vermont, 2003

Raudvere, C. Trolldomr in Early Medieval Scandinavia. In Ankarloo & Clark (ed.) Witchcraft and Magic in Europe. Penn, US, 2002

Solli, B. Seid. Pax forlag, Oslo, 2002

Steinsland, G. Norrøn religion. Pax forlag, Oslo, 2005

Biography

Nicholaj de Mattos Frisvold has a MA in Anthropology and a MA in Psychology. He is currently concluding his doctorate in Psychology at NTNU, Norway. He is a professional traditional astrologer and herbalist and also an initiate into a Scandinavian stream of the *Nameless Art*. His main interest is in Traditional wisdom and metaphysics which lead to initiations to *Houngan Asogwe* in a *Haitian hounfor* and *Awo Ogboni of Ifa* in Abeokuta, Nigeria.

He is also the founder of Institute Chadezoad: *International Society for Traditional Research* and has three books published; *Kiumbanda- A Complete Grammar of the Art of Exu* (Chadezoad: 2006), *Arts of the Night* (Chadezoad: 2009) and *The Craft of the Untamed* (Mandrake of Oxford: 2010). Forthcoming is the title *Invisible Fire: Inner Dimensions of Western Gnosis and Theurgy* (Capall Bann: 2010)

Staving the Hawthorn Tree

Beth Hansen-Buth

"Come Fairies, take me out of this dull world,
for I would ride with you upon the wind
and dance upon the mountains like a flame!"
William Butler Yeats

The snow is sculpted into strange rounded shapes in the moonlight as I gaze on my back yard. It's late winter in Minnesota, and Imbolc just passed to let me know that Spring will be returning, albeit slowly. The energy is beginning to change, at least within me, and I start to dream of digging in the earth. I have been blessed with a large back yard that's perfect for parties with a fire pit, deck, and overgrown and neglected gardens. This is the year to plant something new, to create a space that is both sacred and fun. But the nights are still long, the trees are still bare, and the snow is still piled high around us in great mounds.

The trees are shape changers throughout the year. In spring, they become like children, growing leaves so bright and new that you can't help but smile at all the green buds. They quickly become maidens before it gets too hot, some flowering with rich scents preparing to make their fruits. Then they enter the Mother phase, nourishing others so that new trees can take root and grow. Finally winter returns and the tree seems to die, just bones reaching up to be sculpted against the sky. It's an extraordinary transformation through Maiden, Mother and living Crone that we humans are privileged to witness and learn from year after year.

We are dependent upon trees for their wood to create our shelter and warmth. Even as the birds, squirrels, and countless insects make their homes within the living trees, we create our homes from their wood after their death. Our furniture is sculpted from their limbs, creating a new beauty. Trees and humans have an extraordinary partnership beyond the physical as well.

This was recognized by the Druids of old, and they created the *Ogham* (pronounced *Ohm*) alphabet which has been used for teaching, divination, and communication for centuries. The letters themselves look like simplified trees with a trunk and straight branches off the side. There are twenty main letters, broken up into four sets of five. Each *Ogham* letter is associated with a particular tree, color, and animal. Used in divination, the patterns they create tell a story. Used in healing, each one carries the energy of the tree, connecting the person to both *Earth* and *Sky* to find the unity within.

I have a strong affinity with the *Ogham*; my first name, *Beth*, corresponds with the first letter of the *Ogham*: *Beith*, which represents Birch. It is the first tree to re-populate after a forest fire. Quick to grow, the bark of the paper birch is used around the world in crafts of native people, and was used by the Celts for recording the alphabet on. Birch is the Goddess as the Flower Maiden. First to bloom in springtime, birch lends itself to starting new projects, and bringing new life to old ideas. Diving into the lore of the *Ogham* for the first time a decade ago was a delightful journey of self-discovery. Working with them now in healing, I find I am discovering new abilities in my old friends the trees.

As I contemplate my garden, I find it hard to find focus. But with gardens come *fairies*, so I know where I can find guidance within all the possibilities my yard provides. I turn to the *Ogham*, through the use of *Volva Stav*, to seek the wisdom of the Hawthorn tree.

I study *Volva Stav* with Kari Tauring, who has pioneered this shamanic technique that utilizes wood to create a rhythm for song, dance, and metaphysical travel to the *Otherworld* seeking answers to questions. Calling on the blood of my Norwegian and Finnish ancestors, I take up my rough maple wood *stav (staff)* and apple wood *tien (wand)*. Together, they carry me, and work wonderfully with the *Ogham*, tapping my way to the root of *Huathe*, the Hawthorn tree.

Sacred to *faeries* and pagan through and through, the Hawthorn stands between our world and the realm of enchantment. I've walked this way before, by candlelight with my eyes closed, deep in meditation as part of my journey with the Celtic *Ogham* alphabet. *Huathe*, or Hawthorn, is the first of the second set of the *Ogham*.

So I light my candles and incense, pick up my *stav*, and begin chanting to each of the directions: *Austri Vestri Sudri Nordri*—East West South North in Old Norse. They are the names of the *four dwarves* that hold up the world. As my *stav* hits the floor there is a satisfying *doum*, and as my wand taps against the *stav* it makes a happy *tek* sound. Feeling the smooth bark on my *stav* and my *tien* I feel a connection with the energy of the Tree as I sent my awareness deep into the earth. My spine becomes the trunk and I sway gently from side to side.

Doum, tek, doum, tek, doum doum tek...the rhythm changes and my voice changes as I walk from East ... to West ... to South ... to North. It is the heartbeat of Mother Earth, and it fills the air with vibration. I call out to *Austri*, and the spirits of the air come in and share their lightness. Laughter and joy fill my mind as I move to the west, *Vestri*. My voice soars and floats in my upper register as I feel warmth and love flowing into the room.

I step over to the South and call upon *Sudri*. My voice gains strength and power, and my *staving* goes wild with *doum doum tekka tekka, tek, doooum*. I sing out *"Gifu gifu mannaheim komme komme alle"* strong and loud. Then I turn to the North, crossing through the center once again. Cold and darkness fill my mind and my voice deepens in the presence of earth and stone. As I *stav* I see the caves of *Nifelheim* in my mind. *"Nordri come, spirits of earth, come in peace and stav with me."*

All the while singing *"komme komme alle"*—come come everyone—I welcome the spirits of each direction into the room. I move to the center and there stands *Yggdrasil*, the World Tree. All four directions are connected as the wheel of the world spins around me and my stav. I ride my *stav* up to the top branches above the clouds, and then down, deep down into *Urd's Well*. Surrounded by darkness and silt, I *stav* some more and rise up again, facing the tree until it takes the form of Hawthorn: *Huathe*. As I close my eyes I see the Grey Lady who guards the entrance to *Faery*. Last time I met her she challenged me:

Before me stood Huathe—dressed in tattered grey with long grey hair, this grand faery was tall and slender.
She asked me "Who comes before me to pass the gateway of Hawthorn?"
I said "I am Beth daughter of Fern, a healer and an empath."
"What do you seek beyond my tree from the realm of faerie?"
"I seek the wisdom of the Ogham for use in healing."
She said "You may pass, but you must bring back all that is given you and share it with those who wish to learn..."

And I did learn much on that journey. On this particular journey she bade me lay down and let inspiration flow through me. I set down my *stav* and *tien* and laid down. My breathing slowed as I allowed my awareness to be in that world and this one at the same time. That's how it is with *Volva Stav*; I remain present at all times so that I may learn and grow from the journey.

The thorns pricked at my *Otherworld* palms, and at my heart, until I laid quietly at the foot of the Hawthorn tree. Eyes closed in this world, but opened to the *Otherworld*, I viewed my back yard in my mind. As I did, images of weeds, dry patches, and piles of brick started changing. There was a path before me and I followed the path to the center of the yard.

In my center this is where Spirit resides, and so for the yard that's where the fire pit is. And that's when I saw the connection to each direction. For each direction was a path leading to a separate garden celebrating the four directions and their corresponding elements.

In the North stood the *Greenman* and the kitchen garden. The sun was shining and a variety of vegetables and berries grew in chaotically organized plots. Life was happening, and it was very good. I knew now that this most obvious of solutions was the best one for me. The garden is the world itself representing and providing a home for the nature spirits, Gods and guides that I'm working with on this path. North is Earth and provides nourishment to us all.

East was filled native plants of Minnesota, and a waterfall and pond was bejeweled with the flashing wings of dragonflies. My husband has had the dream of having a dragonfly hatchery in the yard, as they are called *witches needles*. Their bright colors and iridescent wings make me think of the flying faeries. Honoring the place we are, I knew it was a blessing to invite them with a habitat at the back of the yard.

In the West, there was a small fountain among flowers and a brick patio just off the deck with plenty of places for friends to sit. Next to the house, by the deck, there is a bench painted bright blue surrounded by flowers and foliage in shades of blues, greens, and whites. The colors of the sea. Here we will dine and look over the rest of our gardens. It is a place for love and laughter to ebb and flow.

I turn to the South and find myself walking past brilliant Asian Lilies and into a labyrinth. My joy at this discovery drives me to continue on my path, walking and learning and turning. South is for fire and action, the passion of doing. Here there is also a bench, this one painted bright red with tiki torches on either side.

In this world, my cat Caruso laid down on top of me and began to purr. He loves prowling the yard, and it will be so much fun to dig and plant and nurture this space while he's there looking on. From this final garden of the South, I now know what Hawthorn had to teach me. That I can create a circle of life, a living temple to the elements to dance and sing and play and dig in.

When the vision of my garden was complete, I knew it was time to go. Caruso had started getting restless and pricking me with his claws. As I came up and out of my trance, I rose and picked up my *tien* and my *stav*. I then gently *tekked* and *doumed* myself away from the Hawthorn tree, thanking all the directions and the Tree Herself for helping me with this lesson. I feel calm and relaxed, yet rejuvenated after my journey. As I set aside my tools and blow out the candles, I have time to reflect on what I have experienced and learned.

What began as an exercise of Air—my scattered thoughts—ended in the place of Fire and the consuming passion to make this vision a reality. I have much planning ahead of me, and that is part of the gift of *Huathe*. Sacred to the *faeries*, hawthorn is often planted near a body of water, so I'm glad to have the opportunity to create a pond for them to visit when they come to my garden. Associated with the Goddess in her Crone aspect, *Huathe* guides me on my path of oneness of body, mind, and spirit. I call upon *Huathe* for knowledge, but I'm often surprised to find a riddle or task to teach me wisdom. This time it's to plan out all the details of my new gardens, focusing on the directions and their purpose. So I'll be researching which plants I can grow from seed indoors, because I just can't wait until the snow is gone before I get started!

Like most Norse traditions, *Volva Staving* is completely practical. It took my jumble of thoughts and simplified them by focusing my body, mind, and spirit. Songs and vocalizations surprised me in their intensity, and I hope those melodies that I sang gave joy to the elements that came to watch. The role of the *stav* carrier is to bring back wisdom and healing that can be used in the real world. I am grateful to my teacher Kari Tauring, who carries her *stav* with great grace and an infectious enthusiasm. Practicing *Volva Stav* is the closest I have ever come to flying on a broom, and each journey teaches me more about myself and how thin the *veil* between the worlds really is. A wand and staff are all I need and I'm on my way.

Doum, tek, doum, tek, doum doum tek.

Biography

Beth Hansen-Buth is a painter, writer, singer, Volva Stav carrier, gardener, Reiki Master, Faerie Oracle reader, autoharpist, and pagan of many colors. With so many hats to wear, it's a good thing that she's also an identical twin born under the sign of Gemini for both sun and moon. Otherwise, all things creative could get a little out of hand. With two black cats and two calico cats to keep her in line, Beth happily *stavs* her way through Paganistan into the *Otherworld* and back again as often as possible. Did we mention the belly dancing? Yeah, that too.

All this and much more can be found at her website: www.reikiartist. com. You can also visit shop.reikiartist.com for t-shirts and gifts for people with open hearts and open minds, featuring original designs by Beth. Because she designs stuff, too.

Showcased in *FATE* magazine's March 2006 issue as painter to the faery court, Beth's connection to the *Otherworld* is evident in her artwork. Always mindful to show respect for her subjects, Beth is aware of their sometimes perilous nature. *"There are good faeries and bad faeries, but the good faeries aren't all good and the bad faeries aren't all bad. They might just take you somewhere unexpected."* Prints of Beth's artwork are available through her website under *Wyrdhaven Print Shop*.

Two of Beth's works of art can be found in this book.

The Beast and the Bride: The Divine Marriage, Fetchwork, and the Feri Tradition

Elise Stewart

The *hierogamos* is the term referring to the *Divine Marriage*, seen in myth through the union of Gods. Many in the pagan community see it as the joining of the divine masculine to the divine feminine in a sexual or romantic union, perpetuating the cycles of fertility. Others see the *Divine Marriage* as a reconciliation of the masculine and feminine aspects of self that leads to a more *"enlightened"* state of being. In some traditions of crafting, this concept is embodied in the coming together of the souls—fetch beast and fetch mate. This concept is complicated further in some traditions such as the Anderson Feri Tradition, which works with the triple soul—fetch, talker, and daemon. Before going into the specifics, let's address the general nature of the *hierogamos*.

The nature of the *Divine Marriage* is seen as the joining of the Gods in sexual union. The story of Diana and Lucifer from the Gospel of Aradia illustrates this nicely. It is Diana, representing the wilderness and the tamer of the wilderness, who lusts after her brother Lucifer, representing the civilized light-bearing principle. From the internalized approach of masculine/feminine balance, this could be seen purely in metaphor. In such instances, it has been said that one *"tames the wilderness of their mind and being to become a more enlightened individual"* through this internal union.

Just the opposite is true. In the thralls of passion, Diana is no more civilized in her lustful manner. It is Lucifer who gives in to wild abandon as he lay with his sister. The *"light-bearing"* divine aspect takes on the bestial traits of the wilderness during their congress. This is the true nature of the *hierogamos*.

In the Feri tradition, the alignment of the souls (*and thus the hierogamos*) is connected to the Blue God, *Dian y Glas*. He is the son/lover of the Star Goddess, the central deity of Feri who is frequently referred to as God *Herself. Dian y Glas* is also seen as the embodiment of the Godself or fetch mate. This doesn't make *Him* any less of a separate being, or lessen *His* individual nature. This joint nature of being both my Godself, your Godself, an expression of the Star Goddess as *Her* consort/son, and an individual independent deity in *His* own right is one of the many *"paradoxes"* of Feri, though it isn't the only instance that a divinity is pulling *"double duty"* so to speak. *(In the Chaldean Oracles, Hekate is referred to as an individual deity, as well as the Soul of the World.)*

The Feri Tradition is an American born tradition of non-Gardnerian witchcraft whose practices are ecstatic and involve jumping the Hedge. The name of the Feri Tradition came out of a roundabout situation. The Grandmaster Victor stated that, as witches, we are on the road to Faery. The tradition then began to be confused with other traditions that took the name Faery or Fairy. The name was then changed to the Feri Tradition *(and is still frequently referred to as the Anderson Feri Tradition)* to avoid confusion. As you can see, connection with the *Otherrealms (specifically the land of Faery)* is implicit in the name of the Feri Tradition.

The *Divine Marriage*, as it applies to *hedgeriding*, is in reference to the joining of the fetch beast and the fetch mate. These are extensions of what you would refer to as yourself. It is stated in this way because while they are an aspect of you, they are equally independent, functioning for many years without your awareness or intervention. Do not make the mistake of thinking that you can *"buy your inner child a toy,"* then be the best of friends!

The fetch selves are far from some pop-psychology aspect of the personality. Understanding the roles of the fetch beast and fetch mate are essential to understanding who they are, as well as their union.

There is some discussion as to what the fetch actually is. The main schools of thought would either classify the natures of the beast and bride as aspects of consciousness or parts of the soul. In the Feri Tradition, they are considered souls. Consciousness can be shared with these *"selves,"* but they function whether or not we are aware of them.

The fetch beast has been referred to as the *fyalgja* or more commonly just as the *fetch. Fetch* is animalistic and childlike, and governs much of the vital energies necessary for our survival. *Fetch* is most interested in conservation of energetic resources. The witch will oftentimes encounter the *fetch* in an animal form. The form will usually be a representation of an unknown aspect of the witch's nature, feral and instinctual. It can be a terrifying experience if the witch isn't fully prepared.

Bestial and childlike are words that have come to be used to describe the nature of the fetch, but instinctual is a better description. This can be seen in the affiliation the *fetch* has to the lower abdomen and the genitals. Food and sex are two of the stronger instinctual drives that we experience as human beings, both of which could be seen as expressions of *fetch*-nature.

The *fetch* is less connected with the external drives for food to fill the belly, or for copulation with another person, as it is with the storage of etheric energy. It isn't the food itself—it's the energy behind it that interests the *"lower"* nature. It is the *fetch* that generates or is connected to the etheric body that emanates about an inch from the physical body, and it is the energy produced by food that is ingested, air that is breathed, and the energy generated during sex that is the *"sticky stuff"* found in the etheric body.

Communicating with fetch can prove difficult. This is another reason as to why fetch is frequently seen as an animal of some sort. The interactions that we have when establishing communication with this soul is similar to the interactions we experience in trying to communicate with an animal. *Fetch* speaks in symbols and this can make communication tricky. Understanding what is said by fetch can frequently read like the interpretation of a dream. Likewise, expressing your perceived needs and goals to fetch can be just as challenging.

In some branches of the Feri Tradition, fetch is referred to as the Sticky One. This refers to the nature of the fetch's energy *"sticking"* to the physical body. *Fetch* is connected to or *"housed in"* what has been called the physical or visceral aura—the energy field that extends about an inch to an inch and a half from the physical body. It *"sticks"* tightly to the physical form. This reiterates the *fetch's* connection to physical vitality.

Fetch has strong interactions in the realm of *Other*. It interacts and experiences the world that underlies the world we see physically. The interactions that fetch experiences are on a more subtle realm than that of our own gross reality. The *fetch* can journey into the deepest parts of the Other planes, usually while we sleep. It tends to be a nocturnal creature, though it doesn't necessarily sleep while we are consciously wakeful. It just remains mostly quiet, rising up on occasion through feelings, intuitions and pangs.

In the Feri tradition, it is also generally held that when a person dies, their *fetch (or Sticky One)* can remain earthbound. This is the generally accepted cause for angry spirits and ghosts according to this line of thought. If the souls are aligned upon death, though, the *fetch* *"follows"* the Talker (*soul of consciousness*) into the afterlife.

The *fetch* mate or *fetch* bride is a more deified aspect of the soul. It is the Godself, the *holy daemon*, or the *holy guardian angel*. This is the part of the soul that knows and touches the realms of the divine. This soul knows no distinction between itself, the Gods, or itself as a God. It is truly divine and wholly human.

The *holy daemon* is just as tricky to understand as the *fetch* is. The very nature of the *daemon* is benevolent and self-actualized, but at the same time distant and hard to connect with. Most find it difficult to connect directly with the *daemon*, and it does require regular practice. There are several grimoires of antiquity dedicated to the conversation with the *holy guardian angel*, an operation requiring many months *(if not years)* to accomplish by the methods contained within these texts.

The connection with the *holy daemon* can usually be felt through the crown of the head, but is actually centered a bit beyond the physical body. The energetic field most associated with the Godself is that of the *"halo"* of saints and holy men. The connection with the head and upper body that the *halo* would show us is that this soul-self is conceptual and rational in the way that we experience it. It also shows a separation from the instinctual and emotive nature of the *fetch* beast.

The *holy daemon* functions as a translator and emissary to the Gods, higher spirits and, some would say, the ancestors. This is not to say that the *daemon* isn't powerful in it's own right, as it possesses the capabilities and skill to rise above *"fate"* and to alter our environmental situations. What it lacks is the energy resources or drive to do so.

Much like the *fetch* beast, the *holy daemon* has interactions in the energetic realms of the *Otherworlds*. The big difference in the interactions had by the *fetch* and *daemon* is that the *daemon* works in the realm that is termed the *"Upper Realm"* in many of the shamanic texts, whereas the *fetch* works in the *"Lower Realm."* These realms are in actuality occupying the same space, but the lower worlds are just denser and frequently connected energetically to the world of matter. The upper worlds are linked more readily to the Gods and other beings, concepts, and places well beyond the comprehension of those of us with physical bodies.

In most lines of Feri, the fetch mate is referred to as the Godself, *daemon*, bird-self or sacred dove. This sacred dove is seen as *"occupying"* a *halo* of energy around or above the person's head. Many see it as being relatively separate from the energies of the other auras, at least until alignment is made.

In Feri, one other soul is mentioned. This is the Talker. Talker is the soul of every-day consciousness. *Fetch* is concerned with the vital energies of the body, and interacting with the Lands Below as well as the holy *daemon*. *Daemon* is concerned with interactions in the Worlds Above, as well as with celestial or God spirits. *Talker* is concerned with interacting with the *World Before Us*, the external world.

Talker is connected with our conscious thoughts and actions in the mundane or physical world. It is interested in how we interact with others like ourselves. *Talker* works with the energy of thought and perception. If *fetch* and *daemon* are being coupled, *Talker* is the matchmaker. *Talker* holds the impetus and desire for growth experienced through the *hierogamos*.

Both the *fetch* and the *daemon* can seem archaic and mysterious, so much so that many people and traditions no longer recognize them as aspects of the self. The key to understanding their connection to you is to understand your conscious self, or your *Talker*. *Talker* is the name of the soul-self that is conscious within us, fully experiencing our flesh and thought. Some say *Talker* is the consciousness, though others feel that *Talker* is more of an observer of consciousness. From either vantage, *Talker* is the aspect of self that experiences the interactions with the *fetch* and bride.

The *Talker* is connected to your consciousness, and is engaged when interacting with the outside tangible world and the people in your life. *Talker* can readily communicate with fetch, though usually only does so out of necessity and doesn't inherently know how to listen to *fetch* most of the time, making the communications seemingly one way. *Fetch* communicates through symbol and instinct.

Fetch is all about drives and survival, basal needs. *Fetch* can also communicate with the *holy daemon*, whereas it is more difficult for *Talker* to make such a connection. *Holy daemon* approaches from a more abstract understanding, which lends itself more readily to *fetch's* symbolic language than it does to *Talker's* rational conversation. This is why conversation with the *holy guardian angel* is said to take so long—the Godself must find a way to quantify the innumerable and give words to experience well beyond *Talker's* current understanding.

Now that we've discussed the players, let's get to the game. The *hierogamos* or *Sacred Marriage* is the alignment and joining of these three soul parts. The first part of the process usually involves establishing a working relationship with the fetch. This can be done through pathworking, energy work, or ritual such as the Housle or Red Meal *(making an offering to the fetch)*. During this stage, you may begin to work with *fetch-flight*, "*riding*" the fetch into the *Otherworld*. You will start to work on different aspects of your relationship with *fetch*, both energetically and through communication, which is truly the key to workings of this nature.

After you establish a strong relationship with your *fetch*, then you may begin to notice the presence of the *holy daemon*. You can ask the *fetch* to *"introduce"* you to the *Godself.* You may also follow the guidance of one of the many texts on achieving conversation with your *holy guardian angel,* either simultaneously or after you've connected with *fetch.* Then the *hierogamos* is just a matter of time.

This isn't the only method of achieving the *Sacred Marriage.* In the Anderson Feri Tradition, the *fetch* and *daemon* are usually addressed very early in the training. Aligning the souls is one of the first things taught and is a daily practice. I do not understand this alignment to be the same thing as the *hierogamos,* but it does result in such a prolonged union if practiced regularly enough. The alignment feels very sexual in nature between the fetch and Godself, according to this system of working. There are also many different techniques and methods to help clear *"complexes"* in the energy system that prevent a whole state of being.

Most of the daily practices of Feri *(including the Three Souls Alignment)* are achieved through the *Ha Prayer.* The *Ha prayer* is a fairly simple breath technique taught by Victor Anderson. To perform a soul alignment, first become aware of each of the three souls starting with the *Talker.* You will feel your *Talker's* presence in the heart and throat area. Next bring your awareness down to your *fetch*—located down in your pelvic area. From there, shift your awareness to the point just above your head—the *"location"* of your *daemon.*

After taking a moment to feel the presence in each of those areas, bring your awareness back to *Talker.* Form a symbol of the working's goal in your mind. In this case, choose a symbol of your three souls aligning. This can be as simple as three shapes such as a square, a circle and a triangle aligning and combining into a single image. It can be equally as complex, such as envisioning images from the tarot *(such as the Fool, the Devil and Judgment cards)* merging together into a single image. The goal is to communicate your intention effectively to *fetch.*

Once you've formed the symbol solidly in your mind, send the symbol down to fetch along your spinal column, through your breath. Once the symbol is *"rooted"* in your pelvic region, begin taking deep breaths to charge the symbol with vital energies. You will feel the symbol become charged with energy *(or perhaps even see it engulfed in the blue flames of your energy).* You then tilt your head back and exhale the symbol up through your breath to your *daemon* by making the sound *"Ha."*

The symbol/energy will reach the *daemon* fully charged. A glowing pearlescent light will then descend and surround you in your inner vision. You will then begin to feel the *daemon* and the *fetch* reaching to join together. The attraction will feel like sexual arousal and a tingling at the crown of the head for most people. They will reach through you, and eventually come together in your heart.

This technique leads to a healthy holistic approach to working with *Sacred Marriage*, which is a state of being in Feri called the *Black Heart of Innocence*. The *Black Heart of Innocence* is a state of purity and mindful awareness of the present. It approaches a state of being *"in the crossroads,"* with a foot in each world while remaining grounded in the present. It is about not just speaking truth, but being truth.

The *Ha Prayer Technique* can be used to work just about any form of simple magic that you can get your fetch and daemon to agree to, just by changing the symbol to communicate your desire. Traditionally, the prayer is done in breath sets of four *(i.e. once you've sent your symbol down to fetch, you would exhale the Ha to your daemon on the 4th, 8th, 12th, etc. breath)*.

The process of soul alignment in particular is traditionally marked by an incantation or poetic statement of intention. Victor himself taught the Flower Prayer for daily recitation for the alignment of the souls:

> *"Who is this flower above me? And what is the work of this god? I would know myself in all my parts."* [1]

Various cultures and systems also acknowledge the *hierogamos* in different forms, and the *hedgewitch* could benefit from a study of some of these cultural views. One such understanding is that of *shaktiput*, or *kundalini rising* of Vedic origin. *Kundalini* is the flow of vital energy that follows the spine in a weaving, snake-like manner. It ascends to the top of the head *(the crown chakra)* before mushrooming out and showering down, which can result in a state of enlightenment if done with the proper training. Side effects of this process are spiritual powers called *siddhis*, which are strikingly similar to the powers of the witch.

Shaktiput can occur spontaneously though, which can result in physical illness or madness, another testament to practicing patience and common sense in the craft. This being said, it should also be noted that many practitioners have wrongly assumed that this would mean that achieving *shaktiput* and alignment of the *fetch* beast and mate are the same thing. This is most definitely not true. They exist side by side, of the same nature within different currents of knowledge.

While such comparisons are excellent for helping a person to understand the entirety of a system on an intuitive level, more often than not these well meaning teaching tools aren't given with enough explanation to squelch misunderstandings. Bear this in mind as you research various systems.

---

1. Victor H. Anderson

It is important to note that achieving the sacred union isn't always a song and a dance. *(Regardless of tradition, nothing in hedgeriding is very "happy fuzzy Disney" if you get my drift.)* The *hierogamos* can result in some unwanted circumstances, difficulty in directing your vital energies, health problems *(especially headaches and insomnia)*, and sometimes even madness. This process is best undertaken over time, not to be hurried into some frenzied pace so that you can catch up to the level of the rest of your coven-mates. There are also practices that help to mitigate some of these side effects.

In Feri, some of these practices are running energy through the Iron Pentacle, Kala water cleansing rite, and daily meditation practices. The focus of the Iron Pentacle is the reclaiming and calibration of our energies as they manifest in our bodies and environments. These energies are exemplified by sex, pride, self, power, and passion in the Iron Pentacle. This pentacle evolves into the Pearl Pentacle as our energies are examined, as they interact beyond ourselves, and the points are changed to indicate the change of focus. The rite of Kala is used to clear our *fetch* of energetic, mental, and emotional complexes by transmuting those complexes back into pure vital energy. These are just some of the more common practices that the Feri tradition uses to further psychic, spiritual, and energetic wellness.

So, we've gone round and round, covering the who's and what's of the *Sacred Marriage*, but we still haven't addressed a vital question: why? Why would this practice be so essential for the *hedgewitch*? What is the benefit?

In *hedgeriding*, we must learn to jump the Hedge to achieve journeys in the *Otherrealms* for magic and healing, and to connect with various beings and spirits of the dead. When we achieve the union of the *daemon* and *fetch*, we experience the full spectrum and breadth of the *Otherworld*. It is through the communications between the souls that we attain the witch's sight, that we work our *thaumaturgy*, and commune with the Gods! *Fetch* flight, in the sense of astral or etheric projection becomes possible. A fuller experience of the *Otherworld* awaits.

Think about it: our consciousness or *Talker* must talk to *fetch* through symbol. *Daemon* is addressed either through discourse with *fetch*, or directly by *Talker*, but still through symbolism. Aligning the souls is akin to holding a conference to negotiate a contract between several parties. The *hierogamos* is when these separate parties merge into a single corporation.

When we jump the Hedge into the Other realms, our consciousness is riding *fetch* into *Elphame* or the *Under-lands*. Many *(if not most)* people do this through dreams. That is why dreams are riddled with symbolism, and it is also why the memories of dreams slip away so easily. The perception through *fetch* is incredibly instinctual, intuitive, and symbolic—all information that is usually discarded by the rational mind as useless.

The alignment of the souls get all the players on the same page creating a common vocabulary and helping the conscious mind to remember and fully experience the journey. *Hierogamos* is also akin to embodying the *Godself*—the piece of you that is of your patron and matron. So, in a sense, when you achieve the *sacred union*, you bring divinity into the flesh. You allow a greater discourse of the mundane world for your Godself, which is connected to/part of your patron and matron deities. This is a very empowering, if not harrowing, experience.

While divinity is brought closer to our everyday world, so are we brought closer to them. The alignment of souls allows for a much easier transition of journey into the *Other*, especially the *Over Realms*. This can increase our Second Sight (*both on an everyday and ritual level*), help us to communicate with spirits and the Land, as well as boost the level of energy that we are able to affect through our workings.

The alignment of the triple soul is paramount to being able to connect with the Otherrealms safely and effectively in Feri. Trance work and ecstatic experiences are central to workings of this tradition that embraces all paths that lead to the Land of Stars within the Earth, called *Elphame* in other traditions. None of this is possible without a strong relationship with all parts of self, whether viewed as the Triple Soul, or as the Beast and the Bride, or even as the Drake Self and the *Holy Guardian Angel*.

By aligning the souls and striving towards the *hierogamos*, the hedgewitch is in essence searching to know themselves in their entirety. This knowledge not only supports and enriches the journeys into the Other, but allows for a more full experience of life. This holy union of opposites grounds us into the existence and experience of the dense outer world while simultaneously allowing us to experience the fullness of the divine in all that we do. Empowerment and wisdom are the trade of the *Hedgerider*, regardless of the tradition that they come from. Working with the *Fetch Selves* is just one of the many practices to get there.

For more information on the Anderson Feri Tradition, visit http://www.feritradition.org

Selected Bibliography

Anderson, Cora, *Fifty Years in the Feri Tradition*. Acorn Guild Press. Albany, CA, 1994.

Anderson, Victor H., *Etheric Anatomy: The Three Selves and Astral Travel.* 2004. Acorn Guild Press, Albany, CA, 2004.

Coyle, T. Thorn, *Evolutionary Witchcraft*, Penguin Group. New York, NY, 2004

Coyle, T. Thorn, *Kissing the Limitless: Deep Magic and the Great Work of Transforming Yourself and the World*, Red Wheel/Weiser. San Francisco, CA, 2009.

Faerywolf, Storm, *The Stars within the Earth*, Faerywolf/Carnivalia. Walnut Creek, CA, 2009.

Faerywolf, Storm, personal correspondence via email and Skype, 2009/2010.

Hedgewitchery in Traditional Craft: Historical Implications and Modern Applications

John Pwyll

> The balance of power between the sorcerer and the spirits is precarious;
> it must be maintained with great care and tact.
> In return, the spirits enable the sorcerer to traverse the webs
> that lead into all worlds: of the gods, Middle-Earth, and the dead.
> - Brian Bates, The Way of Wyrd[1]

We who follow the ways of traditional witchcraft abide by a practice that is deep, organic, and powerful. We pride ourselves on historical accuracy, cultural integrity, and hard work. We scour manuscripts and literature for hints of ancestral wisdom. Our traditions are not based on fear but rely on courage and experience. We might be found deep in the forest during the darkness of the new moon making offerings or waiting at dawn for low tide, gathering the last component for a spell. We delve into the full potential of witchcraft as a spiritual path and a way of life. And for most of us, we dare to cross the Hedge and explore the world of spirits and Gods, only to return changed each time.

A signature of Traditional Witchcraft is the use of visionary and ecstatic techniques, hedge-witchcraft, to develop a personal relationship with the Gods, ancestors, and spirits of the land. Any witch worth his or her salt incorporates shamanic techniques in their practice.[2] In fact, the integration of shamanism and trance is considered one of the core distinctions between Traditional Witchcraft and Wicca.[3] Doreen Valiente, for example, when comparing Gardnerian Wicca with the craft of Roy Bowers (*Robert Cochrane*), noted the more extensive shamanic elements of Cochrane's rituals.[4] It is unsurprising, therefore, that some feel the terms *"traditional witchcraft"* and *"hedge-witchcraft"* are somewhat synonymous, for it is said no one can truly call themselves a witch and have never crossed the Hedge.[5]

How does hedgewitchery fit into the traditional witchcraft paradigm? For some, hedge-witchcraft is used solely to define Germanic shamanism.[6] Although hedge-witchcraft's etymological origins are indeed Germanic, its modern usage is quite different. Word origins do not necessarily determine definitions. For example, the old English term *"witch"* has a much more cosmopolitan use than its original definition in Germanic culture. Similarly, the Tungusic word *"shaman"* no longer refers to the practitioners found in just the indigenous tribes of North and Central Asia.[7] If etymology, then, is not a reliable basis for definition, is it possible that the concept of *"hedgewitch"* may include more than Germanic shamanism?

In many currents of modern traditional witchcraft, we define hedge-witchcraft as the various trance and shamanic techniques to gain entrance into the Otherworld. But did this type of witch practice really exist in history, and if so, can we reconstruct the image of a hedgewitch from these sources? Where was shamanism practiced in other parts of Europe, and how does this practice relate to today's traditions?

Shamanism and cunning-folk have naturally been intertwined with witchcraft, and these connections have been debated in both academic and pagan circles for quite some time and for good reason. The human need to definitively categorize people, places, and things can cloud our ability to recognize overlap. The shaman, according to preeminent researcher Mircea Eliade, is an individual in society that interacts in both this world and the Otherworld through ecstatic techniques. It is through this interaction that the shaman performs healings, divination, ancestral communication and propitiation.[8] Shamans function within the cultural framework of their society, and although shamanism in its strictest sense refers to specific indigenous tribes, shamanic elements can be found in many cultures worldwide.[9]

Cunning folk provided a range of services to their community including divination, healing, finding treasure, and the curing of and protection from curses through magick.[10] Although most cunning-folk are thought to have used natural or folk *(low)* magick, some English cunning-folk incorporated ceremonial *(high)* magick into their practice.[11] Note the similarity in the roles that shamans and cunning-folk play in their society, despite the important differences in their methodologies. An overlap between the two practices should not be surprising, and the presence of folk magic and shamanism practiced together would expand our current view of hedgewitch practices. Academics currently debate the extent to which shamanic elements from the pre-Christian past lingered in various European cultures, but evidence has been growing that its presence remained in many regions and in various stages of continued existence.

Iron Age Celtic tribes practiced their own form of ecstatic and visionary techniques, examples of which can be found in the myth cycles.[12] Much of this shamanic tradition faded as Christianity gained prominence, but some hints of the practice can be teased out of later folklore and cultural anomalies. Poets in Scotland and Ireland into the 18th century isolated themselves in darkness for long periods, most likely to enter an altered state of consciousness and gain inspiration for their poetry.[13] These bards were known to take up the mantle of tradition bearers after the loss of the druid order.

Fragments of this shamanic practice can also be found in some historic collections of fairy-faith.[14] The Scottish Highlands have a rich tradition of charms, spells, healing, and interactions with the Fairies—a diverse host of spirits of the land, sidhe mounds and the Otherworld. Despite the overlay of Christianity to the region, pagan beliefs were slow to fade and pre-Christian traditions were difficult to quell. The possession of the Second Sight (an dá shealladh), the ability to see and interact with spirits, fetches, fairies, and ghosts, is very similar to the abilities of shamanic cultures throughout the world.[15] Fairy encounters often occurred while sleeping on cnocs, hills, or sidhe mounds, perhaps allowing for an altered state of consciousness. Spirit possession, shape shifting, and ceremonies such as the taghairm, in which the Devil was summoned through a variety of means, are considered other remnants of shamanic tradition.[16] Slipping into a trance state to commune with fairies has also been recorded in Ireland and Scotland.[17] Fairy encounters may be equated with shamanic spirit allies, which we will examine in further detail.[18]

Hungary, as another example, has a rich tradition of both folk magic and shamanic practice. Different types of cunning-folk specialties existed up to the early 20th century, such as the *táltos (similar to shaman), garabonciás (wandering magickal scholar), halottlátó (necromancer)*, and others. However, these professions were not necessarily restricted by the methods of their services.[19] For example, a *táltos* or a *halottlátó* might use herbal or folk magic practices for healing or trance to provide spirit assistance.[20] Divination was also practiced by Hungarian cunning-folk, and their methods included both shamanic work and folk magick techniques, such as pouring wax or lead and reading bean patterns in sieves.[21] Cunning-folk were certainly not excluded from performing the folk magick practices that were widespread in eighteenth century Hungary, and the same could be said for the Celtic regions above. The tradition of shamanic night battles to protect the community from evil forces and spirits found in the Balkans also appears here, and was an important service for a táltos.[22] Flying, riding poles or reeds, shape shifting into animals or wheels of fire, and multiple soul belief are just a few examples of classic shamanic practice and theory found in the Hungarian cunning-folk of the recent past.[23]

In the seminal work Practical Magic, Davies extensively summarizes cunning-folk practice in early modern England. While Davies expertly provides a comprehensive perspective of the history and mechanics of cunning-folk, he remains unconvinced that shamanic elements were used in their magick.[24] Davies prefers to categorize the *táltos* of Hungary as cunning-folk rather than *shaman*. One argument for this categorization is that the *táltos*, as well as the *benandanti*, the shamanic warriors of Northern Italy, interact with the *Otherworld* at night, and therefore their ecstatic experiences could be attributed to dreaming.[25]

However, shamanic practitioners, including *hedgewitches*, are well aware of the power darkness provides to spiritual journeying. The importance of darkness in shamanic practice has been noted in both indigenous shamanic practice and in core shamanism.[26] Although Davies is skeptical of the *táltos* being *shamans* in the strictest sense, the evidence for them retaining at least some shamanic elements *(i.e. "peripheral shamanism")* is undeniable.[27] Whether a *táltos* was more *cunning-folk* than *shaman* or more *shaman* than *cunning-folk* is difficult to say, but it is critical to note that they performed both folk magic and shamanic techniques to accomplish their service.

In contrast to Davies, Emma Wilby believes that interacting with the spirit realms lingered in early modern England, and evidence can be found of this in the confessions of certain *cunning-folk* during the witch trials. Again, we see individuals using both folk magic and shamanic practices together to provide services to the community.[28] One of Wilby's most influential arguments is the ubiquitous presence of the familiar, the spirit ally or helping spirit, that is common to both the English witch and many indigenous shamanic cultures.[29] It is through their familiar that witches conducted much of their work and received their knowledge. Encounters with *spirits* or *fairies* allowed *cunning-folk* to perform healings, divination, and necromancy.[30] Possible *spirit* encounters included animals, fairies, and demons, a diverse host of entities similar to other shamanic experiences in other cultures. The implications of Wilby's work are extensive, and we can conclude that Wilby's theories present remnants of shamanic practice in another region of Europe.

Celtic, Hungarian, and English historical evidence for remnants of shamanism and its use with folk magic by no means exhausts our European examples. In addition to the Anglo-Saxon influences of England, Germanic lore includes both natural magic and shamanism,[31] although the extent to which shamanism existed, as in all of our examples, is still being debated.[32] This skepticism may come from the perceptions of historians that originate outside of the magickal and shamanic context that was so prevalent through human history.[33] Current research, which investigates events such as witch trials through the eyes of the people and the worldview of that time, is beginning to shed new light on these topics.

A few conclusions can be drawn from the brief synopses above that are pertinent to hedge-witchcraft. First, folk magic and shamanic techniques are inextricably linked. *Cunning-folk* art often consisted of both natural magick and shamanic elements in a seamless blend. Most likely, a *witch, cunning-man* or *wise-woman* used the method which was most appropriate or with which they were most skilled. Eventually, Christianity gained a stronger hold on rural folk, and interaction with the *spirit* world decreased. As animistic and polytheistic realities were discouraged, so, too, did the relevance for shamanism.[34] However, the use of shamanism by *witches* is historically accurate, and the practice of shamanic techniques included in modern witchcraft is absolutely appropriate. The *hedgewitch*, therefore, encompasses many of the quintessential *witch's folk magick* practices *(spells, divination, healing, cursing, necromancy, wild-crafting, etc.)* united under a shamanic framework.

Second, the use of both natural magic and ecstatic trance is not isolated to one European location or culture. As in other indigenous cultures, shamanism did not exist in a vacuum. The folk magic and shamanic practices reflected the culture, ebbing and flowing with the fluidity of cultural change. Whatever the origins of shamanic types of work throughout Europe, they were embedded in the culture and magick of the people, lingering in various states depending on the region, but longest in poor, rural communities. Therefore, cultural appropriation of shamanism in modern traditional witchcraft is not only immoral but unnecessary.[35] The fact that different European cultures maintained similar shamanic techniques, such as *soul flight, pole-riding (be it farm instrument, broom, or stang), spirit* communication, *shape-shifting*, etc. is intriguing to say the least. Whether these practices originated from one source and dispersed or evolved convergently is a matter for debate, but they were used and retained because they were woven into the culture and effective.

So, if similar practices are found throughout Europe, should the term *hedgewitch* refer only to Germanic shamanism? Like the words *shaman* and *witch*, *hedge-witchcraft* could certainly apply to the shamanic aspects of our practice. Visionary and ecstatic techniques, shamanism in its broadest sense, are not only appropriate but indispensable in traditional witchcraft. Although our methods of crossing into the *Otherworld* may differ by tradition and culture, a unifying term such as *hedge-witchery* provides a way of cross-communication between traditions. The contemporary use of *hedge-witchery* or *hedge-riding* to describe shamanic workings may be justified.

Therefore, it would seem that if a *hedgewitch* emphasizes shamanism in their witchcraft, then anyone other than a *hedgewitch* using trance work is using *hedge-witchery*. Each of the currents that make up the diverse mosaic of traditional witchcraft can reclaim shamanic practices that are intrinsic to their tradition. Only time will tell how the term *hedgewitch* will evolve in traditional craft vocabulary. Regardless, it is time to reconnect with and embrace our true magickal heritage, the *witch* as *spell-caster, seer, healer* and *shaman*.

Shamanic practice is the result of animistic beliefs, in which the natural world and the Otherworld are full of Gods and spirits.[36] Animism continued in Europe despite the acceptance of Christianity, and the persistence of animism can be seen throughout the early modern period.[37] As Christian doctrine strengthened and replaced folk beliefs, animistic perceptions declined. The *cunning-folk* studied by Davies and Wilby were Christian and lived within a Christian paradigm, thus, their connection to the *spirits* became distorted in the religious conflicts that ensued and began to evaporate.[38] The modern pagan *hedgewitch*, however, does not suffer this clash in beliefs and interacts with the spirit world freely. They experience a profound, intimate connection to the natural world, where it is possible to commune with the *spirits* of the land and the Gods that reside there on a very deep, physical level.

Traditional crafters have emphasized that *hedge-witchery* refers to a shamanic practice rather than a user of natural magic. This has been a reaction to yet another use of the term *hedgewitch*: a solitary, rural Wiccan. For some, this form of *witchcraft* will be the extent of both their connection to the *spirit* world and to *nature*. True trance working and *hedge-crossing* is not for the faint-hearted or the poorly prepared. However, to deny the essential connections between the traditional *hedgewitch* and the *wilds beyond the Hedge* is to deny the very nature of natural magic and animistic belief. As we have seen, the practices of natural magick and *hedgewitchery* are tightly wound, and the true *hedgewitch* is intimately connected to the land as a source of magick and sacred interaction. In our determination to separate ourselves from this Wiccan practice, we cannot lose the importance of our connection to *nature* and its *spirits*.

History, tradition, and modern witchcraft combine to form for us a picture of the *hedgewitch.*

We are *cunning-folk,*
and we provide the services needed
through magick *and* shamanic work.

We are *seers,*
and will *throw the bones* for predictions
as easily as we call on our spirit allies to foretell the future.

We are *spell-casters,*
and will tie the rowan and red thread for your protection
or curse your neighbor for thievery.

We are *wild-crafters,*
and will trek deep into the wood
and provide an offering to the forest *spirits*
before harvesting our components at the auspicious times.

We are *shamans,*
and are ready to fly by night and do battle for your soul
and heal you from those who wish you ill.

We are *hedge-crossers,*
and leave our bodies under the protection of our *spirit guardians*
to join our familiars and explore the *Otherworld.*

We are *necromancers* and *psychopomps,*
leading the dead to their place of rest
and consulting the ancestors for answers.

We are *wisdom-seekers,*
and use the knowledge that has been handed down to us
with the insight we retain from our journeys in *Twilyte.*

We are *pagans,*
and feel the forces of nature
ebb and flow through the cycles of the year
and commune with the *Gods, ancestors,*
and *spirits* of the land directly.

We are *witches,*
in the deepest sense of the word,
we who *cast, heal, curse, divine,*
and journey to the *Otherworld.*

*N*otes

All of these works are excellent resources
and recommended for further information.

1 Brian Bates, The Way of Wyrd (Carlsbad: Hay House, 2005), p. 121.
2 Eric de Vries, Hedgerider (Los Angeles: Pendraig, 2008), p. 17.
3 Gwyn, Light from the Shadows (Berks: Capall Bann, 1999), p. 23.
4 Doreen Valiente, The Rebirth of Witchcraft (London: Robert Hale, 2007), pp. 125, 193.
5 Nigel G. Pearson, Treading the Mill: Practical CraftWorking in Modern Traditional Witchcraft (Somerset: Capall Bann, 2007), p. 119.
6 de Vries, Hedgerider pp. 20-23.
7 Mircea Eliade, Shamanism: Archaic Techniques of Ecstasy (Princeton: Princeton University, 1992), p. 4.
8 Eliade, Shamanism: Archaic Techniques of Ecstasy, p. 3-8.
9 Eliade, Shamanism: Archaic Techniques of Ecstasy, p. 6.
10 Owen Davies, Popular Magic: Cunning-folk in English History (New York: Hambledon Continuum, 2007), pp. VII, 196; John Gregorson Cambell, The Gaelic Otherworld. Ronald Black, ed. (Edinburgh: Birlinn, 2005), pp. 199-200.
11 Davies, Popular Magic: Cunning-folk in English History p. ix-xi, 119.
12 Sharynne MacLeod NicMhacha, Queen of the Night: Rediscovering the Celtic Moon Goddess (Boston: Weiser, 2005), pp. 34-53.
13 NicMhacha, Queen of the Night (Boston: Weiser, 2005), pp. 37-38.
14 Campbell, The Gaelic Otherworld p. lxxvii.
15 Campbell, The Gaelic Otherworld p. 241; Eliade, Shamanism: Archaic Techniques of Ecstasy, p. 6.
16 Campbell, The Gaelic Otherworld pp. 56, 57, 298, 309, 423, 427.
17 W.Y. Evans-Wentz, The Fairy Faith in Celtic Countries (New York: Citadel, 1994), pp. 34, 65, 69; Robert Kirk, The Secret Commonwealth of Elves, Fauns, and Fairies (Mineola: Dover, 2008), p 84.
18 For an example of one author's perspective on the Celtic links to shamanism, please see Harris-Logan, Singing with Blackbirds: the Survival of Primal Celtic Shamanism in Later Folk-Traditions.

19 Tekla Dömötör, Hungarian Folk Beliefs (Bloomington: Indiana University Press, 1981), p.128-142.

20 Dömötör, Hungarian Folk Beliefs p. 134, 136, 157.

21 ?va Pócs, Between the Living and the Dead (Budapest: Central European University Press, 1999), p.145; Dömötör, Hungarian Folk Beliefs pp. 197-206.

22 Pócs, Between the Living and the Dead, p.87, 134.

23 Eliade, Shamanism: Archaic Techniques of Ecstasy, p. 126, 174; Dömötör, Hungarian Folk Beliefs p.30, 134.

24 Davies, Popular Magic: Cunning-folk in English History p. 178-185.

25 Davies, Popular Magic: Cunning-folk in English History p. 182.

26 Michael Harner, The Way of the Shaman (New York: Harper Collins, 1990) p. 24.

27 Pócs, Between the Living and the Dead p. 15; Dömötör, Hungarian Folk Beliefs p. 128-165.

28 Emma Wilby, Cunning Folk and Familiar Spirits: Shamanistic Visionary Traditions in Early Modern British Witchcraft and Magic (Portland: Sussex Academic Press), pp. 41-51.

29 Wilby, Cunning Folk and Familiar Spirits: Shamanistic Visionary Traditions in Early Modern British Witchcraft and Magic, pp. 46-58.

30 Wilby, Cunning Folk and Familiar Spirits: Shamanistic Visionary Traditions in Early Modern British Witchcraft and Magic, pp. 67-70.

31 Please see Stephen Pollington, Leechcraft: Early English Charms, Plant-lore, and Healing (Norfolk: Anglo-Saxon Books, 2008) and Jenny Blain, Nine Worlds of Seid-Magic: Ecstasy and Neo-Shamanism in North European Paganism (New York: Routledge, 2002) for examples on Germanic folk magick and shamanism (respectively).

32 Bill Griffiths, Aspects of Anglo-Saxon Magic (Norfolk: Anglo-Saxon Books, 2006) p. 110.

33 Wilby, Cunning Folk and Familiar Spirits: Shamanistic Visionary Traditions in Early Modern British Witchcraft and Magic, pp. 123-127, 190.

34 Davies, Popular Magic: Cunning-folk in English History p. 183.

35 de Vries, Hedgerider p. 17.

36 Wilby, Cunning Folk and Familiar Spirits: Shamanistic Visionary Traditions in Early Modern British Witchcraft and Magic, p. 128.

37 Wilby, Cunning Folk and Familiar Spirits: Shamanistic Visionary Traditions in Early Modern British Witchcraft and Magic, pp. 14, 15, 17; Dömötör, Hungarian Folk Beliefs pp. 12, 80-87; Harris-Logan, Singing with Blackbirds: the Survival of Primal Celtic Shamanism in Later Folk-Traditions, p. 79.

38 Davies, Popular Magic: Cunning-folk in English History p. 196.

Biography

John has been practicing Pagan witchcraft for over 20 years. As a distinct, separate tradition, he also practices Celtic shamanism and reconstruction, in which he is a student of and assistant to shaman-priestess and scholar Sharynne Macleod NicMhacha. For over two years John lived with the Chewa and Yao tribes in rural Malai, and has participated in and witnessed indigenous rites and ceremonies in Africa, Asia, and the South Pacific. He holds a Masters degree in biology and teaches at the secondary and college levels. He currently resides in the forests of New England with his wife and son.

Elder Visions

Ingredients for a Scrying Wreath:
Elder branches
Red thread (cotton or *silk is best*)
Ingredients for a Scrying Altar:
Elder branches or leaves
Red thread
A black bowl or black mirror
Two candles (one red and one white or one black and one white)
Water (preferably rain water or spring water)

Mother or Frau Holle is the Goddess of the Hollow, the Lady of the elder tree. She can appear as a woman from the front, but as a hollow tree from the back. She is a Goddess of the wild places, of death and, also, of life—for what She gives, She can also take away. As the Lady of the elder, Her tree is linked to the rites and remembrance of the dead and to the attaining of visions, in particular of the Underworld.

The elder is a Faery tree and a witch tree and has a history of being used in brooms, as riding poles, and to make actual hedgerows. A riding pole of elder can carry you far, deep into the Underworld. A broom of elder can also be used for flight, or to sweep away all that has grown outworn, even if the process might not always be a comfortable one. Brooms made from different trees all have within them different powers, including how they sweep a space "clean" and how they take you on the spirit flight.

Be sure that before you harvest the branches from the elder, to ask the Lady of the Elder for permission and make an appropriate offering. Never take something from nature without giving something in return. This is part of the ever-renewing bond with the land and with the spirits of the land. Wine, cream, and honey are always good offerings, but its how you make the offering and what lies in your heart that counts the most.

To make use of it for visions during your dreams, you can put together a small wreath of branches bound with red thread. This wreath can then be laid beneath your pillow when you go to sleep, though you shouldn't leave it there all the time. It may also be worn during ritual, in particular when you desire to look into Faery, to see the land of the dead. In fact, to stand beneath an elder tree could sometimes afford a glimpse of the Wild Hunt passing by on All Hallow's. After all, you would be standing by a tree of the Hedge, the boundary marker between worlds.

If you want to use the wreath—or the leaves of the elder—you can also choose to set it around a black bowl filled with rain or spring water or a black mirror. If you intend to just use the leaves, lay them one a time around the bowl of water or the mirror, concentrating on receiving the gifts of the Elder Mother. One lit candle can be set on either side of the bowl or mirror and the two candles bound together by red thread. One candle represents this world and one candle symbolizes the Otherworld.

If desired, you can use the charm:

Mother Holle
Mother Holle
Red thread, breath and blood
Elder flower, berry and branch
Weave and spin
Two into one
Weave and spin
Two into one
Red thread
Elder branch
Mother Holle
Thee I call

Or a shorter version:

Mother Holle
Breath and bone
Red thread
Elder branch
Thee I call
Mother Holle

An added bonus is that elder can also be used for protection as well as for flight and visions. A bundle of elder bound up over the door can keep ill-wishes out. Pray to Mother Holle when you place it, asking Her to please watch over the household. It would a good idea, thereafter, to make an offering to Her at least once a year, in particular during the Yuletide season or at All Hallows, any traditioal time of transition.

To Fly

Listen--
Listen to the whispers
Of the wide places
The sound that comes in the night
The cry of the souls
Who dare to travel the dark.
Night flyers
Birds whose wings are black
As the abyss
Whose eyes shimmer
With the light of the first moonrise
They hold the spark
Within the altar of their own bodies
and are attracted to all that
Glimmers and glitters
Especially the brightest of witches
When they cast themselves
To the arms of the fire
To call them forth
To call them near.

A soul in a red gem
The fire in the blood
Ruby and garnet spilled
They steal the stones revealed
And carry them far to distant lands
And to places never known before
To ride the winds
To fly as jewels
Tendered in the heart of terror
Rushing screaming
A whirl a shrill a scream
Beyond all measure
Afraid and yet fearless of the fall.
The bird and the witch
Are one.

Conclusion

"Quhan we wold ryd,
we tak windle-straws,
or been-stalks and put them betwixt owr foot,
and say thryse,
Horse and Hattok,
horse and goe,
Horse and pellattis,
ho! ho!
and immediatlie, we flie away
whair euir we wold..."
-Isobell Gowdie, 1662

What does it take to be a *hedgewitch*? To be someone who rides the night and who journeys into strange realms. Who lives half in one world and half in another. It takes courage, perhaps even to the point of foolhardiness, and it takes curiosity. A fine blend of fixed will and resolve and a propensity for the mystical and poetic. A sensitivity that occasionally flirts with outright insanity. The strength to keep going and a dedication to the purpose at hand, plus the vision to glimpse what that purpose will resolve itself into in time. It takes a skill set built up from years of experience, one intimately bound to the raw talent born in the body and in the blood.

A *hedgewitch* must not just know how to stand in two worlds, to maintain a dynamic balancing act, but to actually prosper from it and share that prosperity with the rest of the community. The vision of the *hedgewitch* must encompass the land within and without the *Hedge*. We must be split and whole at the same time in order to function as a shaman must function—channeling energy and information back and forth between the *Otherworld* and this world, acting as the point of intersection, becoming a bridge, an *axis mundi*.

Does one need an awareness of death in order to have an awareness of life? One thing defines the boundaries of another. So does not death form the boundaries of life, even as life forms the boundaries of death? One way of looking at it is as twin pillars, one white and one black, one day and one night, one God and one Goddess, one male and one female or, as in some paths, mercy and severity. The door that they form is the gate between. It is the place that is not a place, a place between the worlds of life and death. It is the thin line that shamans and hedgewitches walk, belonging to both worlds and to neither.

It's an act of sheer will to return from the *Otherworld*, an act of self-knowledge. To be torn asunder, only to be put back together again in a new configuration, is part of what creates someone who can walk in many worlds. If the essence of the soul is lost in the process, then there is a hole in the center of the *shaman* or *hedgewitch* instead of a light. And this darkness may well consume all. For it is the darkness of the void, the nothingness from which all first sprang. For this reason, the *hedgewitch* must win knowledge and trust in their own spark, their light, the source of the foundation of being.

The universe itself was created from an act of will. When one goes into the void, one must recreate one's self again—rising up from the ashes of the old self, which has been destroyed. This takes both will and faith. In the process you must be both destroyed and yet not destroyed. The seed must remain, the egg, the spark from which all rises again. The seed contains all possibility, all that you may be or aspire to be. Just as all the universe is contained in each seed, all possibility, waiting for the act of will to spring forth and take form. Waiting to take the leap of faith to take it to the light, to creation.

Those who have gone over fully to the realms of death, to the *Underworld*, to *Faery*, must remain there. They have eaten of the food of that world and taken it into themselves. The *hedgewitch* or the *shaman* is he or she who returns to the sun-lit world of the living and whose insights and even their particular shade of "madness" has been gained for use by the land and the community. It's not enough to be just a bit crazy around the edges if you're a *hedgewitch*; that crazy must always serve a purpose.

Its not always a simple or easy task and it can even sometimes be thankless. For one thing, most *"modern"* societies don't accept or support the role of the *shaman*, the double-spirited, those who ride the edge of madness for a reason. Add to that, the problem that there aren't too many readily available groups or teachers to help guide a fledgling *hedgewitch*. The lucky few may find a good teacher, but generally we must learn to rely on our spirit contacts. After all, that's what they're there for, to be our guardians and our guides to the other side. But in order to trust them, we must first trust ourselves and know how to listen to our instincts and sort out true perceptions from those that might be misleading.

It's definitely a proving ground, a school of hard-knocks, where you may be tested again and again. But like all those called by the spirits, such adversity creates strength. As *hedgewitches* and *hedgeriders*, we traverse the edges and may well bloody our feet on them, and yet how can we not walk? Someone must go there, no matter the cost, and those who are drawn to go there quite often pay the cost. It is who we are and we can do no less. We are made for the task, even if we must rediscover it for ourselves within the ashes of the past, rebuilding the flame and raising the phoenix. We must go. We must be free to go. We must be willing to go and find what we need to find. We must be strong to bring it back again.

What a *hedgewitch* does reverberates across many worlds. To comprehend what effect those ripples may have takes the innate and occasionally overwhelming touch known as the Second Sight. It requires an intimate link to spirits and entities of all sorts, allowing us to see as they see and know as they know, to be able to not just think outside the box, but to get outside the box. We have to be both well grounded in this world and within ourselves, and yet remain capable of walking free of our bodies and flexible in our definition of what is and what isn't.

We have to come to an inner balance and accord or we can easily be pulled off balance by the needs and requirements of this world and the *Otherworld*, by the paradoxes such a double existence can create, and by the powers that we are playing with and calling up. For example, one of the necessities of gaining the Second Sight is to find a way to not only turn it on when needed, but to be able to turn it off, as well. Otherwise, it can making living in this world difficult, if not outright impossible. We also have to make sure we are not so drawn by the lands beyond the *Hedge* that we lose sight of this one, of our responsibilities here, or we could become not crazy in a good way, but crazy in a no longer able to take care of ourselves way.

The tools for this lie both within and all around us. Not only do we need to find them, but use them wisely to unlock the gate—the gate to *Faery* and the *Underworld* and the gate inside us, for each reflects the other. As we walk, we walk with shadows and spirits. As we fly, we taste real freedom. We know the sharp joy and pain of life and we know what it is to commune with death. We find the secret rose within and unravel the secrets that can never be told, save to those who have walked that way before us and those who will come after.

Once *out there*, we seek to tap into that secret river, that hidden current, out of which comes the wellsprings of each time. Ages and cultures live and die, and so the aspect of the wellspring that feeds and serves it. Yet what lies beneath it all is deeper and darker and more mysterious still. We travel to touch that darkness and we journey to know mystery, to find within it the sparks, the seeds of might be, could be, should be, and to bring them back. The serpent's egg. The brightest star in the heavens. The phoenix flame. The wine within the cup. What lies behind the bright, dread mask of Medusa. The hidden face of Hela.

The sunlit human world is not the only one and the darkness that lies beyond what is known draws us. The strange twilight land of the *Elves*, of *Gods* and *Giants*, calls to us, and who are we to deny that call? We cannot. We dare not. The boundaries, the *hedges*, that enclose the human world, must be breached and the *wildest powers of Wyrd*, of the *beyond*, be allowed to come pouring in. The storms of change must pass, washing away the old and giving rise to the new.

We have a part to play in that, for we have seen that tangled wilderness past the *hedgerows*, the beautiful and deadly road least chosen, the road to *Elphame*, the dark heart of the Craft, and have decided to embrace. No matter where it may lead...to the depths of the *World Mountain* or to the heights, the tallest branches of the *World Tree*. We seek the ecstasy, the sharp rush of freedom, and the strange and bittersweet knowledge at journey's end. Its almost addictive and so we go and return, traveling elsewhere and elsewhen and coming home again. Until we finally take the road and chose to remain, to become one with the flight, with the drifting shadows and the secret company.

One with the beloved dead and the shining ones of old.

*S*trix

Red cap
White spatter
Night dreaming;
To eat the visions
Is to eat your own heart.

To consume the mushroom
To hear the cry of the night-fliers
Shakes the soul loose from its underpinnings,
Leaving it wandering in a world
Of fear and pain and joy
Beyond normal understanding,
One foot on the path and one
Foot on never...

The Strix cry and wail
Black winged black eyed jagged pieces
Of night and beyond and clatter
As they sweep down to steal the heart,
Taking it unto themselves
As you would a small and
Precious thing.

Would you not know
The price of flight,
Are you not willing to pay,
As you have paid many times before.

They who would drink of your blood
Will to give of their wings
To change and to become as them,
And so learn at last how to travel.
Together as one to rise
High and so very higher

Until the sun burns away
All that needs not remain;
For even the Gods remember
What it is to burn.

Growing upon the moss of the soul,
A tattered leaf,
A stolen jewel
Red as blood and twice as golden,
The spring that wells up in the center
Of the woodlands
Renders eternal all who drink
Even though it means
They shall never return again.
It is there that the flying ones pause,
Black birds gathered
Like a broken rosary around a pool
Of liquid light,
And like a rosary their prayer
Is beaded into a single voice,
Much like a coven dreams of a single thing,
Each witch a woven jewel,
A budded rose.

What you bring back is always yourself.
The well you drink from you've always known.
As the one who carries you there
Knows well the witches of old,
And knows you among their company
Or else they would not come at all.

Their black eyes dance the light
Of the ancient ways,
Unforgotten and unshriven
And within them lies the precious secret
That lies at heart of every fairytale--
That the red cap is not a Faery hat,
But a Faery cake,
Sprung from stormtide and sacrifice
From love and joy
And loss and pain
A cake of finding and forgetting
Of coming home again.

Author Book Recommendations

Ancient Herbs, Marina Heilmeyer, Getty Publications, 2007

The Art and Practice of Geomancy, John Michael Greer, Weiser Books, 2009

Call of the Horned Piper, Nigel Aldcroft Jackson, Capall Bann Publishing, 1994

Breaking Open the Head: A Psychedelic Journey into the Heart of Contemporary Shamanism, Daniel Pinchbeck, Broadway Books, 2002

Brian Froud's World of Faerie, Brian Froud, Insight Editions, 2007

Catmagic, Whitley Strieber, Tom Doherty Associates Inc, 1986

Chosen by the Spirits: Following Your Shamanic Calling, Sarangerel, Inner Traditions International Ltd, 2001

Crossing the Borderlines: Guising, Masking, and Ritual Animal Disguises in the European Tradition, Nigel Pennick, Capall Bann Publishing, 1998

Cunning Folk and Familiar Spirits: Shamanistic Visionary Traditions in Early Modern British Witchcraft and Magic, Emma Wilby, Sussex Academic Press, 2005

The Dream-Hunters of Corsica, Dorothy Carrington, Weidenfeld and Nicholson, 1995

Druid Priestess: An Intimate Journey Through the Pagan Year, Emma Restall Orr, Thorsons, 2000

Ecstasies—Deciphering the Witches' Sabbath, Carlo Ginzburg, Penguin Books, Random House, 1991

Encyclopedia of Natural Magic, John Michael Greer, Llewellyn Publications, 2005

The Essential Guide to Herbal Safety, Simon Mills and Kerry Bone, Churchill Livingstone, 2004

Faces in the Smoke: An Eyewitness Experience of Voodoo, Shamanism, Psychic Healing, and Other Amazing Human Powers, Douchan Gersi, Jeremy P. Tarcher Inc, 1991

Fire Burn, Ken Radford, Peter Bedrick Books, 1989

Fire in the Head: Shamanism and the Celtic Spirit, Tom Cowan, HarperCollins Publishers, 1993

Green Pharmacy: The History and Evolution of Western Herbal Medicine, Barbara Griggs, Inner Traditions International Ltd, 1997

Hallucinogens and Shamanism, Michael J. Harner (editor), Oxford University Press, 1973

The Healing Power of Celtic Plants: Their History, Their Use, and the Scientific Evidence That They Work, Angela Paine, O Books, 2006

Hedge-Rider, Eric De Vries, Pendraig Publishing, 2008

Herbs of the Northern Shaman: A Guide to Mind-Altering Plants of the Northern Hemisphere, Steve Andrews, Loompanics Unlimited, 2000

Hoodoo Herb and Root Magic: A Materia Magica of African-American Conjure, Catherine Yronwode, Lucky Mojo Curio Co, 2002

In The Dark Places of Wisdom, Peter Kingsley, The Golden Sufi Center, 1999

Into the Green, Charles de Lint, Orb Books, 2001

Lammas Night, Kathryn Kurtz, Ballantine Books, 1983 (fiction)

Learning Their Language: Intuitive Communication with Animals and Nature, Marta Williams, New World Library, 2003

Leechcraft: Early English Charms, Plant-lore and Healing, Stephen Pollington, Anglo Saxon Books, 2008

Leechdoms, Wortcunning, and Starcraft of Early England: A Collection of Documents, For the Most Part Never Before Printed, Illustrating the History of Science in This County Before the Norman Conquest, Volumes I, II, III, Thomas Oswald Cockayne and Charles Singer, The Holland Press, 1961

The Lost Language of Plants: The Ecological Importance of Plant Medicine to Life on Earth, Stephen Harrod Buhner, Chelsea Green Publishing, 2002

The Magic of Shapeshifting, Rosalyn Greene, Samuel Weiser Inc, 2000

The Magical Garden: Spells, Charms, and Lore for Magical Gardens and the Curious Gardners Who Tend Them, Sophia and Denny Sargent, Andrews McMeel Publishing, 2000

The Meaning of Herbs: Myth, Language & Lore, Ann Field and Gretchen Scoble,

The Earth Path: Grounding Your Spirit in the Rhythms of Nature, Starhawk, HarperCollins Publishers, 2005

The Night Battles—Witchcraft & Agrarian Cults in the Sixteenth & Seventeenth Centuries, Carlo Ginzburg, Penguin Books, 1985

Nine Worlds of Seid-Magic: Ecstasy and Neo-Shamanism in North European Paganism, Jenny Blain, Routledge, 2001

Norron Religion, Gro Steinsland, Pax Forlag, Oslo, 2005

North Star Road—Shamanism, Witchcraft & the Otherworld Journey, Kenneth Johnson, Llewellyn Publications, 1996

Omens, Oghams & Oracles: Divination in the Druidic Tradition, Richard Webster, Llewellyn Publications, 1995

The One-Eyed God, Kris Kershaw, Journal of Indo-European Studies, Monograph #36, Washington DC, 2000

Other Ways of Knowing—Recharting Our Future With Ageless Wisdom, John Broomfield, Inner Traditions International, 1997

The Owl Service, Alan Garner, Ballantine Books, 1967

Plant Spirit Shamanism: Traditional Techniques for Healing the Soul, Ross Heaven, Howard Charing, and Pablo Amaringo, Destiny Books, 2006

The Practical Handbook of Plant Alchemy: An Herbalist's Guide to Preparing Medicinal Essences, Tinctures, and Elixers, Manfred M. Junius, Healing Arts Press, 1985

Psychedelic Shamanism: The Cultivation, Preparation & Shamanic Use of Psychoactive Plants, Jim DeKorne, Loompanics Unlimited, 1994

Reality, Peter Kingsley, The Golden Sufi Center, 2003

Revisioning the Earth: A Guide to Opening the Healing Channels Between Mind and Nature, Paul Devereaux, Fireside, 1996

Riding Windhorses: A Journey into the Heart of Mongoliam Shamanism, Sarangerel, Destiny Books, 2000

Rune Magic: The History and Practice of Ancient Runic Traditions, Nigel Pennick, Thorsons, 1992

Runenmagie-Handbuch der Runenkunde, Karl Spiesberger, Verlag Richard Schikowski, 1954

Runor: Historia, tydning, tolking, Lars Magnar Enoksen, Historica Medica, Sweden, 1998

The Sacred Mushroom: Key to the Door of Eternity, Andrija Puharich, Doubleday & Co, 1959

Seid, Brit Solli, Pax Forlag, Oslo, 2002

The Shaman, Piers Viteb Sky, Duncan Baird Publishers, 2001

Shamanic Journeying: A Beginner's Guide, Sandra Ingerman, Sounds True Inc, 2008

Shamanic Voices: A Survey of Visionary Narratives, Joan Halifax PhD, Arkana Books, 1991

Shamanism: Archaic Techniques of Ecstasy, Mircea Eliade, Princeton University Press, 2004

Shamanism As a Spiritual Practice for Daily Life, Tom Cowan, Crossing Press, 1996

Shamans: Siberian Spirituality and the Western Imagination, Ronald Hutton, Hambledon and London, 2007

Singing the Soul Back Home: Shamanic Wisdom for Every Day, Caitlin Matthews, Connections Book Publishing, 2003

Sorgitzak-Old Forest Craft, Veronica Cummer, Pendraig Publishing, 2008

Spirit Speak: Knowing and Understanding Spirit Guides, Ancestors, Ghosts, Angels, and the Divine, Ivo Dominguez Jr, New Page Books, 2008

The Twelve Wild Swans: A Journey to the Realm of Magic, Healing and Action, Starhawk and Hilary Valentine, Harper One, 2001

Unseen Worlds and Practical Aspects of Spiritual Discernment, Anastacia J. Nutt, R. J. Stewart Books, 2008.

Uthark: Nightside of the Runes, Thomas Karlsson, Ouroboros Produktion, Sweden, 2002

The Veil's Edge-Exploring the Boundaries of Magic, Willow Polson, Citadel Press, Kensington Publishing Corp, 2003.

Veterinary Herbal Medicine, Susan G. Wynn and Barbara Fougere, Mosby, 2006

Werewolves, Bird-Women, Tiger-Men and Other Human Animals, Frank Hamel, Dover Publications, 2007, reprint of Human Animals, Frederick A Stokes Co, 1915

The Wild Plant Companion: A Fresh Understanding of Herbal Food and Medicine, Kathryn G. March, Meridian Hill Publications, 1986

Witchcraft in Britain, Christina Hole, Paladin Grafton Books, 1980

Witchcraft Medicine: Healing Arts, Shamanic Practices, and Forbidden Plants, Claudia Muller-Ebeling, Christian Ratsch, Wolf Dieter Storl PhD, Inner Traditions, 2003

The Witching Way of the Hollow Hill, Robin Artisson, Pendraig Publishing, 2005

Where the Spirits Ride the Wind: Trance Journeys and Other Ecstatic Experiences, Felicitas Goodman, Indiana University Press, 1990

The Woman in the Shaman's Body: Reclaiming the Feminine in Religion and Medicine, Barbara Tedlock, Bantam, 2005

Index

C

F

H

U

V

W

X Y Z

CPSIA information can be obtained
at www.ICGtesting.com
Printed in the USA
BVOW11s0444180817

492246BV00006B/149/P